THE DISORDER OF W

For my mother
Beatrice Kate Bennett

The Disorder of Women

Democracy, Feminism and Political Theory

CAROLE PATEMAN

Polity Press

Essay 1 © 1980 by The University of Chicago
Essay 4 © 1980 Sage Publications, Inc.
Essay 5 © 1975 Butterworths Publishers
This collection and all other essays copyright © Carole Pateman 1989

First published 1989 by Polity Press
in association with Basil Blackwell

Editorial office:
Polity Press,
65 Bridge Street
Cambridge CB2 1UR, UK

Marketing and production:
Basil Blackwell Ltd
108 Cowley Road, Oxford OX4 1JF, UK

ISBN 0 7456 0572 9
0 7456 0789 6 (pbk)

British Library Cataloguing in Publication Data
A CIP catalogue record for this book is available from
the British Library.

Typeset in 11 on 12 point Garamond
by Hope Services
Printed in Great Britain by
Billing & Sons Limited, Worcester

Contents

Acknowledgements

The Introduction was written and this volume compiled during my tenure of the Kerstin Hesselgren Professorship of the Swedish Council for Research in the Humanities and Social Sciences (Humanistisk-Samhällsvetenskapliga Forskningsrådet). I am honoured to have been chosen as the first occupant of the Chair; Kerstin Hesselgren was a champion of women's rights and the first woman member of the Swedish Parliament. I would like to thank the Council for their generous assistance, to thank Olof Ruin and Bo Särlvik for the hospitality of their departments in Stockholm and Göteborg during the first part of my visit to Sweden and my Swedish friends and colleagues for making my stay so enjoyable and fruitful. I also owe thanks to David Held for insisting that I collect my essays together and to Roy for helping me do so.

The essays in this collection previously appeared in the following publications and the author and publishers are grateful for permission to reproduce them here:

1 'The Disorder of Women': Women, Love, and the Sense of Justice. In *Ethics*, 91 (1980), pp. 20–34. Copyright © 1980 by the University of Chicago.
2 The Fraternal Social Contract. In J. Keane, ed., *Civil Society and the State: New European Perspectives*, London and New York: Verso, 1988.
3 Justifying Political Obligation. In A. Kontos, ed., *Powers, Possessions and Freedom*, Ontario: University of Toronto Press, 1979.
4 Women and Consent. In *Political Theory*, 8 (May 1980), pp. 149–68. Copyright © Sage Publications, Inc.
5 Sublimation and Reification: Locke, Wolin and the Liberal–Democratic

Conception of the Political. In *Politics and Society*, 6 (1975), pp. 441–67. Copyright © Butterworth Publishers.

6 Feminist Critiques of the Public/Private Dichotomy. In S. Benn and G. Gaus, eds, *Public and Private in Social Life*, London and New York: Croom Helm, 1983.

7 *The Civic Culture*: A Philosophic Critique. In G. Almond and S. Verba, eds, *The Civic Culture Revisited*, Boston: Little Brown & Co., 1980.

8 The Patriarchal Welfare State. In A. Gutmann, ed., *Democracy and the Welfare State*, Princeton: Princeton University Press, 1988.

9 Feminism and Democracy. In G. Duncan, ed., *Democratic Theory and Practice*, Cambridge: Cambridge University Press, 1983.

Introduction

The essays in this volume were first published between 1975 and 1988 and they appear here in their original form. All the essays deal with aspects of democratic theory and the social conditions necessary for democracy, and several refer to the classic contract theorists, in particular to Locke and Rousseau. My perspective on democratic theory and my reading of the texts has changed in some fundamental respects during these years. The impetus for this theoretical development came from the revival of the organized feminist movement, which provided a new, and in many ways extremely disquieting, view of democracy and political life. Theoretical inquiry is an important part of contemporary feminism and the new feminist scholarship is beginning to reveal that sexual difference and the subordination of women are central to the construction of modern political theory.

Mainstream political theory has also flourished, and over the past five years or so there has been a revival of interest in democratic theory, especially in radical or participatory theory. But democratic theory, like the wider body of political theory, for the most part remains untouched by feminist argument. Feminist theory has been part of the development of modern political theory from the seventeenth century, although feminist writings are excluded from the canon of texts studied under the heading 'political theory'.[1] The existence of feminist argument is not so remarkable in itself, and feminism has always stood in a critical relation to the theories of famous writers. But women were not present in universities in earlier periods, and political theory has not always been a professional discipline, conducted from within the confines of academia. The new development is a sweeping challenge by feminist scholars to the central assumptions and presuppositions of academic political theory. One impetus for the challenge has come from feminist reinterpretations of the classic texts. Some parts of the books admitted to the canon are rarely studied; the sections and chapters that deal with relations between the sexes and the political significance of sexual difference are typically either omitted or merely mentioned in passing, since these matters are dismissed as peripheral to the real business of political theory.

Most current work in political theory repeats the standard readings of the texts, ignores the copious empirical evidence collected by feminist investigators about women's position in all areas of social and political life and shows no interest in the broader body of feminist theory that ranges from epistemological questions and analyses of reason and rationality to arguments about the phallus as a signifier and the institution of hetero-sexuality. This is not to say that the revival of the organized feminist movement has had no impact at all on political theory. The movement has raised numerous issues that political theorists have been able to use in their discussions of, say, rights (e.g. does the foetus have rights?), or justice (e.g. is there a form of injustice that happens to affect women in particular?) or labour (e.g. is there a connection between domestic labour and capitalism?). Such discussions are based on the view that existing theoretical frameworks and modes of argument, whether liberal theories of rights, Rawlsian theories of justice or Marxist theories of capitalism, are entirely adequate to deal with the concerns of feminists. Feminism may generate new issues for discussion, but the underlying assumption is that questions which have been taken up as 'women's issues' can be embraced and incorporated into mainstream theory. For political theorists, feminism raises no distinctive problems of its own and poses no fundamental challenge to the familiar terms of argument.

To discuss 'women's issues' is not the same as engaging with or contributing to feminist theory. Feminist theory brings a new perspective to bear on the relation between 'women's issues' and the staple diet of political theory. Feminists are concerned with democracy and citizenship, with freedom, justice, equality and consent. They are vitally interested in power and the problem of how government can be legitimate, but what feminists mean by 'power' and 'government' and the understanding of these two terms in orthodox political theory is very different. Feminist theory is distinctive because it has raised a new problem; or, more precisely, feminist theorists insist that a repressed problem lies at the heart of modern political theory – the problem of patriarchal power or the government of women by men. Political theorists have deliberated about power and government for at least two thousand years; in the modern period they have engaged in controversies about the legitimacy and justification of the power, for example, of masters over slaves and servants, the rich over the poor, governments over citizens, capitalists over workers, elites over masses, the vanguard party over the proletariat, and technocrats and scientists over laymen. In the texts of the famous theorists there are also discussions of the power of men over women, but contemporary political theory does not acknowledge this form of jurisdiction as *political* power and pays no heed to feminist theorists who attack the legitimacy of patriarchal government.

Contemporary political theorists are able to admit the relevance or significance of feminist questions and criticisms only with great difficulty. Such matters are systematically excluded from their theorizing by the modern patriarchal construction of the object of their studies, 'political' theory itself. Political theorists base their inquiries on the assumption that their subject lies in the public world of the economy and state and that the private realm of domestic, familial and sexual relations lies outside their proper concerns. The classic social contract theorists were of crucial importance in the development of this view of political theory, not least because their arguments about the political meaning of sexual difference were an integral part of the emergence of the idea of a modern 'civil' society that is divided into two contrasting spheres of social life. Contemporary theorists, however, do not examine the texts to see how the classic contract theorists constructed the two categories of public and private; rather, they now read the texts in the light of the structure of argument established in the texts themselves. The political implications of a social order divided between private and public arenas are precluded from critical investigation.

In mainstream political theory, the public sphere is assumed to be capable of being understood on its own, as if it existed *sui generis*, independently of private sexual relations and domestic life. The structure of relations between the sexes is ignored and sexual relations stand as the paradigm of all that is private or non-political. Yet, as attention to the classic texts would show, the meanings of 'private' and 'public' are mutually interdependent; the 'public' cannot be comprehended in isolation. Properly to understand the conception of a public world and the capacities and characteristics that are required to participate within it demands, at the same time, an understanding of what is excluded from the public and why the exclusion takes place. The 'public' rests on a particular conception of the 'private' and vice versa. When the 'public' is analysed in isolation, theorists are able to assume that nothing or no one of significance is excluded; or, to make this point differently, theorists work on the assumption that the public world, and the categories through which it is presented in theoretical argument, are sexually neutral or universal, including everyone alike. On the contrary, the 'individuals' who are so prominent in political theory are sexually indifferent only to the extent that they are disembodied.

I have, along with other theorists, criticized the abstract character of the individual who peoples the pages of much democratic theory, but this criticism has usually been blind to the fact that abstraction from the body is also necessary if the 'individual' is not to be revealed as a masculine figure. One of the major themes that runs through my more recent essays is that women, womanhood and women's bodies represent the private; they represent all that is excluded from the public sphere. In the patriarchal construction of the difference between masculinity and femininity, women lack the capacities necessary for political life. 'The disorder of women' means that they pose a threat to political order and so must be excluded from the public world. Men possess the capacities required for citizenship, in particular they are able to use their reason to sublimate their passions, develop a sense of justice and so uphold the universal, civil law. Women, we learn from the classic texts of contract theory, cannot transcend their bodily natures and sexual passions; women cannot develop such a political morality.

In the story of the creation of civil society through an original agreement, women are brought into the new social order as inhabitants of a private sphere that is part of civil society and yet is separated from the public world of freedom and equality, rights, contract, interests and citizenship. Women, that is to say, are incorporated into the civil order differently from men. But women's inclusion within the private sphere is not the whole story. Women have never been completely excluded from participation in the institutions of the public world – but women have been incorporated into public life in a different manner from men. Women's bodies symbolize everything opposed to political order, and yet the long and often bitterly contested process through which women have been included as citizens has been structured around women's bodily (sexual) difference from men. Women have been included as 'women'; that is, as beings whose sexual embodiment prevents them enjoying the same political standing as men. Women's political position, before and since we have won citizenship, is full of paradoxes, contradictions and ironies, but both women's exclusion from the public world and the manner of our inclusion have escaped the notice of political theorists.

One reason for this blindness is the standard interpretation of the classic texts. In the seventeenth century the notion that men or 'individuals' are born free and equal to each other, or are naturally free and equal, began to gain wide currency, and the idea has now become fundamental to political theory. The classic contract theorists first formulated general theories of social and political life that depended upon the premise of freedom and equality as a birthright, and their texts still inform and help to constitute political theory in the late twentieth century

– but in an emasculated form. The terms 'men' and 'individuals' in their texts are now read as generic or universal, as inclusive of everyone. But this is a misreading. The classic contract theorists (with one notable exception) argued that natural freedom and equality were the birthright of one sex. Only *men* are born free and equal. The contract theorists constructed sexual difference as a *political* difference, the difference between men's natural freedom and women's natural subjection.

The exception among the contract theorists is Hobbes.[2] Hobbes proclaims that in the natural condition women are men's equals and enjoy the same freedom. But commentaries on the texts have nothing to say about the opposition between Hobbes and the other theorists on this fundamental point, or about the importance for their theories of this striking difference in views about men and women. Almost as soon as the idea of natural freedom and equality was formulated, feminist critics began asking, in Mary Astell's words, 'if all Men are born Free, how is it that all Women are born Slaves?'[3] How, if God had made humankind, and endowed them with rationality and other capacities, or how, if freedom and equality were natural attributes of humans, could such a division between the two sexes be justified? Political theorists have not yet acknowledged the existence or relevance of these feminist questions.

The preceeding paragraphs have, of course, been written with the benefit of the hindsight available from over a decade of work on these and related questions on my part. The earliest essays reprinted in this volume contain various references to a problem about women revealed in the texts of political theory, in empirical data and in contemporary argument, but I had not then appreciated quite how fundamental and far-reaching the problem was. My discussions remain framed within prevailing assumptions about the character and scope of political theory. For example, the arguments in the long-standing controversy between advocates of a liberal view of democracy and their radical critics – such as myself – were, and remain, vigorous on both sides. Yet today, from a different vantage point, I am conscious that there are assumptions and premises that unite the antagonists as strongly as those that divide them. Consider the argument about whether the economy and the workplace are private or public and whether democracy in the workplace is feasible or desirable: neither side in the debate questions the exclusive concentration on what I call (in 'Feminist Critiques of the Public/Private Dichtomy') the class conception of 'private' and 'public'. Nothing of significance for democracy is seen in the patriarchal opposition between the 'public' (economy/state) and the 'private' (domestic, conjugal and intimate life), an opposition which is both presupposed and repressed by democratic theorists. The current revival of interest in participatory democratic theory has, so far, gone only a small way in changing this.[4]

I would not have included the earlier essays here if I now thought my arguments completely misguided. I still believe that they capture some important dimensions and problems of contemporary political theory and political life. But I have also included them to provide a concrete illustration of the difference that a feminist perspective makes in political theory. For example, I drew the distinction between the class and patriarchal conceptions of the private and the public partly from a (re)reading of Locke's theory. In the earliest piece published here, 'Sublimation and Reification', I was also concerned with Locke, the private and the public. The essay examines the question of the characterization of the 'political' in liberal-democratic theory, and whether only a liberal-democratic political order is (as is sometimes claimed) appropriately called 'political'. I argue, drawing on an interpretation of Locke's theory, that although liberal theory postulates that individuals have a natural political right, the assumption is always made that the right must be given up. The 'political', represented by the state, then stands over and above the governed, who interact in a depoliticized private sphere. Citizenship is divorced from daily life and becomes what Marx called a 'political lion skin', worn only occasionally and somewhat reluctantly. Yet, as my later analyses of the contract theorists and the development of citizenship show, the political lion skin has a large mane and belonged to a male lion; it is a costume for men. When women finally win the right to don the lion skin it is exceedingly ill-fitting and therefore unbecoming.

In the same essay, I argued that Rousseau's theory provides a clear alternative to Locke's arguments (and I used Rousseau as the exemplar of a participatory democratic theorist, in *Participation and Democratic Theory*). Following standard accounts of his arguments, I overlooked the fact that Rousseau declares that political order depends on the exclusion of women from citizenship. Rousseau's 'democracy' is a masculine preserve in which the political right of self-government is exercised only by men. Nor can his theory simply be revised to include women. The meaning of 'political' and 'democracy' in Rousseau's theory depends upon the meaning he gives to manhood and womanhood. Fully to understand what it means to be an active citizen who is master of himself requires the mirror provided by the private sphere that lies outside citizenship, a sphere in which women are mastered by men. To dismiss Rousseau's or the other contract theorists' arguments about the political significance of sexual difference as irrelevant or merely peripheral to their theories, is to disregard a fundamental feature of the original contract said to create the modern world of citizenship. Women's political disorder means that they must be *excluded* from the original agreement.[5] The original contract is a masculine or fraternal pact.

In my analysis in 'The Fraternal Social Contract', I have amended my earlier argument about the lack of any common bond uniting 'individuals' participating in the economy and the practice of contract. They do have such a bond, a bond consolidated through the original contract; they are united by the interests that they share *as men* in their jurisdiction over women, interests that are protected by the laws and policies of the state. The story of the original contract, political theorists argue, is still important because it allows us to interpret our political institutions correctly as institutions in which the freedom of all is secured. To admit that the story tells of women's subjection as well as men's freedom requires a major transformation of the terms of political inquiry. So it is hardly surprising that students of politics have had enormous difficulty in seeing women's struggles against that subjection, for example, to reform marriage law, to ensure the public and private safety of women and girls, to achieve temperance, to enter higher education, to gain entry to a variety of occupations, to improve their working conditions or to improve the health and welfare of mothers and children, as falling within 'politics'; even the womanhood suffrage movement is neglected.

Until recently, political scientists frequently portrayed women as apolitical, and democratic theorists have asked few questions about empirical studies, such as *The Civic Culture*, that found that women were less likely to feel politically competent or to be active citizens than men. Most empirical studies have focused on conventional, electoral politics in which women have occupied a peripheral position, so that such findings are to be expected. Women, like men, are capable of making a rational assessment of the operation of a political system in which empirical findings show that the benefits of participation tend to go to the better off. In my criticism of *The Civic Culture*, chapter 7, I argue that the gap between the large number of citizens who achieve high scores on scales measuring political competence and the rather small number, drawn largely from the middle classes, who participate can be explained by the fact that working-class citizens reason that it is not worth being active. Similarly, women can perceive that participation helps men more than women, so that it is rational for them to abstain from political activity.

The civic culture is divided along sexual as well as class lines – although, as I discuss in some detail in chapter 7, this is not the way in which the data are presented in the study itself. Ironically, one of the major weaknesses of empirical democratic theory was the interpretation of the empirical findings on which its proponents laid so much stress, an aspect of this genre of theorizing oddly neglected by many of its critics. Because empirical theorists reduced political culture to an aggregation of individual characteristics, they could not explain the social patterns of participation revealed in their data. They merely accepted the social distribution of political activity and inactivity as given or natural; it merely happened that the 'uncivic' citizens, those on the apathetic side of the nice balance between apathy and participation that constituted a civic culture, were disproportionately drawn from lower socio-economic status (SES) groups and women.

Another explanation I offer for the lower activity of working-class citizens, drawing on my argument in *Participation and Democratic Theory*, is that they are systematically deprived of a political education. They do not have the same opportunities as middle-class citizens to learn how to participate; most importantly, as *The Civic Culture* confirms, they are less likely to have opportunities to participate in the workplace. My hypothesis about the link between workplace participation and wider political activity has now received some empirical support (though less research has been undertaken on this question than one might suppose).[6] If the absence of industrial democracy provides a reasonable explanation for the lower political activity of working men, does it also explain the sexual division of the civic culture? In one sense it does; as I note in chapter 9, 'Feminism and Democracy', women in paid employment are likely to be in the low-status, low-skilled jobs that are associated with low political participation. Even in professional occupations, women are concentrated at the lower ends of the occupational hierarchy. In another sense, the argument fails. As in *The Civic Culture*, a 'social fact' is being taken for granted instead of being treated as a problem that requires investigation; in this case, the fact that the public division of labour is sexually segregated.

Men and women do not usually work together; most women in paid employment are concentrated together in a few occupations (typically, they are also supervised by men, and men are likely to be their union leaders and representatives). The sexual segregation of the labour force has been remarkably persistent during this century. The question of *why* this is the case is rarely raised in discussions of workplace democracy, since silence is invariably maintained about this aspect of working life. Students of workplace democracy have little to say about the exclusion of women from certain occupations and the continued separation, even in new 'high tech' industries, of men's from women's work. Women have been in paid employment since the early development of capitalist factories, but it does not follow that they have been incorporated into the workforce in the same way as men. Arguments about and explanations of work and citizenship that centre on male workers – or 'the worker' – cannot, as is usually supposed, merely be extended to women. Women and men stand in a different relation to the work which is undertaken in workplaces. Women do not have the same status as workers as men.

Few questions are asked about the category of 'work' in discussions of industrial democracy. Once again, the tacit assumption is that theoretical argument about the public world (the workplace) can proceed independently of any consideration of the connection between the public and the private. John Stuart Mill (that rare being, a feminist theorist admitted to the canon of political theory, albeit his feminist writings are rarely referred to in standard discussions) provides an instructive example here. In 'Feminism and Democracy', I discuss how Mill's failure to bring together his support for democratic cooperation in the public workplace with his attack on the private tyranny of husbands undercuts his arguments for women's citizenship. The interdependence of public and private – or work and housework, the worker and his wife, men and women – is clear enough when critical attention is given to the 'wage'. The wage is not merely payment for a (sexually neutral) worker's labours, but a 'family wage', i.e. payment that enables a man to support an economically dependent (subordinate) wife and minor children. The wage received for public 'work' presupposes a private world of women and unpaid labour. Recent empirical investigations by feminist scholars also show that the 'worker' is a man, and the workplace is male territory. Women workers are not seen as 'workers' in the same sense as men, by either men or women.[7] 'To go to work' is part of what it means to be a man. To be a woman in a workplace has a rather different meaning, as indicated by the widespread practice of what is now called sexual harassment.

Democratic theorists have concentrated on the link between men's participation in the workplace and their wider political participation. They have had nothing to say about men's position as husbands or breadwinners and how that is connected to their citizenship – or to women's citizenship. The terms of the fraternal pact and the patriarchal criteria for participation in the public world have been embodied in the structure of the workplace and in the structure of the state. Women are now citizens, but the continuing uncertainties and paradoxes of our citizenship have been illustrated in the large body of empirical and theoretical research by feminist scholars into the welfare state. Political theorists still manage to write on the 'normative justification' of democratic citizenship in the welfare state without taking any account of women, the 'feminization of poverty' or feminist arguments.[8] They are still silent about women's indirect constitution as citizens of the welfare state as men's (workers') dependents, and about the fact that women have not been called upon to make the same 'contribution' to the welfare state as men.

Men's 'contribution' derives from their construction as free and equal 'individuals'. As 'individuals' all men are owners, in that they all own the property in their persons and capacities over which they alone have right of jurisdiction; they are self-governing. Work and citizenship come together around the criterion of ownership. A 'worker' is a man who contracts out a specific piece of the property in his person, namely his labour power, and, as owners, all men are able to be incorporated on the same footing as citizens of the welfare state. One of the main arguments advanced by democratic theorists in defence of the welfare state is that all 'individuals' (workers) make a 'contribution' that allows them to be 'insured' against times when they are unable to participate in the labour market. Thus the welfare state provides the resources that (in principle) enable all men to enjoy their citizenship, even if their material circumstances are impoverished through, say, unemployment. All men are thus entitled by right of citizenship to the resources that enable the equal worth or equal enjoyment of their citizenship to be maintained.

The attack from the right on public provision of resources over the past decade has brought renewed interest in political theory in arguments justifying citizenship in the welfare state. But neither these discussions nor radical democratic theory pays attention to the question of women and self-ownership or to women's 'contribution' to the welfare state. The 'contribution' exacted from women by the state has reflected the political significance given to sexual difference. In the case of the welfare state, as I argue in 'The Patriarchal Welfare State', the irony is that women have been required to contribute welfare. The welfare in question is the private, unpaid 'welfare' provided by women in their homes for the young, the aged, the sick and infirm, and for their husbands. More generally, the demands made upon women by the state have always taken a form suited to those held to have their own private tasks and whose status as citizens is thus ambiguous and contradictory. Women's 'contribution' is not seen as part of, or as relevant to, their citizenship, but as a necessary part of the private tasks proper to their sex. Political theorists have not pondered about this state of affairs, even though the complex question of the demands placed upon women and the paradoxes surrounding their public standing is of considerable importance for a problem central to political theory: the issue of what, if any, political obligation is owed to the state by citizens.

There is a large literature on political obligation in the democratic state, but the question of women's obligation in a political order structured by patriarchal power is conspicuous by its absence. This is not the only omission in the discussions. Exactly why there is any general problem at all about political obligation is rarely made explicit, even though the standard discussions are concerned with justifying the power of the state and the obedience of citizens. If there were no problem about what the state may rightfully demand of citizens, the effort devoted to formulating justifications would be pointless. The problem, as I argue in chapter 3,

'Justifying Political Obligation', arises because of the premise that men are born free and equal, or self-governing. If all men have this standing, then it follows that there are no natural relations of superiority and subordination among them and, therefore, any government of one (or one group) by another must be conventional, created by men themselves. The postulate of natural freedom and equality entails that the *only* acceptable justification for government is that men agree to being ruled; they signify their agreement, for example, by making a contract of government or consenting in various ways to be governed. Men must consent to be governed by other men – but women are subordinate to men by nature. Natural sexual dominion is excluded from the conventional relations studied in political theory. Patriarchal government requires no justification.

The ultimate test of men's political obligation, political theorists agree, is that they will, if necessary, be prepared to give up their lives in defence of the state. It has been widely believed that women cannot, and would not be willing to, bear arms, an argument that was central to the fierce opposition to women's enfranchisement and that still finds echoes in the contemporary opposition to women in combat positions in the military. Women do not share men's ultimate obligation. The question of what the corresponding duty might be for women has not been asked by contemporary political theorists, and I have not asked it in these essays, but the answer is not hard to find. Women's duty must be suited to their sex. Men's duty to die for the state is matched by women's duty to give birth for the state.[9]

I argue in Chapter 2, 'The Fraternal Social Contract', that birth symbolizes the reasons why women must be excluded from political life, but women's natural capacity has also been one of the major mechanisms of women's inclusion into the political order. Modern states take an enormous interest in, and are greatly concerned about, the quantity and quality of their population and, as mothers and potential mothers, women are the objects of this interest. 'Motherhood, like 'masculinity' and 'femininity', has a patriarchal political meaning in modern political life, embodying the paradoxes and ironies of women's relation to the political world. The peculiarity of the duty to give birth for the state, like women's 'contribution' of welfare, is that it is a political duty that can be performed whether or not women are citizens. Since at least the 1790s, women have demanded that the performance of their duty should be part of citizenship (although the demand has clearly never been made at sufficient volume to catch the ears of political theorists). The performance of women's duty is vital for the health of the state, yet the duty lies outside citizenship – indeed, motherhood is seen as the antithesis of the duties of men and citizens.

These reflections suppose that men are politically obliged, but the embarrassing question always remains of exactly how, when and in what form the necessary agreement to be governed has been given. No satisfactory answer has been provided to this question and, I argue in 'Justifying Political Obligation', an answer cannot be found without some major theoretical and political changes. But if there is an intractable problem about men's political obligation, the problem of women's obligation is even more complex and difficult. On what grounds can women's political obligation be justified? Women have not been incorporated as citizens in the same way as men; women's 'contribution' is deemed to be private, nothing to do with citizenship; and the benefits of the welfare state have usually been distributed to women not in their own right as citizens, but as dependents of men, as private beings. Once the question of how women agree or consent to be governed is asked, the problem becomes even more difficult. 'Consent' as discussed in democratic theory is about the manner in which (it is held) agreement is given through various (public) indicators of explicit or tacitly given consent, such as voting, the receipt of benefits from the state and participation in fair institutions. Democratic theorists pay no attention to the fact that consent is also held to constitute the relation between the sexes.

For women, consent is something which is at least as, if not much more, important in private as in public life. The problem which I address in 'Women and Consent' is whether, given the patriarchal construction of what it means to be men and women and the present structure of relations between the sexes, 'consent' can have any genuine meaning in private or public life. Unless refusal of consent is possible, talk of consent is pointless. I draw attention in the chapter to the conflicting set of views that are held (in theory and practice) about women and consent. Women's consent in sexual matters is, at one and the same time, both vital and irrelevant, a contradiction that arises from women's exclusion from the category of 'individual' or owner of property in the person. Women's lack of ownership was illustrated very clearly in the common law doctrine of coverture. In the mid-nineteenth century, when a woman married she ceased to have an independent existence; she disappeared from juridical and civil view under the 'cover' of, or into the ownership of, her husband, who gained 'conjugal rights', i.e. right of sexual access to her body whether or not she was willing. Married women have now reappeared as civil beings, but the law of coverture lingers on in marriage. Recent legal reforms in, for example, many states in Australia and the USA have made marital rape a criminal offence, but in other legal jurisdictions, notably in Britain, to consent to become a wife is to give up the right to refuse consent to conjugal relations.

In sexual relations more generally, a woman's refusal of consent – her utterance of the word 'no' or other clear indications of refusal – is systematically invalidated; her refusal is reinterpreted as 'yes'. The view is still widespread that a woman's refusal to consent to sexual intercourse is never to be taken at face value; we all know, do we not, that when women say 'no' what they really mean is 'yes'? If doubts arise on this score they have to be firmly held to survive the message conveyed, for example, by the multi-million dollar sex industry or verdicts in the courts in rape cases. Evidence available since I wrote 'Women and Consent' shows that enforced submission continues to be interpreted as consent.[10] Court cases also reveal a good deal about the modern patriarchal construction of masculinity. In a recent case in Britain, a man who sexually assaulted his mentally retarded step-daughter, aged 12, was merely put on probation because, according to the judge, his wife's pregnancy led 'to a lack of sexual appetite in the lady, and considerable problems for a healthy young husband'.[11] The judge could not have made it plainer that men's government over women, and what it means to be a 'man', includes right of sexual access to women's bodies, a right that precludes refusal by women. How, then, can the practice of consent exist in any genuine sense?

The problem about consent is not confined to relations in the private sphere. I have already mentioned sexual harassment, and men's right of sexual access is upheld in the capitalist market through prostitution and other sectors of the sex industry.[12] The question of women's consent is also of direct importance for democratic theorists' arguments about citizenship. Discussion, speech and deliberation are seen as central to democracy; for example, Michael Walzer states that 'what counts is argument among the citizens. Democracy puts a premium on speech . . . Citizens come into the forum with nothing but their arguments.'[13] And, according to Benjamin Barber, 'give each citizen some control over what the community will mean by the crucial terms it uses to define all the citizens' selves and lives in public and private, and other forms of equality will follow.'[14] But neither theorist has anything to say about the reinterpretation by men of women's refusal of consent. How are women to join in the debate between citizens if their words are meaningless? How can there be participatory democracy when consent is the prerogative of one sex?

This volume may help to explain why, in political theory, feminist argument is to a large extent developing on a parallel track to mainstream discussions. Political theory (and political science) is probably more resistant to feminist argument than some other disciplines because of the character of the orthodox understanding of the subject matter of 'political' inquiry. The power of men over women is excluded from scrutiny and deemed irrelevant to political life and democracy by the patriarchal construction of the categories with which political theorists work. Not surprisingly, feminists and political theorists frequently talk past each other. Feminism does not, as is often supposed, merely add something to existing theories and modes of argument. Rather, feminism challenges the patriarchal construction of modern political theory, and to engage with feminist criticisms political theorists have to be willing to think again about fundamental premises of their arguments. The feminist challenge is particularly pressing in the case of radical democratic theory which argues for the active participation of all citizens, but has barely begun to acknowledge the problem of women's standing in a political order in which citizenship has been made in the male image.

Democratic theorists have not yet confronted the implications of the patriarchal construction of citizenship and so they provide little or no help in elucidating or solving the complex dilemma facing women. The two horns of Wollstonecraft's dilemma (as I label it in 'The Patriarchal Welfare State') are, first, that within the contemporary patriarchal order, and within the confines of the ostensibly universal categories of democratic theory, it is taken for granted that for women to be active, full citizens they must become (like) men. Second, although women have demanded for two centuries that their distinctive qualities and tasks should become part of citizenship – that is, that they should be citizens as women – their demand cannot be met when it is precisely these marks of womanhood that place women in opposition to, or, at best, in a paradoxical and contradictory relation to, citizenship. Women are expected to don the lion's skin, mane and all, or to take their place among, and indistinguishable from, the new men postulated in radical democratic theory. There is no set of clothes available for a citizen who is a woman, no vision available within political theory of the new democratic woman. Women have always been incorporated into the civil order as 'women', as subordinates or lesser men, and democratic theorists have not yet formulated any alternative. The dilemma remains. All that is clear is that if women are to be citizens as *women*, as autonomous, equal, yet sexually different beings from men, democratic theory and practice has to undergo a radical transformation.

The possibility of such a change is more open at the end of the twentieth century than ever before. Patriarchal institutions are less solid than they once were, familiar political arguments look increasingly inadequate in the face of current economic and political changes and feminists have turned the patriarchal separation of private and public into a political problem. But there are anti-democratic trends too, and there can be no confidence or certainty that the outcome will be one that feminists desire. Feminists face the added difficulty that the transformation they seek reaches into the meaning of 'masculinity' and 'femininity', into our very identities as embodied women and men. The changes sought so far by radical democratic theorists have proved very hard to accomplish; to transform personal and public relations between the sexes into genuinely consensual and mutual interaction is an even more enormous task. Nonetheless, the task has to be attempted if 'democracy' is not to remain the preserve of men. Feminist theory has an important part to play, but whether a new, genuinely democratic theory can develop within mainstream political theory remains to be seen.

NOTES

1 Strictly, this use of 'feminism' and 'feminist' is anachronistic. The terms were not used until the latter part of the nineteenth century; see K. Offen, 'Defining Feminism: A Comparative Historical Approach', *Signs*, 14 (1988), pp. 119–57. Anachronism is justified here. Many of the major problems and arguments now called 'feminist' were first raised 300 years ago, and if they are not named, they can more easily continue to be repressed and ignored.

2 I have discussed Hobbes's premise and his endorsement of men's patriarchal right in civil society in '"God Hath Ordained to Man a Helper": Hobbes, Patriarchy and Conjugal Right', in *Feminist Interpretations and Political Theory*, ed. M. Shanley and C. Pateman (Polity Press, Cambridge, forthcoming) and in *British Journal of Political Science* (October 1989).

3 M. Astell, *Some Reflections Upon Marriage* (Source Book Press, New York, 1970), (from 4th ed. of 1730), p. 107.

4 Of the recent books, only P. Green, *Retrieving Democracy: In Search of Civic Equality* (Rowman & Allenheld, Totowa, NJ, 1985), and D. Held, *Models of Democracy* (Polity Press, Cambridge, 1987) have acknowledged that feminism has something of importance to say about democratic theory.

5 For a detailed discussion, see C. Pateman, *The Sexual Contract* (Polity Press Cambridge, 1988; Stanford University Press, Stanford, CA, 1988).

6 See e.g. J. M. Elden, 'Political Efficacy at Work: The Connection between More Autonomous Forms of Workplace Organization and a More Participatory Politics', *American Political Science Review*, 75 (1981), pp. 43–58; E. S. Greenberg, *Workplace Democracy: The Political Effects of Participation* (Cornell University Press, Ithaca and London, 1986), especially chap. 5; E. S. Greenberg, 'Industrial Self-Management and Political Attitudes', *American Political Science Review*, 75 (1981), pp. 29–42; E. S. Greenberg, 'Industrial Democracy and the Democratic Citizen', *Journal of Politics*, 43 (1981), pp. 965–81; R. M. Mason, *Participatory and Workplace Democracy* (Southern Illinois University Press, Carbondale, 1982).

7 See, e.g., M. Porter, *Home, Work and Class Consciousness* (Manchester

University Press, Manchester, 1983); C. Cockburn, *Brothers: Male Dominance and Technological Change* (Pluto Press, London, 1983); J. Wajcman, *Women in Control: Dilemmas of a Worker's Cooperative* (St Martin's Press, New York, 1983); A. Pollert, *Girls, Wives and Factory Lives* (Macmillan, London, 1981); S. Walby, *Patriarchy at Work* (Polity Press, Cambridge, 1986).

8 The most recent example to come to hand is D. S. King and J. Waldron, 'Citizenship, Social Citizenship and the Defence of Welfare Provision', *British Journal of Political Science*, 18 (1988), pp. 415–43.

9 I mention this here to illustrate some of the peculiarities of women's position as citizens. I have said something more about this duty in my most recent paper, 'Women's Citizenship: Equality, Difference, Subordination', presented to the Conference on Equality and Difference Gender Dimensions in Political Thought, Justice and Morality, European University Institute, Florence, December 1988.

10 See, e.g., S. Estrich, *Real Rape* (Harvard University Press, Cambridge, MA, 1987); L. Kelly, *Surviving Sexual Violence* (Polity Press, Cambridge, 1988); D. Russell and N. Howell, 'The Prevalance of Rape in the United States Revisited', *Signs*, 8 (1983), pp. 688–95. On the use of evidence and women's credibility, see L. Bienen, 'A Question of Credibility: John Henry Wigmore's Use of Scientific Authority in Section 924a of *The Treatise on Evidence*', *Californian Western Law Review*, 19 (1983), pp. 235–86.

11 Report in *The Guardian*, 1 December 1988.

12 It is often argued that there is no problem about consent in the sex industry, since women enter prostitution etc. voluntarily, and freely grant access to their bodies, or put their bodies on display, in exchange for payment. As MacKinnon has commented, 'never mind that consent in sex . . . is supposed to mean freedom of desire expressed, not compensation for services rendered': C. A. MacKinnon, *Feminism Unmodified: Discourses on Life and Law* (Harvard University Press, Cambridge, MA, 1987) p. 11.

13 M. Walzer, *Spheres of Justice: A Defence of Pluralism and Equality* (Basic Books, New York, 1983), p. 304.

14 B. Barber, *Strong Democracy: Participatory Politics for a New Age* (University of California Press, Berkeley and Los Angeles, 1984) p. 193.

1

'The Disorder of Women': Women, Love, and the Sense of Justice

In his essay, *Politics and the Arts*, Rousseau proclaims that 'never has a people perished from an excess of wine; all perish from the disorder of women'. Rousseau states that drunkenness is usually the sole failing of otherwise upright, decent men; only the immoral fear the indiscretion that wine will promote. Drunkenness is not the worst of the vices since it makes men stupid rather than evil, and wine turns men away from the other vices so it poses no danger to the polity. In contrast, the 'disorder of women' engenders all the vices and can bring the state to ruin.[1]

Rousseau is not the only social or political theorist to regard women as a permanently subversive force within the political order. Freud (to whose arguments I shall also refer) argues in chapter 4 of *Civilization and Its Discontents* that women are 'hostile to' and 'in opposition to' civilization. In a similar vein, Hegel writes that the community 'creates its enemy for itself within its own gates' in 'womankind in general.' Women are 'the everlasting irony in the life of the community', and when 'women hold the helm of government, the state is at once in jeopardy'.[2] These arguments are by no means of only historical interest. Although women have now been granted citizenship in the liberal democracies, it is still widely believed that they are unfitted for political life and that it would be dangerous if the state were in their hands. This belief is very complex. One of its central dimensions, which I shall begin to explore in this paper, is the conviction that women lack, and cannot develop, a *sense of justice*.

The belief in the essential subversiveness of women[3] is of extremely ancient origin and is deeply embedded in our mythological and religious heritage. However, it is only in the modern world that 'the disorder of women' constitutes a general social and political problem. More specifically, it is only with the development of liberal individualism and the arguments of its democratic and socialist critics that beliefs about women become an acute, though not always acknowledged, problem in social and political theory and practice. In premodern conceptions of the world, animal and human life were seen as part of a divinely or 'naturally' ordered hierarchy of creation; individuals were conceived as born into a natural order of dominance and subordination. Nature and culture were part of a whole in which the hierarchy of social life was grounded in natural differences such as age, sex and strength. Rulers were those whose 'natural' characteristics fitted them for the task. From about the seventeenth century a new and revolutionary conception of social life developed within which the relationship between 'nature' and 'society', and between women and society, became inherently problematic.

Individuals began to be seen as rational beings, born free and equal to each other – or as naturally free and equal – and as individuals who create their social relationships and institutions for themselves. Political institutions, in particular, began to be seen as, properly, based on convention – on contract, consent and agreement. The conception of a conventionally grounded socio-political order brought with it a complex of problems concerning its relation to nature that, three centuries later, is still unresolved. The nature of the individuals who create and take their place within conventional or 'civil' associations is one of these problems. Do all individuals have the requisite nature or natural capacities? Or are there some who lack, or cannot develop, the capacities required for participation in civil life? If these individuals exist, their nature will appear as a threat to social life and there has been wide agreement that women are dangerous for this very reason. Women, by virtue of their natures, are a source of disorder in the state.

'Disorder' can be used in either of two basic senses: first, there is the socio-political sense of 'civil disorder' as in a rowdy demonstration, a tumultuous assembly, a riot, a breakdown of law and order. Second, 'disorder' is also used to refer to an internal malfunction of an individual, as when we speak of a disordered imagination or a disorder of the stomach or intestines. The term thus has application to the constitution of both the individual and the state. In addition, its moral content can also be made explicit when it is used to describe a 'disorderly house' in which decency and propriety are cast aside. Women, it is held, are a source of disorder because their being, or their nature, is such that it necessarily leads them to exert a disruptive influence in social and political life. Women have a disorder at their very centres – in their morality – which can bring about the destruction of the state. Women thus exemplify one of the ways in which nature and society stand opposed to each other. Moreover, the threat posed by women is exacerbated because of the place, or social sphere, for which they are fitted by their natures – the family.

Another of the problems thrown up by the individualist, conventionalist conception of social life is whether *all* social relations are conventional in character. The family is seemingly the most natural of all human associations and thus specially suited to women, who cannot transcend their natures in the manner demanded by civil forms of life. However, if the family is natural, then it is a form of association that stands in contrast to, and perhaps in conflict with, (conventional) social and political life. These two aspects of the problem of the disorder of women are revealed in the writings of the social contract theorists and especially in Rousseau's theory.

The social contract theorists set out the individualist and conventionalist conception of social life with particular clarity. Their arguments depend on, and thus illustrate, all the ambiguities and complexities inherent in the antinomy between nature and 'convention'. Popular contemporary beliefs about women, no less than seventeenth-century patriarchal arguments, rely on an appeal to nature and also on the fact that what is natural or 'ordered according to nature' is widely believed to be good and desirable.[4] The contract theorists appealed both to conceptions of individuals' natures and to the state of nature which natural individuals inhabited – but exactly in what form they inhabited it, and what kind of relationships existed between them, is one of the key questions in the contract story.

Rousseau's version of contract theory highlights the problems in an acute form. He was the only contract theorist willing to pursue the revolutionary implications inherent in the doctrine, but he also believed that women posed a permanent threat to political order. Rousseau's theory contains some profound sociological insights precisely because he was concerned with the interrelations of different dimensions of social life and with transformations of human consciousness. In the *Discourse on Inequality* he attacks the abstract individualism of the liberal contract theorists who postulated a familiar yet natural condition original to humanity. Rousseau argues that, strictly, a natural state is asocial, inhabited only by animals of various kinds, one species of which has the potential to develop into human individuals. That is to say, Rousseau denies that one can draw political conclusions from assertions about the natural characteristics of isolated individuals or individuals seen severally, not collectively. His basic premise is that human life is social life, or sociality is natural to humans. According to Rousseau, and here he agrees with Locke, the social state of nature is inhabited not by (isolated) individuals but by families. He writes that 'the oldest of all societies, and the only natural one, is that of the family'.[5] This is another way of saying that the family precedes, or can exist in the absence of, wider social institutions or 'civil society'; it exists in the natural condition. The family is also grounded in the natural ties of love and affection (which are natural because they are within human capacities as, say, flying is not) and it has its origin in the biological process of procreation, in the natural difference between the sexes. Rousseau argues that the family provides us with a major example of a social institution that follows the order of nature because, in the family, age naturally takes precedence over youth and males are naturally in authority over females. For Rousseau, the family is necessarily patriarchal.

The state of nature stands in contrast to civil society, but the family is common to both forms of existence. The family spans the divide between a condition grounded in nature and the conventional bonds of civil life. Few social and political theorists, with the notable exception of Hobbes,[6] have been willing to present the family as a conventional association. Indeed, in the *Philosophy of Right*, Hegel claims that it is 'shameful' to see marriage and the family as merely contractual associations. The family is widely regarded as the natural basis of civil life. Familial, or domestic, relations are based on the natural ties of biology and sentiment, and the family is constituted by the particularistic bonds of an organic unity. However, the status of the family as the foundation of civil society means that the contrast between the different forms of social life in 'the state of nature' and 'civil society' is carried over into civil life itself. The distinction between and separation of the private and public, or particularistic and universal, spheres of association is a fundamental structural principle of the modern, liberal conception of social life. The natural, particularistic family nestles at the centre of the private sphere, and it throws into prominence and stands opposed to the impersonal, universal, 'conventional' bonds of public life.

Rawls has recently stated that 'justice is the first virtue of social institutions'.[7] Similarly, Freud argues that 'the first requisite of civilization, . . . is that of justice – that is, the assurance that a law once made will not be broken in favour of an individual'.[8] But justice is not the virtue of *all* social institutions. As the preceding discussion suggests, and as Freud (and Hegel) tell us, it is love, not justice, that is the first virtue of the family. The family is a naturally social, not a conventionally social, institution, but justice is a public or conventional virtue. In the family, individuals appear as unique and unequal personalities and as members of a differentiated unity grounded in sentiment. In civil life individuals transcend, or leave behind, the particular and ascribed characteristics which distinguish them in the private sphere and appear as unrelated equals. They enter the sphere of individualism – which is also universalism – as bearers of rights (liberties), as owners of property and as citizens. In a civil association, individuals are bound together and their actions are regulated solely by general or universal rules and laws that apply impartially to all. The rules and laws protect the rights and property of all individuals – providing that all do their share to uphold the rules, that is to say, to maintain justice. Particular or private interests of individuals must be subordinated to the public interest, or to the virtue of justice.

Individuals will more readily uphold the rules of civil association if they develop a sense of justice or a morality of order. Individuals must 'internalize' the universal rules of the socio-political order, understand that they ought to be observed and wish to act accordingly. The sense of justice is fundamental to the maintenance of public order. However, if individuals exist who, like women – according to Rousseau and Freud – are naturally incapable of developing a sense of justice, the basis of civil association is threatened; it contains within itself a permanent source of disorder. The threat is all the greater because the natural morality, or deficiency in moral capacity, of women fits them only for the 'natural society' of domestic life. But the family itself is a threat to civil life. Love and justice are antagonistic virtues; the demands of love and of family bonds are particularistic and so in direct conflict with justice which demands that private interest is subordinated to the public (universal) good. The family is thus simultaneously the foundation of the state and antagonistic to it. Moreover, the presence within it of women who have no sense of justice – and whose natures prevent them from leaving the domestic sphere – can only work against and weaken the sense of justice of their male kin who must uphold justice in civil life. 'Womankind', Hegel states, 'perverts the universal property of the state into a possession and ornament for the family'.[9]

Rousseau and Freud offer a remarkably similar diagnosis of why women are incapable of developing a sense of justice. Both agree that, for women, anatomy is destiny. The biological (natural) differences between the sexes influence and are reflected in their respective moral characters. Rousseau argues that the source of the disorder of women lies in their boundless sexual passion. Women, he claims, foreshadowing Freud, are unable to subdue and sublimate their sexual desires in the same manner, or to the same extent, as men. Men are the active and aggressive sex and are 'controlled by nature'; passive and defensive women have only the control of modesty. There must therefore be a double standard of sexual conduct. If both sexes gave equal rein to their passions 'the men . . . would at last become [the women's] victims, and would be dragged to their death without the least chance of escape'.[10] Modesty is natural to women, but it provides a weak and uncertain control of their sexual desires. Moreover, as Rousseau argues in *Politics and the Arts*: 'even if it could be denied that a special sentiment of chasteness was natural to women, would it be any the less true that in society . . . they ought to be raised in principles appropriate to it? If the timidity, chasteness, and modesty which are proper to them are social inventions, it is in society's interest that women acquire these qualities. . . .'[11] However, even an education specifically designed to foster modesty is not sufficient guarantee against the disorderliness of women. Rousseau spells out this lesson in graphic fashion in *La Nouvelle Héloise*. Julie desires nothing more than to be virtuous and lead an exemplary life as a wife and mother, but she is unable, despite all her efforts and apparent success in passing through the trials set for her by Wolmar, to overcome her passion for Saint Preux. If the good order of Clarens is not to be fatally disrupted, Julie must take the one course left to her; the only solution to the problem of the disorder of women is her 'accidental' death.

Rousseau and Freud argue that this fundamental difference between the sexes has existed since the very beginning of social life and, indeed, has structured it. Both claim that the creation of civil society, or 'civilization', is the work of men. For Rousseau the sexes are equal only when isolated from each other among the animals in the true (asocial) natural condition. Social life develops as family life, and while charting its emergence Rousseau suddenly announces that 'the first difference was established in the way of life of the two sexes, . . . women . . . grew accustomed to tend the hut and the children'.[12] His conjectural history of the development of civil society and the transformation of human nature then continues as a history of male activity and male nature. Freud also presents a conjectural history of the development of civil society (civilization) in *Civilization and Its Discontents*. He argues that once 'the need for genital satisfaction no longer made its appearance like a guest who drops in suddenly',[13] males had a reason for keeping females close at hand and the latter, in their turn, were obliged to comply in order to care for their helpless young. Once the family was established, the development of civilization was the work of men alone because it requires the 'instinctual sublimations of which women are little capable'. Only men are capable of sublimating their passions and thus capable of the justice that civil life demands. Furthermore, men's involvement in public life, and their consequent dependence on other men, means that they have little energy left for their wives and families: 'thus the woman finds herself forced into the background by the claims of civilization, and she adopts a hostile attitude towards it'.[14]

No explanation was available of why women are less able than men to sublimate their passions, or how the 'special stamp to the character of females as social beings'[15] comes about until Freud formulated his psychoanalytic theory. Rousseau can only tell us that men and women differ in this respect – and he prescribes an education for girls that will reinforce their disorderly natures and indifference to justice. Women are 'naturally' made to be 'at the mercy of man's judgement' and 'to endure even injustice at his hands'.[16] (Hegel, it might be noted, was content to leave women in their natural state; women, he says with resignation, are 'educated – who knows how? – as it were by breathing in ideas, by living. . . .')[17] Freud argues that the explanation for women's lack of, or deficiency in, a sense of justice is the differential passage of the two sexes through the Oedipus complex and a consequent difference in the development of their super-egos. The super-ego is the 'representative for us of every moral restriction'[18] and, especially, of the restrictions that justice demands.

Civilization is the work of men in the most profound sense, for it is men alone who possess a fully developed super-ego. The emergence of the super-ego is bound up with (the conjectural history of) the 'original' momentous move from the family to wider communal life. Freud argues that 'originally' the 'first' sons killed the 'first' father, whom they simultaneously loved and hated. Out of the awful act of hatred, remorse and guilt grew from their love, and their subsequent identification with their dead father led to the emergence of the super-ego. The brothers, Freud argues, imposed on each other the mutual restrictions necessary to prevent a repetition of their dreadful deed. Thus the public virtue of justice, or 'the first "right" or "law"' necessary for civil life, was established – by men; women had no part in this development.[19] In our own time the different manner in which little boys and girls pass through the Oedipus complex harks back to the purely masculine 'origin' of justice, political right and the super-ego.

Little boys have a dramatic passage through the Oedipus complex. The threat of castration, the force of which is confirmed when the boy sees the 'castrated' female genitals, impels him to identify with his father, and so the Oedipus complex is 'literally smashed to pieces'.[20] The super-ego, which is 'heir' to the Oedipus complex, then begins its development. The little boy 'assimilates' his father's ego to his own and thereby internalizes all the restraints embodied in the paternal agency. Thus the male infant becomes a moral individual, in due course a 'man', since the creation of the super-ego initiates him into 'all the processes that are designed to make the individual find a place in the cultural community'.[21] For females, however, the process is quite different. Females are already 'castrated' and when they make this terrible discovery by comparing themselves with little boys, their Oedipus complex is created, not destroyed. It is a long and difficult journey through which the little girl comes to take her father as her object – in fact, she may never surmount the Oedipus complex. The result is that women lack or, at best, have a much weaker super-ego than men. Freud writes that 'for women the level of what is ethically normal is different from what it is in men. Their super-ego is never so inexorable, so impersonal, so independent of its emotional origins as we require it to be in men. . . . They show less sense of justice than men, . . . they are less ready to submit to the great exigencies of life, . . . they are more often influenced in their judgements by feelings of affection or hostility. . . .'[22]

Freud argues that the creation and dissolution of the Oedipus complex is a universal feature of human existence. The difference in moral capacity between the sexes must, therefore, be accepted. In Rousseau's terms, it is a social reflection of the order of nature. Freud emphasizes the costs of creating civilization,[23] but he has no suggestions for containing the disorderliness of women. Rousseau, however, concludes that the only way in which the state can be protected from the impact of women is through strict segregation of the sexes in their activities, including, as at Clarens, in domestic life. Sexual separation is necessary because even modest (good) women are a corrupting influence on men. Their disorder leads them always to pull men away from civic virtue and to mock at justice. But segregation is only a preventive measure; it does nothing to cure the disorder of women.

This is shown when the separation of the sexes is taken to its logical limit – the seraglio. The seraglio appears to be a secure 'asylum against the onslaughts of vice', and the one place where a woman can 'be sure about [herself], where there are no dangers to fear.'[24] Nevertheless, as Usbek discovers, disorder can break out even in the seraglio. In La Nouvelle Héloise, the presence of Wolmar, who epitomizes the qualities of a wise man with a highly developed sense of justice, is not enough to protect Clarens. Julie states that Wolmar never violates 'conjugal solemnity', and that even his passion for her is of a kind in which he 'loves only as much as he wishes to and . . . he wishes to only as much as reason permits.'[25] Yet Julie's passion triumphs over Wolmar's justice. Neither the seraglio nor Clarens can provide a true asylum or substitute for a weak super-ego and natural lack of capacity for sublimation. In any social context 'the life of a good woman is a perpetual struggle against self.'[26] Julie says everything when she writes on her death-bed that 'I dare pride myself in the past, but who might have been able to answer for my future? One day more, perhaps, and I might be guilty!'[27]

Rousseau presents us with many insights into the problem of the disorder of women. However, he is, very surprisingly, far less aware of the problem posed by the family. Rousseau's political theory highlights the conflict between the private interests of sectional associations and the general will (or principles of justice) that governs the political order. However, he fails to see that the family, too, is a sectional association that threatens justice. Rousseau pictures the family, the little commonwealth with the father at its head, as the foundation of the state: 'Will the bonds of convention hold firm without some foundation in nature? Can devotion to the state exist apart from the love of those near and dear to us? Can patriotism thrive except in the soil of that miniature fatherland, the home? Is it not the good son, the good husband, the good father, who makes the good citizen?'[28] Perhaps – if the father's sense of justice is strong enough to override his love for his family, his desire to protect its interests and the baleful influence of his wife. Freud argues that the conflict between love, whether sensual or 'aim-inhibited', and public life cannot be avoided: 'love comes into opposition to the interests of civilization; . . . civilization threatens love with substantial restrictions'. The more closely that family members are attached to each other, the harder it is for them to enter into public life.[29] Freud might have added that the more diligently husbands and fathers work for the interests of their families, the more likely it is that they will put those interests before the requirements of justice. There can be no easy reconciliation of the virtues of love and justice.

Paradoxically, because the family is the 'foundation' of social life in the sense that it is the point of 'procreative origin'[30] of society and because it stands directly at the border with nature, women are seen as guardians of order and morality as well as inherently subversive. It is women who reproduce and have the major responsibility for educating the next generation; it is the mother who turns asocial, bisexual babies into little 'boys' and 'girls'. Rousseau glorifies women's task as mothers. He was one of the first writers to emphasize the moral implications of breast-feeding, and he is careful to stress, for example, that when Julie constructs her natural garden retreat she does not allow the work to interfere with her duties as a mother. (However, it should be noted that the mother's task is completed in the early years; a male tutor takes over from her.) Women's guardianship of order reaches beyond motherhood. Within the shelter of domestic life women impose an order, a social pattern, and thus give meaning to the natural world of birth and death and other physical processes, of dirt and raw materials, that is integral to domestic life. Women are direct mediators between nature and society. However, because women face nature directly, and because, in giving birth and in their other bodily functions, they appear as part of nature, they exemplify the ambiguous status of the family as both natural and social.[31] Women impose order and foster morality; but they are also in daily contact with dirt and with natural processes only partly under our control. They cannot escape being tainted by this contact or completely transcend the naturalness of their own being. Hence they represent both order and disorder, both morality and boundless passion.

It is worth remarking here that one way in which women (and their male kin and keepers) attempt to hide this contact with nature, their own natural functions, and hence their potential for disorder, is through cleanliness – presented as purity. In the *Persian Letters*, the chief eunuch stresses to Usbek that he has always been trained to keep the women in the seraglio 'absolutely clean . . . and [to take] an infinite amount of care over it'.[32] Rousseau proclaims that 'nothing could be more revolting than a dirty woman, and a husband who tires of her is not to blame'. Emile will never find this fault in Sophy: 'things are never clean enough for her. . . . She has always disliked inspecting the kitchen-garden . . . the soil is dirty, . . . absolute cleanliness . . . has become a habit, till it absorbs one half of her time and controls the other; so that she thinks less of how to do a thing than of how to do it without getting dirty. . . . Sophy is more than clean, she is pure'.[33]

The profound insights into the contradictions and antagonisms in the dialectic between individuals and their social relations, and between the family and civil society, to be found in the work of thinkers of the stature of Rousseau and Freud, are sadly neglected (or not even recognized) in most contemporary work on the subject of justice and in much feminist writing. In part, this reflects the consolidation of liberal theory over three centuries as the ideology of the liberal capitalist state, centred on the separation of the political and private spheres. The problems which appear explictly at the origins of liberal theory in the arguments of the social contract theorists and their critics are now either ignored or regarded as unproblematic. In particular, the tension between nature and convention or love and justice is continually glossed over or suppressed.

Early liberal feminist writers such as Mary Wollstonecraft and John Stuart Mill, for example, who agree that women lack a sense of justice, offer a much more superficial diagnosis of the problem than Rousseau (though that is not to underestimate their achievement). They see it primarily as a matter of extending the liberal principles of freedom, equality and rationality to women through a process of education. In the *Vindication*, Wollstonecraft appeals for the 'rights of men and citizens' to be extended to both sexes; reason has no sex. It appears that the virtues are sexually differentiated because women have been turned into 'artificial' creatures. Their education (or, more accurately, lack of it) enforces their dependence on men and makes them mean and selfish, narrowing the range of their concerns to exclude the wider community so that they cannot develop a sense of justice. Similarly, in *The Subjection of Women*, Mill argues that we cannot say that women are 'naturally' fit only for subordination because we know nothing of what they might become if the principles of freedom and equality, now governing the rest of our social institutions, were extended to sexual relations. Mill argues that individuals develop a sense of justice through participation in as wide a range of public institutions as possible; confined to the family – which the law allows to be a 'school of despotism' – women can never learn to weigh the public interest against selfish inclination.

The obvious problem with Mill's and Wollstonecraft's arguments is that although they both advocate a proper education for women and a widening of opportunities to enable them to be economically independent of men, they also assume that the opportunities will be largely irrelevant for the majority of women. Most women will continue working within the home since child-rearing will remain their major responsibility. But this means that, despite legal and educational reforms, men's moral understanding will continue to be more highly developed than women's. Women will not obtain within the family the breadth of social experience and practical education that will develop their sense of justice and allow them, with safety, to participate in political life. The problem of the disorder of women, while mitigated by education, remains unresolved. These feminist arguments assume that the family can become the bedrock on which the liberal state is raised, but they also contain a hint that love and justice can conflict. Mill implies that education is the answer here too; educated persons of both sexes should be able to control and subdue their 'lower' passions.[34] Wollstonecraft contrasts love, that is, sexual passion, with friendship and mutual respect between equals, and she argues that the latter is the only true basis for marriage and family life. Rousseau, also, thought it 'an error' to see sexual passion as the basis of domestic life (he makes it clear that Saint Preux, Julie's lover, would not make a good husband). He claims that: 'people do not marry in order to think exclusively of each other, but in order to fulfill the duties of civil society jointly, to govern the house prudently, to rear their children well. Lovers never see anyone but themselves, they incessantly attend only to themselves, and the only thing they are able to do is love each other.'[35]

However, given Rousseau's conception of women's nature and his plan for their education, it is impossible that marriage could be placed on this footing – as he shows clearly enough in his story of Wolmar's virtue and Julie's love. To state that sexual attraction is not the proper foundation for marriage solves nothing if it is also believed that women are naturally creatures governed wholly by their sexual passions. More generally, the liberal feminists' recognition that the relationship between the sexes contradicts basic liberal principles and their proposals for social reforms fail to get to the heart of the problem of the disorder of women. Their argument is undercut by the acceptance of the separation of domestic from civil life, which is also a sexual separation; women and love are irrevocably set in opposition to justice. Liberal theory presupposes the opposition between nature and convention but the opposition can be neither admitted nor its implications pursued. The account of the development of the sense of justice in Rawls's extremely influential *A*

Theory of Justice shows how liberal theorists consistently obscure one of the major problems in their arguments.

Rawls states that he has drawn on both Rousseau and Freud, but he gives no indication that he has appreciated the relevance of their insights into sexual relationships for the question of justice. Rawls presents an apparently sexually undifferentiated account; arguing that 'our moral understanding increases as we move in the course of life through a sequence of positions'.[36] The sense of justice develops in three stages; first, the child learns the 'morality of order' from its parents. Then the 'morality of association', a morality characterized by the cooperative virtues of justice and impartiality, is developed when the individual occupies a variety of roles in a range of institutions. Finally, we reach the stage of the 'morality of principles' in which we understand the fundamental role of justice in the social order and we wish to uphold it; the sense of justice is attained. Now this account, of course, has the same obvious failing as the liberal feminist arguments – only if men *and* women can move 'through a sequence of positions' will both sexes develop the sense of justice. Rawls, not surprisingly, rejects cries to 'abolish the family', but he has nothing to say about the sexual division of labour or the conviction that domestic life is the proper sphere for women. On the contrary, he remarks that if a publicly recognized concept of justice regulates social life it will 'reconcile us to the dispositions of the natural order'.[37] And what is more natural, or in accordance with the order of nature, than the division of social life and its virtues between the sexes: conventional political life and justice belong to men; domestic life and love belong to women?

One reaction from the feminist movement to the problems sketched in this chapter has been a call for the last vestiges of nature to be swept away. In the *Dialectics of Sex*, Firestone claims that the problem of women and nature can be solved through artificial reproduction which will allow all relationships, including those between adults and children, to be based on convention or to be freely chosen. However, this is to argue that the whole of social life could be fashioned in the image of a philosophically and sociologically incoherent abstract, possessive individualism. It is a 'solution' based on a continuing opposition between nature and society rather than an attempt to recreate this relationship. Another feminist response to claims about the disorder of women has been to argue that, since 'justice' is the work of men and an aspect of the domination of women, women should reject it totally and remake their lives on the basis of love, sentiment and personal relations. But this no more solves the problem than a declaration of war on nature; neither position breaks with liberal conceptions or can take account of the dialectic between individual and social life, between the particular or personal and the universal or political. To attempt technologically to banish nature or to deny that justice has any relevance is to try to wish away fundamental dimensions of human life. Rather, the extraordinarily difficult and complex task must be undertaken of developing a critique of the liberal and patriarchal conception of the relation between nature and convention that will also provide the foundation for a theory of a democratic, sexually egalitarian practice.

The insights and failings of the theorists discussed in this chapter provide one starting point for such a critique. I have concentrated on 'love', that is to say, sexual passion. However, one of the most urgent tasks is to provide an alternative to the liberal view of justice, that assumes that 'a' sense of justice presently exists, developed through the smooth passage of all individuals through social institutions. This claim rests on the uncritical acceptance that the structure of liberal capitalist institutions allows both men and women, working class and middle-class, to develop in the same fashion. It ignores the reality of institutions in which the subordination of women and the 'despotic organization of production'[38] are seen as natural. Rousseau's critique of abstract individualism and the liberal theory of the state can assist in building a critical theory, just as his many insights into the relationship between sexual and political life, disentangled from his patriarchalism, are essential to a critical theory of the relation between love and justice. Similarly, Freud's psychoanalytic theory is indispensable, but must be used carefully as part of an account of the historical development of civil society – which includes a specific form of domestic association and 'masculine' and 'feminine' sexuality – and not, as Freud presents it, as an abstract theory of the 'individual' and 'civilization'.[39] This project may sound daunting, even completely overwhelming. Yet once the problem of the disorder of women begins to be seen as a question of social life, not as a fact that confronts us in nature, the reality of the structure of our personal and political lives is beginning to be revealed within the appearance presented in liberal and patriarchal ideology, and the task has already begun.

NOTES

1 J.-J. Rousseau, *Politics and the Arts: A Letter to M. D'Alembert on the Theatre*, tr. A. Bloom (Cornell University Press, Ithaca, NY, 1968), p. 109. Rousseau also notes that wine attracts old men because youth have other desires; beliefs about the subversiveness of youth are outside the scope of this paper.

2 G. W. F. Hegel, *The Phenomenology of Mind*, tr. J. B. Bailie (Allen & Unwin, London, 1949), p. 496; *Philosophy of Right*, tr. T. M. Knox (Oxford University Press, Oxford, 1952), addition to par. 166. N. O. Keohane ('Female Citizenship: "The Monstrous Regiment of

Women"') (paper presented at the annual meeting of the Conference for the Study of Political Thought, New York, 6–8 April 1979) discusses various aspects of the belief that women should not enter the political sphere, with particular reference to ancient Greece and Bodin's theory.

3 Women have also been perceived from ancient times as guardians of morality and order. This contradictory view is briefly discussed below, but it should be noted that the two conceptions of women are not straightforwardly opposed to each other. The 'morality' and 'order' represented by women is not the same as the 'order' of the political sphere.

4 But compare Nietzsche: 'You desire to *live* "according to Nature"? Oh, . . . what fraud of words! Imagine to yourselves a being like Nature, boundlessly extravagant, boundlessly indifferent, without purpose or consideration, without pity or justice, at once fruitful and barren and uncertain: imagine to yourselves *indifference* as a power – how *could* you live in accordance with such indifference?' (F. Nietzsche, *The Complete Works*, ed. O. Levy (Foulis, London, 1911), vol. 12, *Beyond Good and Evil*, tr. H. Zimmer, chap. 1, par. 9). The same ambiguities and contradictions in our perception of women also surround 'nature'. Social life can, for example, be regarded as properly a reflection of the harmony in nature or the 'order of nature'; alternatively, nature can be seen as the sphere of the uncontrolled, the arbitrary, the capricious, the indifferent that must be transcended in social life. A discussion of various meanings attributed to 'natural' in relation to women can be found in C. Pierce, 'Natural Law Language and Women', in *Women in Sexist Society*, ed. V. Gornick and B. K. Moran (Basic Books, New York, 1971).

5 J.-J. Rousseau, *The Social Contract*, tr. M. Cranston (Penguin Books, Harmondsworth, Middlesex, 1968), bk 1, p. 50.

6 Hobbes's view of the family is discussed in T. Brennan and C. Pateman, '"Mere Auxiliaries to the Commonwealth": Women and the Origins of Liberalism', *Political Studies* 27 (1979), pp. 183–200.

7 J. Rawls, *A Theory of Justice* (Oxford University Press, Oxford, 1971), p. 3.

8 S. Freud, 'Civilization and Its Discontents', in *The Standard Edition of the Complete Psychological Works*, tr. J. Strachey (Hogarth Press, London, 1961), vol. 21, p. 95.

9 Hegel, *The Phenomenology of Mind*, p. 496.

10 J.-J. Rousseau, *Emile*, tr. B. Foxley (Dent, London 1911), p. 322.

11 Rousseau, *Politics and the Arts*, p. 87.

12 J.-J. Rousseau, 'Discourse on the Origin and Foundations of Inequality', in *The First and Second Discourses*, tr. R. D. Masters (St Martin's Press, New York, 1964), p. 147. The speculations of classic theorists about the 'natural condition' and 'the origin of society' should be compared with the speculations of scientists studying

animal life. See the fascinating discussion by D. Haraway, 'Animal Sociology and a Natural Economy of the Body Politic, Part II: The Past Is the Contested Zone: Human Nature and Theories of Production and Reproduction in Primate Behavior Studies', *Signs*, 4 (1978), pp. 37–60.

13 Freud, 'Civilization and Its Discontents', p. 99.

14 Ibid., pp. 103–4.

15 S. Freud, 'Female Sexuality', in *On Sexuality*, ed. A. Richards, (Penguin Freud Library, Harmondsworth, Middlesex, 1977), vol. 7, p. 377.

16 Rousseau, *Emile*, pp. 328, 359.

17 Hegel, *Philosophy of Right*, addition to par. 166.

18 S. Freud, 'The Dissection of the Psychical Personality', in *New Introductory Lectures on Psychoanalysis*, ed, J. Strachey (Penguin Freud Library, Harmondsworth, Middlesex, 1973), vol. 2, p. 98.

19 Freud, 'Civilization and Its Discontents', pp. 101, 131–2.

20 Freud, 'Some Psychical Consequences of the Anatomical Distinction between the Sexes', in Richards, ed., vol. 7, p. 341.

21 Freud, 'Female Sexuality', p. 375.

22 Freud, 'Some Psychical Consequences of the Anatomical Distinction between the Sexes', vol. 7, p. 342.

23 Cf, 'Society cannot be formed or maintained without our being required to make perpetual and costly sacrifices. Because society surpasses us, it obliges us to surpass ourselves, and to surpass itself, a being must, to some degree, depart from its nature.' (E. Durkheim, 'The Dualism of Human Nature and Its Social Conditions', *Essays on Sociology and Philosophy*, ed. K. H. Wolff (Harper & Row, New York, 1964), p. 338).

24 Montesquieu, *Persian Letters*, tr. C.J. Betts (Penguin Books, Harmondsworth Middlesex, 1973), letter 20, p. 68; letter 26, p. 76.,

25 J.-J. Rousseau, *La Nouvelle Héloise*, tr. J. H. McDowell (Pennsylvania State University Press, University Park, 1968), pt 2, letter 20, p. 260.

26 Rousseau, *Emile*, p. 332.

27 Rousseau, *La Nouvelle Héloise*, pt 4, letter 12, p. 405.

28 Rousseau, *Emile*, p. 326. I was first alerted to this point by the excellent discussion of Rousseau in S. Okin, *Women in Western Political Thought* (Princeton University Press, Princeton, NJ, 1980).

29 Freud, 'Civilization and Its Discontents', pp. 102–3.

30 I am indebted for the phrase to A. Yeatman's unpublished paper, 'Gender Ascription and the Conditions of Its Breakdown: The Rationalization of the 'Domestic Sphere' and the Nineteenth-Century "Cult of Domesticity"'.

31 On these points see M. Douglas, *Purity and Danger* (Penguin Books, Harmondsworth, Middlesex, 1970); S. B. Ortner, 'Is Female to Male as Nature Is to Culture?', in *Women, Culture and Society*, ed. M. Rosaldo and L. Lamphere (Stanford University Press, Stanford, CA, 1974); and L. Davidoff, 'The Rationalization of Housework', in

Dependence and Exploitation in Work and Marriage, ed. D. L. Barker and S. Allen, (Longmans, London, 1976). (On purity, see also Ortner's suggestive sketch 'The Virgin and the State', *Feminist Studies*, 8 (1978), pp. 19–36.)

32 Montesquieu, letter 64, p. 131.
33 Rousseau, *Emile*, pp. 357–8.
34 Victorian arguments about women's lack of sexual feeling, while oppressive, could also be used to women's advantage. There is an excellent discussion of this area in N. F. Cott, 'Passionlessness: an Interpretation of Victorian Sexual Ideology, 1790–1850', *Signs*, 4 (1978), pp. 219–36.
35 Rousseau, *La Nouvelle Héloise*, pt 3, letter 30, pp. 261–2.
36 Rawls, p. 468. The discussion here draws generally on secs. 70–2.
37 Ibid., p. 512.
38 The phrase is taken from B. Clark and H. Gintis, 'Rawlsian Justice and Economic Systems', *Philosophy and Public Affairs*, 4 (1978), pp. 302–25. This essay forms part of the 'left' critique of Rawls which, so far, has largely ignored the sexual (in contrast to the class) dimension of subordination and its relevance for justice.
39 See M. Poster, *Critical Theory of the Family* (Pluto Press, London, 1978), chap. 1 (though women are relegated to a footnote); and 'Freud's Concept of the Family', *Telos*, 30 (1976), pp. 93–115.

2

The Fraternal Social Contract

The sons form a conspiracy to overthrow the despot, and in the end substitute a social contract with equal rights for all . . . Liberty means equality among the brothers (sons) . . . Locke suggests that the fraternity is formed not by birth but by election, by contract . . . Rousseau would say it is based on will.

Norman O. Brown, *Love's Body*

The stories of the origins of civil society found in the classic social contract theories of the seventeenth and eighteenth centuries have been repeated many times. More recently, John Rawls and his followers have given new lease of life to the story of the contract that generates political right. But in all the telling of the tales, and in the discussion and argument about the social contract, we are told only half the story. Political theorists present the familiar account of the creation of civil society as a universal realm that (at least potentially) includes everyone and of the origins of political right in the sense of the authority of government in the liberal state, or Rousseau's participatory polity. But this is not the 'original' political right. There is silence about the part of the story which reveals that the social contract is a fraternal pact that constitutes civil society as a patriarchal or masculine order. To uncover the latter, it is necessary to begin to tell the repressed story of the genesis of patriarchal political right which men exercise over women.

Most discussions of contract theory accept uncritically the claim that the stories successfully show why the authority of the state is legitimate; but the critical failure to recognize the social contract as fraternal pact is of a different kind. Only half the story appears in commentaries on the classic texts or in contemporary Rawlsian arguments, because modern political theory is so thoroughly patriarchal that one aspect of its origins lies outside the analytical reach of most theorists. Political theorists argue about the individual, and take it for granted that their subject matter concerns the public world, without investigating the way in which the 'individual', 'civil society' and 'the public' have been constituted as patriarchal categories in opposition to womanly nature and the 'private' sphere. The civil body politic created through the fraternal social contract is fashioned after only one of the two bodies of humankind.

The patriarchal character of civil society is quite explicit in the classic texts – if they are read from a feminist perspective. In this chapter, I can draw attention to only a few of the implications of such a reading and to some of most obvious omissions in standard discussions of contract theory.[1] For instance, civil society is public society, but it is not usually appreciated that feminist arguments refer to a different sense of the separation of 'public' and 'private' from that typically found in discussions of civil society.

The meaning of 'civil society' in the contract stories, and as I am using it here, is constituted through the 'original' separation and opposition between the modern, public – civil – world and the modern, private or conjugal and familial sphere: that is, in the new social world created through contract, everything that lies beyond the domestic (private) sphere is public, or 'civil', society. Feminists are concerned with *this* division. In contrast, most discussions of civil society and such formulations as 'public' regulation versus 'private' enterprise presuppose that the politically relevant separation between public and private is drawn *within* 'civil society' as constructed in the social contract stories. That is to say, 'civil society' has come to be used in a meaning closer to that of Hegel, the social contract theorists' greatest critic, who contrasts the universal, public state with the market, classes and corporations of private, civil society.

Hegel, of course, presents a threefold division between family, civil society, state – but the separation between the family and the rest of social life is invariably 'forgotten' in arguments about civil society. The shift in meaning of 'civil', 'public' and 'private' goes unnoticed because the 'original' creation of civil society through the social contract is a patriarchal construction which is also a separation of the sexes. Political theorists have repressed this part of the story from their theoretical consciousness – though it is implicit in the assumption that civil life requires a natural foundation – and thus liberals and (non-feminist) radicals alike deal only with the liberal understanding of civil society, in which 'civil' life becomes private in opposition to the public state.

Perhaps the most striking feature of accounts of the contract story is the lack of attention paid to fraternity, when liberty and equality are so much discussed. One reason for the neglect is that most discussions pass over the insights about fraternity found in Freud's versions of the contract story. Fraternity is central to socialism, and nineteenth- and twentieth-century liberalism, as a recent study has shown, relies heavily on fraternity as a crucial bond integrating individual and community. However, discussions of fraternity do not touch upon the constitution of the 'individual' through the patriarchal separation of private and public, nor upon how the division within the (masculine) 'individual' includes an opposition between fraternity and reason. Fraternity comes to the fore in liberals' attempts to formulate a more sociologically adequate account of the individual than is found in the abstract conceptions of classic liberal contract theory. But for feminists explicit recourse to liberal or socialist fraternal bonds merely exposes the patriarchal character of ostensibly universal categories and calls attention to the fundamental problem of whether and how women could be fully incorporated into a patriarchal civil world.

A feminist reading of the contract stories is also important for another reason. The contemporary feminist movement has brought the idea of patriarchy into popular and academic currency, but confusion abounds about its meaning and implications and recently some feminists have argued that the term is best avoided. 'Patriarchy' is, to my knowledge, the only term with which to capture the specificities of the subjection and oppression of *women* and to distinguish this from other forms of domination. If we abandon the concept of patriarchy, the problem of the subjection of women and sexual domination will again vanish from view within individualist and class theories. The crucial question, therefore, is the sense in which it can be said that our own society is patriarchal.

Two popular feminist claims about patriarchy add to the confusion. The first is that the literal meaning of 'patriarchy', rule by fathers, is still relevant. To insist that patriarchy is nothing more than paternal rule is itself a patriarchal interpretation, as an examination of the classic texts reveals. The second claim is that patriarchy is a timeless, human universal, which obviously rules out the possibility that men's domination of women takes different forms in different historical periods and cultures. More precisely, neither claim about patriarchy can acknowledge that our own momentous transition from the traditional to the modern world – a transition which the contract stories encapsulate theoretically – involved a change from a traditional (paternal) form of patriarchy to a new *specifically modern* (or fraternal) form: patriarchal civil society.

Few of the participants in recent feminist debates about patriarchy seem aware of the significance of patriarchal political theory in the classic sense: that is, the patriarchalism of Sir Robert Filmer and other less well-known writers of three centuries ago. Nor have they taken account of the theoretical and practical significance of the battle waged between the patriarchalists and the social contract theorists. Zillah Eisenstein has done so, but on the other hand Jean Elshtain's references to patriarchal theory merely reiterate the standard view in political theory that patriarchalism had suffered a fatal defeat by the end of the seventeenth century.[2] This is far from the case, and an understanding of the exact sense in which, and the limits within which, the contract theorists emerged victorious over the patriarchalists is central to an appreciation of how a specifically modern form of patriarchy was brought into being.

Patriarchal political theory had little in common with the ancient tradition of patriarchalism that took the family as the general model for social order and made claims about the emergence of political society from the family, or the coming together of many families. In *Patriarchalism in Political Thought*, Schochet emphasizes that patriarchal theory was formulated explicitly as a justification for political authority and political obedience, and – as he also stresses – it was systematized in opposition to the social contract theories that were developing at the same time and challenging (one half of) the patriarchalists' most fundamental assumptions.[3] Patriarchalism developed, and was 'defeated', in a specific historical and theoretical context.

The standard interpretation of the conflict between the patriarchalists and the contract theorists treat it as a battle over paternal rule and focuses on the irreconcilable differences between the two doctrines over the political right of fathers and the natural liberty of sons. The patriarchalists claimed that kings and fathers ruled in exactly the same way (kings were fathers and vice versa); that family and polity were homologous; that sons were born naturally subject to their fathers; and that political authority and obedience and a hierarchy of inequality were natural. The contract theorists rejected all these claims: they argued that paternal and political rule were distinct; that family and polity were two different and separate forms of association; that sons were born free and equal and, as adults, were as free as their fathers before them; that political authority and obligation were conventional and political subjects were civil equals.[4] It is true that in this particular controversy the patriarchalists were defeated. The theoretical assumptions of the contract theorists were an essential part of the transformation of the traditional order and the world of father-kings into capitalist society, liberal representative government and the modern family.

However, this familiar version of the story in which the sons gain their natural liberty, make the contract and create liberal civil society, or Rousseau's participatory civil order, is only half the tale. It is a patriarchal reading of the texts which identifies patriarchy with paternal rule; it therefore omits the story of the real origin of political right. Patriarchalism has two dimensions: the paternal (father/son) and the masculine (husband/wife). Political theorists can represent the outcome of the theoretical battle as a victory for contract theory because they are silent about the sexual or conjugal aspect of patriarchy, which appears as non-political or natural and so of no theoretical consequence. But a feminist reading of the texts shows that patriarchalism was far from defeated. The contract theorists rejected paternal right, but they absorbed and simultaneously transformed conjugal, masculine patriarchal right.

To see how this came about – and hence to take a necessary first step towards elucidating some of the characteristics of modern patriarchy – it is necessary to begin with the patriarchal story of monarchical fatherhood exemplified in the writings of Sir Robert Filmer. Although Filmer's father is overthrown in the story of the social contract, his sons receive a vital inheritance that is, paradoxically, obscured by the doctrine of paternal right.

Filmer's aim was to show the awful error of the contract theorists' claim that men were by nature free and equal, a claim he saw as the 'main foundation of popular sedition'.[5] Filmer argued that all law was of necessity the product of the will of one man. All titles to rule devolved from the original divine grant of kingly right to Adam, the first father. The ground was immediately swept from under the feet of the proponents of the doctrine of the natural freedom of mankind once it was recognized that 'the natural and private dominion of Adam [is] the fountain of all government and propriety'.[6] Filmer writes that 'the title comes from the fatherhood';[7] Adam's sons, and hence all succeeding generations of sons, were born into political subjection by virtue of Adam's 'right of fatherhood', his 'fatherly power' or the 'power of the fatherhood'.[8]

At the birth of his first son, Adam became the first monarch, and his political right passed to all subsequent fathers and kings. For Filmer, fathers and kings ruled by virtue of their fatherhood and all fathers were monarchs in their families: 'the Father of a family governs by no other law than by his own will.'[9] Filmer argued that no government could be a tyranny because the king's will was law; similarly, the will of the father was the absolute, arbitrary will of the *patria potestas* who, under Roman law, had the power of life and death over his children. Laslett comments that Filmer 'did not adopt the capital punishment of children by their fathers, but he quoted examples of it from Bodin with approval.'[10]

Filmer's view of the origin of political right seems, therefore, to be unmistakable: it derives from fatherhood. But patriarchy, even in its classical formulation, is more complex than its literal meaning suggests. Fatherly power is only one dimension of patriarchy, as Filmer himself reveals. Filmer's apparently straightforward statements obscure the foundation of patriarchal right. Paternal power is not the origin of political right. The genesis of political power lies in Adam's conjugal or sex right, not in his fatherhood. Adam's political title is granted *before* he becomes a father. Sons, as Filmer caustically reminds Hobbes, do not spring up like mushrooms. If Adam was to be a father, Eve had to become a mother and if Eve was to be a mother, then Adam must have sexual access to her body. In other words, sexual or conjugal right must *necessarily precede* the right of fatherhood.

Filmer makes it clear that Adam's political right is originally established in his right as a husband over Eve: 'God gave to Adam . . . the dominion over the woman', and 'God ordained Adam to rule over his wife, and her desires were to be subject to his'.[11] However, sexual or conjugal right then fades from view in Filmer's writings. After proclaiming that Adam's first dominion or political right is over a woman, not another man (son), Filmer then subsumes conjugal right under the power of fatherhood. Eve and her desires are subject to Adam but, Filmer continues, 'here we have the original grant of government, and the fountain of all power placed in the Father of all mankind'. Recall that in the Bible story in the Book of Genesis, Eve is created only after Adam and the animals have been placed on earth. Moreover, she is not created *ab initio* but *from* Adam, who is thus in a sense her parent. Filmer is able to treat all political right as the right of a father because the patriarchal father has the creative powers of both a mother and a father. He is not just one of two parents; he is *the* parent.

The patriarchal image of political fathers (here in Locke's words) is that of 'nursing Fathers tender and careful of the publick weale'.[12] The patriarchal story is about the procreative power of a father who is complete in himself. His procreative power both gives and nurtures physical life and creates and maintains political right. Filmer is able to dismiss Adam's power over Eve so easily because, in the story, women are procreatively and politically irrelevant. The reason Adam has dominion over 'the woman' is, according to Filmer (here following a very ancient notion), that 'the man . . . is the nobler and principal agent in generation'.[13] Women are merely empty vessels for the exercise of the father's sexual and procreative power. The original political right which God gives to Adam is, so to speak, the right to fill the empty vessel.

There is therefore no question to be asked, or error to be corrected, about women's natural freedom. Filmer invokes women merely to highlight the folly of the doctrine of the natural liberty of sons. The contract theorists' argument about natural freedom entails that 'there can be no superior power'. The full absurdity of that conclusion is revealed for Filmer in its corollary that 'women, especially virgins, [would] by birth have as much natural freedom as any other, and therefore ought not to lose their liberty without their own consent.'[14]

Filmer could present the natural freedom of women as the *reductio ad absurdum* of the contract argument because there was no controversy between the patriarchalists and contract theorists about women's subjection. The contract theorists' aim was theoretical parricide, not the overthrow of the sexual right of men and husbands. Both sides agreed, first, that women (wives), unlike sons, were born and remained naturally subject to men (husbands); and, second, that the right of men over women was *not political*. Locke, for example, concurred with Filmer's view that a wife's subjection has a 'Foundation in Nature'. The husband is naturally 'the abler and the stronger', so he must rule over his wife.[15] Rousseau, the vehement critic of the fraudulent liberal social contract that brings into being a corrupt civil society of inequality and domination, is no less insistent that women must be 'subjected either to a man or to the judgements of men and they are never permitted to put themselves above these judgements'. When a woman becomes a wife, she acknowledges her husband as 'a master for the whole of life'.[16]

The contract theorists' 'victory' hinged on the separation of paternal from political power, so they could not, like Filmer, subsume sexual under paternal – that is, political – rule. Instead, the social contract story hides original political right by proclaiming sexual or conjugal right as *natural*. Men's dominion over women is held to follow from the respective natures of the sexes, and Rousseau spells out this claim in detail in Book V of *Emile*. Locke has no quarrel with Filmer about the *legitimacy* of sexual, patriarchal right; rather, he insists that it is not political. Eve's subordination.

> can be no other Subjection than what every Wife owes her Husband, . . . Adam ['s] . . . can only be a Conjugal Power, not Political, the Power that every Husband hath to order the things of private Concernment in his Family, as Proprietor of the Goods and Land there, and to have his Will take place before that of his wife in all things of their common Concernment.[17]

Both sides in the seventeenth-century controversy – unlike contemporary political theorists – were well aware that the new doctrine of natural freedom and equality had subversive implications for *all* relationships of power and subordination. The patriarchalists claimed that the doctrine was so absurd that the problems it raised of justifying, say, the power of a husband over his wife were immediately shown to be figments of the contract theorists' disordered imaginations. But if the contract theorists were content with conjugal patriarchy, the individualist language of their attack on paternal right meant that they had (as Sir Robert Filmer argued) opened the thin ends of numerous revolutionary wedges, including a feminist wedge. Women almost at once seized on the contradiction of an 'individualism' and a 'universalism' which insisted that women were born into subjection and that their subjection was natural and politically irrelevant. By the end of the seventeenth century, for example, Mary Astell was asking: 'If all Men are born Free, how is it that all Women are born Slaves?'[18]

The difficulty for the contract theorists was that given their premises, an answer to the question was impossible. Logically, there is no reason why a free and equal female individual should always (contract to) subordinate herself to another free and equal (male) individual upon marriage. The difficulty, however, was easily overcome. Political theorists, whether liberal or socialist, absorbed masculine right into their theories and 'forgot' the story of the origin of patriarchal power. Natural subjection was seen in terms of paternal power and three centuries of feminist criticism – whether written by women whose names never appear in political theory textbooks, by the cooperative or utopian socialists, or by the otherwise acceptable philosopher, John Stuart Mill – was suppressed and ignored.

The standard view that the rise of social contract theory and the development of civil society was also a defeat for patriarchalism has meant that some vital questions about the construction of the civil body politic have never been asked. One problem about the social contract that has received some attention is the question of exactly who makes the agreement. Many commentators talk uncritically of 'individuals' sealing the pact, but Schochet, for example, points out that in the seventeenth century it was taken for granted that fathers of families entered the social contract.

When I first began to think about these matters from a feminist perspective, I assumed that the social contract was a patriarchal contract because it was made by fathers whose agreement was taken to bind their families. Certainly, 'individuals', in the universal sense in which the category is usually used to mean anyone and everyone, do not make the social contract. Women have no part in it: as natural subjects they lack the requisite capacities and abilities. The 'individuals' of the stories are *men*, but they do not act as fathers. After all, the stories tell of the defeat of the father's political power. Men no longer have a political place as fathers. But fathers are also husbands – Locke's friend Tyrrell wrote that wives were 'concluded by their Husbands'[19] – and, from yet another viewpoint, the participants in the social contract are sons or brothers. The contract is made by brothers, or a *fraternity*. It is no accident that fraternity appears historically hand in hand with liberty and equality, nor that it means exactly what it says: brotherhood.

If 'patriarchy' is all too often interpreted literally, 'fraternity' is usually treated as if its literal meaning had no relevance today and as if the terms in the revolutionary slogan, 'Liberty, Equality, Fraternity', unquestionably applied to us all, not only to men joined by fraternal bonds. Bernard Crick has recently pointed out that fraternity has been relatively little analysed, even though, he says, 'fraternity with liberty is humanity's greatest dream'.[20] When it is mentioned, fraternity is usually presented as an expression of community; it is seen as 'at bottom, a certain type of social co-operation . . . a relation between a group of equals for the utmost mutual help and aid'.[21] Or as Crick argues, addressing his fellow socialists, fraternity is an ethic and social practice that 'goes with simplicity, lack of ostentation, friendliness, helpfulness, kindliness, openness, lack of restraint between individuals in everyday life and a willingness to work together in common tasks'.[22] The general acceptance that 'fraternity' is no more than a way of talking about the bonds of community illustrates how deeply patriarchal conceptions structure our political theory and practice. Feminists have long appreciated the extent to which socialist solidarity and community has meant that women are little more than auxiliaries to the comrades and that women's political demands must wait until after the revolution. But the problems women have in finding a language in which to make their demands is illustrated by the final words of Simone de Beauvoir's *The Second Sex*, where she states that 'men and women [must] unequivocally affirm their brotherhood.'[23]

The fact that the social contract is not an agreement between individuals, fathers or husbands, but a fraternal pact, becomes particularly clear in Freud's versions of the social contract story. Freud's account of the murder of the primal father by his sons is not usually considered in discussions of the social contract. Yet, as Brown states, 'the battle of books re-enacts Freud's primal crime.'[24] And Rieff treats Freud's myth of the parricide as a version of the social contract, to be considered as part of the same tradition as the theories of Hobbes, Locke or Rousseau.[25] The best warrant of all is available for this interpretation. In *Moses and Monotheism* Freud refers to the pact made by the brothers after their dreadful deed as 'a sort of social contract'.[26]

But, it could be objected, Freud's myth is about the origins of society itself. Freud claims – and this is taken at face value by Juliet Mitchell's *Psychoanalysis and Feminism*, which has been very influential among feminists – that the parricide ushers in 'civilization': that is, human society. However, the classic social contract theorists are also sometimes read in the same way; the passage from 'the state of nature' can be seen as the transition from nature or savagery to the first human social order. In neither case is there good reason to accept a universal reading that identifies 'civilization' or 'civil society' with society itself. When the form of the laws instituted by the brothers is examined, it is clear that the stories are about the origin of a culturally and historically specific form of social life. The close connection between 'civil society' and 'civilization' is suggested too by the fact that the term 'civilization' came into general use only towards the end of the eighteenth century, 'to express a particular stage of European history, sometimes the final or ultimate stage'.[27] 'Civilization' expressed the 'sense of modernity: an achieved condition of refinement and order'.[28]

In her interpretation of Freud, Mitchell claims that the 'law of the father' is established after the parricide. On the contrary: the law of the father, the absolute rule of one father-king, holds sway before his murder. The crucial point about the contract is that it takes place after the death of the father and abolishes his arbitrary right. Instead, the brothers (sons), prompted by remorse for their dreadful deed, by love and hatred and by a desire to prevent parricide in future, establish their *own* law. They establish justice, 'the first "right" or "law" '[29] – or civil society. The law, or arbitrary will, of the father is overthrown by the combined action of the brothers, who then place mutual restrictions on themselves, establishing an equality which, Freud states, 'saved the organization which had made them strong'.[30] A contract between free and equal brothers replaces the 'law of the father' with public rules which bind all equally. As Locke makes clear, the rule of one man (father) is incompatible with civil society, which requires an impartial, impersonal set of rules promulgated by a collective body of men who stand to the law and each other as free equals, as a fraternity.

At this point the objection might be raised that even if brothers enter the contract, they cease to be brothers once the pact is concluded. In the act of contracting they constitute themselves as equal, civil 'individuals' and thus cast off familial and, hence, fraternal ties. The fundamental distinction between the traditional patriarchy of the father and modern patriarchy is precisely that the latter is created in separation from, and opposition to, the familial sphere.

However, it does not follow that all ascriptive ties are therefore abandoned and that the term 'fraternal' ceases to be appropriate. Brown claims that there is an 'inner contradiction' in the trilogy of liberty, equality, fraternity: 'without a father there can be no sons or brothers.'[31] However, as recent accounts of fraternity make clear, the concept covers much more than bonds of kinship. 'Individuals' can be part of a fraternity or a brotherhood – a 'community' – even though they are not brothers (sons of a father or kin). The father is dead and the participants in civil society have left kinship behind them, but as civil individuals they still share an ascriptive bond – a bond *as men*.

Freud's story of the parricide is important because he makes explicit what the classic tales of theoretical murder leave obscure: the motive for the brothers' collective act is not merely to claim their natural liberty and right of self-government, but *to gain access to women*. In the classic theorists' state of nature the 'family' already exists and men's conjugal right is deemed a natural right.[32] Freud's primal father, his *patria potestas*, keeps all the women of the horde for himself. The parricide eliminates the father's political right, and also his *exclusive* sexual right. The brothers inherit his patriarchal, masculine right and share the women among themselves. No man can be a primal father ever again, but by setting up rules that give all men equal access to women (compare their equality before the laws of the state) they exercise the 'original' political right of dominion over women that was once the prerogative of the father.

Freud writes of the brothers' 'renunciation of the passionately desired mothers and sisters of the horde.'[33] This is misleading. The fraternity do not renounce the women, but each gives up the desire to put himself in the place of the father. As part of the fraternal social contract the brothers institute what Freud calls the law of exogamy or kinship. In historically specific terms, the brothers create the modern system of marriage law and family and establish the modern order of conjugal or sexual right. The 'natural foundation' of civil society has been brought into being through the fraternal social contract.

The separation of 'paternal' from political rule, or the family from the public sphere, is also the separation of women from men through the subjection of women to men. The brothers establish their own law and their own form of sexual or conjugal dominion. The fraternal social contract creates a new, modern patriarchal order that is presented as divided into two spheres: civil society or the universal sphere of freedom, equality, individualism, reason, contract and impartial law – the realm of men or 'individuals'; and the private world of particularity, natural subjection, ties of blood, emotion, love and sexual passion – the world of women, in which men also rule.

In short, the contract constitutes patriarchal civil society and the modern, ascriptive rule of men over women. Ascription and contract are usually seen as standing at opposite poles, but the social contract is sexually ascriptive in both form (it is made by brothers) and content (the patriarchal right of a fraternity is established). Civil individuals have a fraternal bond because, *as men*, they share a common interest in upholding the contract which legitimizes their masculine patriarchal right and allows them to gain material and psychological benefit from women's subjection.

One important question raised by the contract stories is exactly how the 'foundation in nature', which upholds the subjection of women, should be characterized. Locke tells us that the strength and ability of the man (husband) is the natural basis of the wife's subordination: a view which becomes absorbed into patriarchal liberalism, but also opens the way for liberal feminism. Feminists began to criticize the argument from strength long ago,[34] and although the claim is still heard today, historically it has become less and less plausible to rely on strength as the criterion for masculine political right. Contemporary liberal feminists, following the lead of much earlier writers like Mary Astell and Mary Wollstonecraft, have attacked the alleged lesser ability and capacity of women as an artifact of defective education, as a matter of deliberate social contrivance, not a fact of nature.

The difficulty for the liberal feminist argument is that education cannot be equal while men and women remain differentially positioned within their 'separate spheres', but the patriarchal division between the private family and public, civil society is a central structural principle of liberalism. Moreover, the problem runs deeper than a liberal perspective suggests. Liberal feminism assumes that the relevant political problem is to show that women possess the capacities men possess and can do what men can do. However, this also assumes that there is no political significance to the fact that women have one natural ability which men lack: women, but not men, are able to give birth.

Now, it may be claimed that this provides no 'foundation in nature' for women's subjection because birth (unlike child-rearing) is ultimately irrelevant to the development of the capacities of civil beings. The difficulty with this argument is that it, too, ignores the story of the 'origin' of patriarchal political right, and thus the importance of birth for patriarchal civil society. The ability to give birth, both actually and metaphorically, is central to patriarchal theory.

Filmer's argument shows that Adam's right of domination over Eve is the right to become a father: a right to demand sexual access to Eve's body and to insist that she give birth. Eve's procreative, creative capacity is then denied and appropriated by *men* as the ability to give *political birth*, to be the 'originators' of a new form of political order. Adam and the participants in the fraternal social contract gain an amazing patriarchal ability and become the 'principal agents' in political generation. Moreover, in patriarchal argument birth also symbolizes and encapsulates all the reasons why it has been claimed that women must be bodily removed from civil society.[35]

Some of the murky depths become clearer in the stories told by Rousseau and Freud. Women, they insist, are unable to transcend their bodily natures in the manner required of 'individuals' who are to participate in civil life and uphold the universal laws of civil society. The female body, subject to uncontrollable natural processes and passions, deprives women of the reason and moral character which can be educated for civil society. (In another chapter I began to explore one aspect of this perception of women and its corollary, that we pose a permanent threat to civil life.[36])

Rousseau's solution is that the sexes must be segregated to the greatest possible extent, even in domestic life. Significantly, in *Emile* Rousseau allows the tutor to give only one direct command, in which he sends Emile away from Sophie for an extended period to learn about politics and citizenship before he is permitted to claim her body as a husband. Freud offers no solution but states explicitly that from the 'beginning' – from the original parricide in which women are at stake, and which is endlessly reproduced through the Oedipus complex – women continue to have 'a hostile attitude towards' civil society.[37] Or, as Mitchell interprets Freud, a woman 'cannot receive the "touch" of the law, her submission to it must be in establishing herself as its opposite.'[38]

Women are 'opposite' to and outside the fraternal social contract and its civil law in two senses. First, they are 'originally', necessarily, excluded from an agreement through which the brothers inherit their legacy of patriarchal sex right and legitimize their claim over women's bodies and ability to give birth. Second, the civil law encapsulates all that women lack. The civil law stems from a reasoned agreement that it is to the rational mutual advantage of the participants to the contract to constrain their interactions and desires through a law equally applicable to all. Women's passions render them incapable of making such a reasoned agreement or of upholding it if made. In other words, the patriarchal claim that there is a 'foundation in nature' for women's subjection to men is a claim that women's bodies must be governed by men's reason. The separation of civil society from the familial sphere is also a division between men's reason and women's bodies.

Feminist scholars are now showing how, from ancient times, political life has been conceptualized in opposition to the mundane world of necessity, the body, the sexual passions and birth: in short, in opposition to women and the disorders and creativity they symbolize.[39] In Filmer's classic patriarchalism the father is both mother and father and creates political right through his fatherhood, but Filmer's account is only one version of a long Western tradition in which the creation of political life has been seen as a masculine act of birth: as a male replica of the ability which only women possess.

The fraternal social contract is a specifically modern reformulation of this patriarchal tradition. The father is dead, but the brothers appropriate the ability specific to women; they, too, can generate new political life and political right. The social contract is the point of origin, or birth, of civil society, and simultaneously its separation from the (private) sphere of real birth and the disorder of women. The brothers give birth to an artificial body, the body politic of civil society; they create Hobbes's 'Artificial Man, we call a Commonwealth,' or Rousseau's 'artificial and collective body', or the 'one Body' of Locke's 'Body Politick'.

The 'birth' of the civil body politic, however, is an act of reason; there is no analogue to a bodily act of procreation. The social contract, as we are all taught, is not an actual event. The natural paternal body of Filmer's patriarchy is metaphorically put to death by the contract theorists, but the 'artificial' body that replaces it is a construct of the mind, not the creation of a political community by real people. Whereas the birth of a human child can produce a new male or female, the creation of civil society produces a social body fashioned after the image of only one of the two bodies of humankind. Or, more exactly, the civil body politic is fashioned after the image of the male 'individual' who is constituted through the separation of civil society from women. This individual has some singular – and largely unrecognized – aspects precisely because his defining characteristics are thrown into relief only through the contrast with the womanly nature that has been excluded from civil society.

The abstract character of the individual in liberal contract theory has been criticized from the left ever since Rousseau's initial attack. But because the critiques invariably pass silently over the separation of male reason from female body in the original creation of the civil individual, one of his most notable features has also silently been incorporated by the critics. The 'individual' is disembodied. For three centuries the figure of the individual has been presented as universal, as the embodiment of all, but it is only because he is disembodied that the 'individual' can appear universal. Like the new body politic he, too, is 'artificial': he is nothing more than a 'man of reason'.[40]

In the most recent rewriting of the liberal contract story, *A Theory of Justice*, Rawls claims that his parties in their original position know none of the essential facts about themselves. Thus it might seem that Rawls's parties are truly universal and that the original choices include a choice between the two bodies (sexes) of humankind. The fact that Rawls ignores this possibility, and writes that the parties can be seen as heads of families,[41] shows how deeply entrenched are patriarchal assumptions about the proper characteristics of the 'individual'. Moreover, the attributes of the parties and their original position illustrate the fact that Rawls stands at the logical conclusion of the fraternal contract tradition. The original position and its choices are explicitly hypothetical (logical) and the parties are nothing more than disembodied entities of reason; otherwise they could not help but know the natural facts about themselves, inseparable from their bodies, such as the facts of sex, age and colour.[42]

Ironically, the disembodiment necessary to maintain the political fiction of the universal civil individual poses profound problems for fraternity. For individualist liberals the problems are part of their wider difficulties over the self, and involve an opposition within the individual between fraternity and reason. The opposition between reason and fraternity is an opposition between the public and the private. But this is not the patriarchal opposition between 'private' and 'public', between family (women) and civil society (men); instead, the relevant division between public and private is the other opposition to which I referred earlier: the opposition located within 'civil society' as I am using the term.[43] For liberals relying on a social view of the self or for socialist critics of liberalism the problems arise because in the 1980s an emphasis on fraternity begins to reveal the patriarchal character of their theories. To preserve universality, '*the* individual' must be abstracted even from his masculinity and fraternity, so that the individual has no body and, hence, no sex.

The creation of the 'individual' presupposes the division of rational civil order from the disorder of womanly nature. It might thus seem that the civil individual and the body politic made in his image would be unified. Indeed, they are so presented in liberal theory, but its critics from Rousseau onward argue that the individual and civil society are inherently divided, one from the other and within themselves. The individual is torn between *bourgeois* and *citoyen*, or between *Homo economicus* and *Homo civicus*, and civil society is divided between private interest and the public universal interest, or between 'civil' society and state. The point about such critiques, however, is exactly that they are concerned with extrafamilial social life and with the individual as an inhabitant of the public world.

The liberal opposition between private and public (like the patriarchal opposition between the sexes) appears in a variety of guises: for example, society, economy and freedom stand against state, public and coercion. Liberals see these dualities as posing important problems of freedom, since the private sphere of civil society must be protected from the coercive intrusions of the state, and they now spend a good deal of time and effort trying to sort out where the dividing line plausibly can be drawn. Their critics, on the other hand, argue that the opposition between private and public poses an insoluble problem; that it is an unbridgeable structural fissure at the centre of liberalism. I agree with the critics; but the criticism does not go far enough because it takes no account of the 'original' patriarchal division and thus leaves the critics' own conception of the 'individual' and 'civil society' untouched.

In *Knowledge and Politics*, Robert Unger presents a comprehensive discussion and critique of the liberal dichotomies, but even his analysis of the division between fact and theory, values and rules, desire and reason, ignores the fact that it also represents the opposition between the sexes. The 'self' is implicitly taken to be masculine. The reference to 'men' must be taken literally when he writes: 'The dichotomy of the public and private life is still another corollary of the separation of understanding and desire . . . When reasoning [men] belong to a public world. . . . When desiring, however, men are private beings.'[44] In Unger's account, the 'desire' and associated disorder represented by women and their private world has been 'forgotten'. The 'self' has beome that of the male individual in civil society, an individual torn between the claims of public interest ('reason') and private or subjective interest ('desire'). The opposition between women, bodies, passion, and men, reason, rational advantage, is repressed and replaced by the dichotomy between the individual's private interest and the claims of the public interest or universal law.

In this form, the dichotomy is also expressed as an opposition between the fraternity and reason of civil individuals. The only ties between the individuals of liberal contract theory are those of self-interest. The individual is, as it were, a collection of pieces of property that can, through rational calculation of the mind, be made the subject of contract. The individual thus enters into only certain kinds of relationship and this limitation gives rise to another familiar difficulty within liberal theory: that of presenting a coherent conception of citizenship or the political. The liberal individual's political bonds with other citizens are merely another expression of the pursuit of self-interest; *Homo civicus* is absorbed into, or is nothing more than one face of, the 'private' *Homo economicus*. However, this view of the individual as citizen – as public or civil individual – systematically undermines one of the most significant expressions of fraternity.

Liberal individuals interact in a benign public world. They compete one with the other, but the competition is regulated and the rules are fair; the only coercion required is to enforce the rules. Hence the division between private and public as an opposition between society and state is often presented as between freedom and coercion. Currently this position is associated with the New Right, but in the past *le doux commerce* could be offered as the antithesis of violence and the idealist liberals, claiming to have reconciled the oppositions, could assert that will, not force, is the basis of the state.

On the other hand, it is also clear that the individual can be required to protect his protection (as Hobbes put it) by something more than mere obedience to the law. He may have to surrender his body in defence of the state. Indeed, this has always been seen as the ultimate act of loyalty and allegiance, the truly exemplary act of citizenship. However, it is also an act which will never be to the rational advantage of a liberal individual, as Hobbes's logical working out of radical individualism reveals. In the clash between private and public interest, the private claim always has the rational advantage. It is not in the individual's self-interest to be a soldier; thus reason is torn apart from the fraternity on which citizenship, in the last analysis, depends. Of all the male clubs and associations, it is in the military and on the battlefield that fraternity finds its most complete expression.

The opposition between the figure of the soldier and the figure of the individual, or between fraternity and reason, is unique to liberal civil society. In many respects the fraternal contract story transforms ancient patriarchal themes into a specifically modern theory, but the conception of a liberal individual breaks with older traditions in which citizenship has involved a distinctive form of activity and has also been closely tied to the bearing of arms. Feminist scholars are now showing that from ancient times there has been an integral connection between the warrior and conceptions of self-identity, sexuality and masculinity, which have all been bound up with citizenship. The peculiarity of the liberal individual is that although he is male he is also defined – unlike either his predecessors in the traditional world or the 'individuals' that appear in social-liberal and socialist theory – in opposition to the political and the masculine passions that underlie the defence of the state by arms.

Although our consciousness is informed by the liberal individual's image, and many of our social practices and institutions presuppose that we are motivated by self-interest (the contemporary preoccupation with freeriders is no accident), the state has never relied on rational self-interest as the basis for socio-political order. Nor did most classic theorists, except Hobbes, have the courage of their theoretical convictions on this point. Hobbes's conclusion that Leviathan's sword was the only alternative to an inherently insecure 'artificial' ground for order was rejected in favour of such devices as natural law, sympathy, benevolence or hidden hands – and socialists have appealed to solidarity, comradeship and community or, in a word, to *fraternity*. Historically, obedience and loyalty to the state have been fostered by appeals not to individual rational advantage but to ascriptive, psychological bonds, especially to nationalism, patriotism and fraternity. These are ties of a much more full-blooded character than, for example, Rawls's sense of justice and, most importantly, they appeal directly to the masculine self's sense of identity. However, the real and ideological basis for the motivating force of self-interest means that it is hard to eliminate the opposition between fraternity and reason.

When some liberals over the past century attempted to develop an adequately social and developmental conception of individuality, one that restored the affective ties of community that had been stripped away in liberal contract theory, they also turned to the idea of fraternity. In the eyes of these liberals, Gaus states, fraternity is the 'most powerful of communal bonds'.[45] The ideal of fraternity provides the 'pre-eminent conception of communal bonds in modern liberal theory', so that Dewey, for example, wrote of a 'fraternally associated public', and Rawls sees his difference principle as a 'natural meaning of fraternity'.[46]

The explicit use of 'fraternity' in both social-liberal and socialist attempts to reintegrate the civil individual and the community (or to reintegrate the liberal division between private and public) means that the patriarchal character of civil society begins to come to the surface. Moreover, the masculine attributes of the individual begin to be exposed. The universalism of the category of the 'individual' can be maintained only as long as the abstraction from the body is maintained. 'The individual' is a fiction: individuals have one of two bodies, masculine or feminine. But how can the feminine body become part of a (liberal or socialist) fraternal body politic?

Citizenship has now been extended formally to women, raising the substantive problem of how we can become civil 'individuals' made in the masculine image. The importance, in practice, of the intimate connection between masculinity, citizenship and bearing arms became explicit when women, taking the universalism of the principles of civil society at face value, demanded to be enfranchised. The 'jewel' in the armoury of the anti-suffragists was the argument from physical force.[47] Women, it was claimed, were naturally unable and unwilling to bear arms or use violence, so that if they became citizens, the state would inevitably be fatally weakened.

Now that women are enfranchised (and are even prime ministers) the same patriarchal view of citizenship is still found. In the British House of Commons in 1981, in a debate on the Nationality Bill, Enoch Powell argued that a woman should not pass on her citizenship to her child because 'nationality, in the last resort, is tested by fighting. A man's nation is the nation for which he will fight.' The difference between men and women, which must be expressed in citizenship, is that between 'fighting on the one hand and the creation and preservation of life on the other'.[48] It is true that women are now included as members of the armed forces but they are still excluded from combat units, which exemplify fraternities in action.[49]

'Men are born free': the rejection of (masculine) natural subjection generated the revolutionary claim that will, not force, is the basis of the state. One of the major successes of the fraternal contract story is the way it has helped to obscure coercion and violence in civil society and the manner in which 'will' is determined within relations of domination and subjection. Critics of contract theory have said a good deal about the inequality of parties to contracts and exploitation, but less about the consequences of contract and subordination. Only rarely have they discussed how contract gives the appearance of freedom to sexually ascriptive domination and subjection. Contract also hides the figure of the armed man in the shadows behind the civil individual. Foucault has counterposed a 'military dream' of a society against the original contract (what is presented as the original pact in the familiar stories), but the two are not so far apart as they may seem.

Foucault writes that the military dream looked, 'not to the state of nature, but to the meticulously subordinated cogs of a machine, not to the primal social contract, but to permanent coercions, not to fundamental rights, but to indefinitely progressive forms of training, not to the general will but to automatic docility.'[50] Automatic docility and the disciplines of the body portrayed by Foucault are part of the consequences of the fraternal social contract. Foucault states that 'the development and generalization of disciplinary mechanisms constituted the other, dark side' of the development of a 'formally egalitarian juridical framework'. However, it is less that the disciplines 'distort the contractual link systematically'[51] than that discipline in civil society, *which is also patriarchal discipline*, is typically established through contract. The forms of subjection specific to civil society are, as Foucault emphasizes, developed by the complicity of subordinates as well as by force – complicity made all the easier (as, importantly, is resistance) when consciousness is informed by patriarchal forms of liberty and equality. For example, when 'individuals' have a free choice of marriage partner, publicly recognized by a free contract, it is made harder to acknowledge that the marriage contract is a political fiction which ceremonially recognizes the patriarchal subjection of a wife and the masculine privileges of a husband.[52]

The modern discipline of the body is aided by political theory that has already separated reason from the body and the reason of men from the bodies of women. Foucault ignores the significant fact that the 'military dream' is a dream of men, whereas the fraternal social contract is also a dream of women. But the women's dream cannot be fulfilled, although the ostensibly universal categories of the contract make it always enticing. The history of liberal feminism is the history of attempts to generalize liberal liberties and rights to the whole adult population; but liberal feminism does not, and cannot, come to grips with the deeper problems of *how* women are to take an equal place in the patriarchal civil order.

Now that the feminist struggle has reached the point where women are almost formal civil equals, the opposition is highlighted between equality made after a male image and the real social position of women *as women*.

Women have never, of course, been excluded entirely from civil life – the two spheres of the modern civil order are not separate in reality – but our inclusion has been singular. In a world presented as conventional, contractual and universal, women's civil position is ascriptive, defined by the natural particularity of being women; patriarchal subordination is socially and legally upheld throughout civil life, in production and citizenship as well as in the family. Thus to explore the subjection of women is also to explore the fraternity of men. Recent feminist research has begun to uncover – despite the important divisions between men of different classes and races (and associations and clubs where fraternity is given explicit expression are usually so divided) – how men, *as men*, maintain the power and privileges of their patriarchal right throughout the whole of socio-political life.

The fraternal social contract story shows that the categories and practices of civil society cannot simply be universalized to women. The social contract is a modern patriarchal pact that establishes men's sex right over women, and the civil individual has been constructed in opposition to women and all that our bodies symbolize, so how can we become full members of civil society or parties to the fraternal contract?

The contradictory answer is that women in civil society must disavow our bodies and act as part of the brotherhood – but since we are never regarded as other than women, we must simultaneously continue to affirm the patriarchal conception of femininity, or patriarchal subjection.[53] The peculiar relation between civil society and women and our bodies is illustrated by the fact that few legal jurisdictions have abolished the right of a husband to use his wife's body against her will, that coercive sexual relations ('sexual harassment') are part of everyday working life; that women's bodies are sold in the capitalist market;[54] that women, until 1934 in the USA and 1948 in Britain, lost their citizenship if they married foreigners; that only in 1983 did all British women citizens win the right to pass on their citizenship to their husbands and so enable them to live in Britain;[55] and that welfare policies still do not fully recognize women's status as individuals.

The theoretical and social transformation required if women and men are to be full members of a free, properly democratic (or properly 'civilized') society is as far-reaching as can be imagined. The meaning of 'civil society' (in both senses discussed here) has been constructed through the exclusion of women and all that we symbolize. To 'rediscover' a patriarchal conception of civil society will do little to challenge men's patriarchal right. To create a properly democratic society, which includes women as full citizens, it is necessary to deconstruct and reassemble our understanding of the body politic. This task extends from the dismantling of the patriarchal separation of private and public, to a transformation of our individuality and sexual identities as feminine and masculine beings. These identities now stand opposed, part of the multi-faceted expression of the patriarchal dichotomy between reason and desire. The most profound and complex problem for political theory and practice is how the two bodies of humankind and feminine and masculine individuality can be fully incorporated into political life. How can the present of patriarchal domination, opposition and duality be transformed into a future of autonomous, democratic differentiation?

The traditional patriarchy of the fathers was long ago transformed into the fraternal, modern patriarchy of civil society. Perhaps there is hope, since these observations could be written only under the shadow of the owl of Minerva's wings. Alternatively, perhaps the time for optimism is past; feminism may have re-emerged at a point in the crisis of patriarchy in which the figure of the armed man – now armed not with the sword but with plastic bullets, cluster bombs, chemical, biological and nuclear weapons – has totally obliterated the figure of the civil individual. Perhaps, as Mary O'Brien suggests, 'the brotherhood have gone quite mad and lost control of their creations in some cosmic sorcerers' apprenticeship.'[56]

NOTES

1 A more extensive and detailed feminist reading of the contract stories and of their significance for the marriage contract and other contracts, such as that between prostitute and client, is presented in my book, *The Sexual Contract* (Polity Press, Cambridge, 1988: Stanford University Press, Stanford, 1988).

2 Z. Eisenstein, *The Radical Future of Liberal Feminism*, (Longman, New York, 1981), chap. 3, but Eisenstein develops her argument in a different direction from my own; J. Elshtain, *Public Man, Private Woman: Women in Social and Political Thought* (Princeton University Press, Princeton, 1981), chap. 3. More recently, see L. Nicholson, *Gender and History: The Limits of Social Theory in the Age of the Family* (Columbia University Press, New York, 1986).

3 G. Schochet, *Patriarchalism in Political Thought: The Authoritarian Family and Political Speculation and Attitudes Especially in Seventeenth Century England* (Basil Blackwell, Oxford, 1975).

4 This brief summary highlights the essential points of conflict between the protagonists, and thus glosses over the differences among theorists on both sides. Hobbes, for instance, saw paternal and political rule as homologous, but rejected patriarchal claims about paternity.

5 Sir R. Filmer, *Patriarchia and Other Political Works*, ed. P. Laslett (Basil Blackwell, Oxford, 1949), p. 54.

6 Ibid., p. 71.

7 Ibid., p. 188.

8 Ibid., pp. 71, 57, 194.

9 Ibid., p. 96.
10 Laslett, 'Introduction', *Patriarchia*, p. 28. Filmer writes (p. 256): 'where there are only Father and sons, no sons can question the Father for the death of their brother.'
11 Filmer, *Patriarchia*, pp. 241, 283.
12 J. Locke, *Two Treatises of Government*, ed. P. Laslett, 2nd ed., (Cambridge University Press, Cambridge, 1967), II, §110.
13 Filmer, *Patriarchia*, p. 245.
14 Ibid., p. 287.
15 Locke, *Two Treatises*, I, §47; II, §82.
16 J.-J. Rousseau, *Emile, or On Education*, tr. A. Bloom (Basic Books, New York, 1979), pp. 370, 404.
17 Locke, *Two Treatises*, I, §48.
18 M. Astell, *Some Reflections Upon Marriage* (Source Book Press, New York, 1970), p. 107 (from the 1730 ed., first published 1700). On analogies drawn between the marriage contract and social contract and powers of husbands and kings, see M. Shanley, 'Marriage Contract and Social Contract in Seventeenth Century English Political Thought', *Western Political Quarterly*, 32(1), 1979, pp. 79–91.
19 Cited by Schochet, *Patriarchalism in Political Thought*, p. 202. I have discussed liberty, equality and the social contract in *The Problem of Political Obligation*, 2nd ed. (Polity Press, Cambridge, 1985; University of California Press, Berkeley, CA, 1985).
20 B. Crick, *In Defence of Politics* 2nd ed. (Penguin Books, Harmondsworth, Middlesex, 1982), p. 228.
21 E. Hobsbawm, 'The Idea of Fraternity', *New Society*, November 1975, cited in M. Taylor, *Community, Anarchy and Liberty* (Cambridge University Press, Cambridge, 1982) p. 31.
22 Crick, *In Defence of Politics*, p. 233. Crick (p. 230) suggests that 'sisterhood' is 'in some ways truly a less ambiguous image of what I am trying to convey by "fraternity".' Although he notes the relation between fraternity, the 'aggressive brothers' band' and 'stereotypes' of manliness, he argues that it is better to 'try to desex, even to feminize, old "fraternity", rather than to pause to rewrite most languages'; which exactly misses the point that language expresses and forms part of the patriarchal structure of our society ('language is a form of life').
23 S. de Beauvoir, *The Second Sex*, tr. H. M. Parshley (Penguin Books, New York, 1953), p. 732. But of course we must remember that de Beauvoir was writing without the support of the organized feminist movement. Today, feminists have devoted a good deal of attention to language – and have provided some fascinating accounts of how, in practice, fraternity has shaped the working class and the labour movement, so that the 'worker' is a man and a member of the 'men's movement'; see especially C. Cockburn, *Brothers: Male Dominance and Technological Change* (Pluto Press, London, 1983), also B. Campbell, *The Road to Wigan Pier Revisited: Poverty and Politics in the 80s*

(Virago Books, London, 1984) (The term 'men's movement' is Beatrix Campbell's.)

24 N. O. Brown, *Love's Body* (Vintage Books, New York, 1966), p. 4. I am grateful to Peter Breiner for drawing my attention to Brown's interpretation in *Love's Body*. A similar point is made, though its implications for patriarchy are not pursued, by M. Hulliung, 'Patriarchalism and Its Early Enemies', *Political Theory*, 2(1974), pp. 410–19. Hulliung (p. 416) notes that there is no reason why the parricide 'cannot just as well be turned into a morality play on behalf of . . . democratic ideals' and that 'the assassins are "brothers" towards each other, and brothers are equal.'

25 P. Rieff, *Freud: The Mind of the Moralist* (Methuen, London, n.d.), chap. VII.

26 S. Freud, *Moses and Monotheism*, tr. K. Jones (Vintage Books, New York, 1939), p. 104.

27 S. Rothblatt, *Tradition and Change in English Liberal Education* (Faber & Faber, London, 1976), p. 18.

28 R. Williams, *Keywords: A Vocabulary of Culture and Society*, revised ed. (Oxford University Press, New York, 1985), p. 58. I am grateful to Ross Poole for drawing my attention to the emergence of 'civilization'.

29 S. Freud, *Civilization and its Discontents* (W. W. Norton & Co., New York, n.d.), p. 53.

30 S. Freud, *Totem and Taboo*, tr. A. Brill (Vintage Books, New York, n.d.), p. 186.

31 Brown, *Love's Body*, p. 5.

32 Again, Hobbes is an exception. There are no families in his radically individualist state of nature; women are as strong as men. However, he merely assumes that in civil society women will always enter a marriage contract that places them in subjection to their husbands.

33 S. Freud, *Moses and Monotheism*, p. 153.

34 For example, Mary Astell sarcastically remarks (*Reflections Upon Marriage*, p. 86) that if 'Strength of Mind goes along with Strength of Body, [then] 'tis only for some odd Accidents which Philosophers have not yet thought worthwhile to enquire into, that the Sturdiest Porter is not the wisest Man!' Or consider William Thompson, *Appeal of One Half of the Human Race, Women, Against the Pretensions of the Other Half, Men, to Retain them in Political, and Thence in Civil and Domestic, Slavery* (Source Book Press, New York, 1970; originally published 1825), p. 120: 'If strength be the superior title to happiness, let the knowledge and skill of man be employed in adding to the pleasurable sensations of horses, elephants, and all stronger animals. If strength be the title to happiness, let all such qualifications for voters as the capacity to read and write, or any *indirect* means to insure intellectual aptitude be abolished; and let the simple test for the exercise of political rights, both by men and women, be the capacity of carrying 300lbs weight.'

35 This helps to explain why we do not have 'a philosophy of birth'; see M. O'Brien, *The Politics of Reproduction* (Routledge & Kegan Paul, London, 1981), especially chap. 1.

36 See chap. 1.

37 S. Freud, *Civilization and Its Discontents*, p. 56.

38 J. Mitchell, *Psychoanalysis and Feminism* (Penguin Books, Harmondsworth, Middlesex, 1975), p. 405.

39 See for example N. Hartsock, *Money, Sex and Power: Towards a Feminist Historical Materialism* (Northeastern University Press, Boston, MA, 1983), chap. 8; O'Brien, *The Politics of Reproduction*, chaps. 3, 4; Elshtain, *Public Man, Private Women*, chap. 1; H. Pitkin, *Fortune Is A Woman: Gender and Politics in the Thought of Niccolo Machiavelli* (University of California Press, Berkeley, CA, 1984).

40 For his history, see G. Lloyd, *The Man of Reason; 'Male' and 'Female' in Western Philosophy* (Methuen, London, 1984). On the Cartesian 'drama of parturition', see S. Bordo. 'The Cartesian Masculinization of Thought', *Signs*, 11(3), (1986), pp. 439–56.

41 J. Rawls, *A Theory of Justice* (Harvard University Press, Cambridge, MA, 1971), p. 128.

42 It will probably be objected that one can look younger or older than one's real age, or be convinced that one is in the 'wrong' body, or 'pass' as white. However, these examples all depend on the knowledge of age, sexual and colour differences and the specific meaning given to them in different cultures. One cannot, say, be a transsexual without already being fully aware of what 'masculine' and 'feminine' involve and how these are integrally connected to bodies. That Rawls's arguments, despite his apparently sexually undifferentiated 'parties', presuppose a sexually differentiated morality is shown in D. Kearns, '*A Theory of Justice* and Love: Rawls on the Family', *Politics*, 18(2), (1983), pp. 36–42.

43 This division between private and public is constituted in the second stage of the familiar story of the social contract (Locke's theory shows this clearly); see my book, *The Problem of Political Obligation*, chap. 4; and chap. 6 of the present book.

44 R. M. Unger, *Knowledge and Politics* (Free Press, New York, 1976), p. 45. Unger has little to say about women or the family, but his comments (like those on the division of labour) illustrate that his critique is not the 'total critique' at which he aims. He notes, for example, that the family 'draws men back into an association that competes with loyalties to all other groups' (p. 264) – but it 'draws back' only those who go into civil society.

45 G. F. Gaus, *The Modern Liberal Theory of Man* (Croom Helm, London, 1983), p. 90.

46 Gaus, *Modern Liberal Theory*, p. 94; he cites Dewey and Rawls on pp. 91 and 94.

47 The description comes from B. Harrison, *Separate Spheres: The Opposition to Women's Suffrage in Britain* (Holmes & Meier, New

York, 1978), chap. 4. Women were once an essential part of armies, but by the First World War 'the once integral place of women in Western armies had faded from memory' (like so much else about women!); see B. C. Hacker, 'Women and Military Institutions in Early Modern Europe: A Reconnaissance', *Signs*, 6(4), (1981), pp. 643–71 (the quotation is from p. 671).

48 Cited in *Rights*, 4(5), (1981), p. 4.

49 On women, the military and combat, see J. Stiehm, 'The Protected, The Protector, The Defender', *Women's Studies International Forum*, 5(1982), pp. 367–76; and 'Reflections on Women and Combat', Postcript to *Bring Me Men and Women: Mandated Change at the US Air Force Academy* (University of California Press, Berkeley, CA, 1981).

50 M. Foucault, *Discipline and Punish: The Birth of the Prison*, tr. A. Sheridan (Vintage Books, New York, 1979), p. 169.

51 Foucault, *Discipline and Punish*, pp. 222–3.

52 See C. Pateman, 'The Shame of the Marriage Contract', in J. Stiehm, ed., *Women's View of the Political World of Men* (Transnational Publishers, Dobbs Ferry, NY, 1984).

53 Mrs Thatcher provides a fascinating illustration. On the one hand she is 'the best man in the Cabinet', the victor of the Falklands War, accomplice of Reagan's state terrorism against Libya, and is photographed with weapons. On the other hand she talks to the press about 'feminine' matters (such as having her hair tinted), draws headlines like 'Four Years on and looking Ten Years Younger', and uses the language of good housekeeping to talk about cuts in social welfare spending (see A. Carter, 'Masochism for the Masses', *New Statesman*, 3 June 1983, pp. 8–10).

54 For a critique of a contractarian defence of prostitution, see my 'Defending Prostitution: Charges Against Ericsson', *Ethics*, 93 (1983), pp. 561–5, and *The Sexual Contract*, chap. 7.

55 The right is still hedged with immigration restrictions that make it hard for black British women to exercise it; for an account of the interaction of sex and race in British law, see Women, Immigration and Nationality Group, *Worlds Apart: Women Under Immigration and Nationality Law* (Pluto Press, London, 1985). For the USA, see V. Sapiro, 'Women, Citizenship and Nationality: Immigration and Naturalization Policies in the United States', *Politics and Society*, 13(1) (1984), pp. 1–26.

56 O'Brien. *The Politics of Reproduction*, p. 205.

3

Justifying Political Obligation

Political theorists today usually agree that political obligation poses a problem in the sense that it requires justification. Yet they are also almost unanimously agreed that there are no really serious or intractable difficulties in providing a justification for the authority of the liberal-democratic state or the political obligation of its citizens. Indeed, a few theorists have even gone so far as to claim that to suggest that political obligation requires a justification, to suggest that it genuinely does pose a general problem, is to show oneself as conceptually confused and in a state of philosophical disorder. I have taken issue with the latter claim elsewhere.[1] In this chapter I shall argue that not only is it a mistake to suppose that few problems exist in justifying political obligation in the liberal-democratic state, but that the justifications most frequently offered do not provide a solution to the problem. Political theorists typically appeal to voluntarist arguments that are, as I shall show, integrally bound up with the valued liberal principles of individual freedom and equality. These arguments cannot provide a justification of political obligation in the liberal-democratic state. Instead, they lead to the conclusion that it is only within a participatory or self-managing form of democracy that a justified political obligation can exist.

In discussing political obligation in the liberal-democratic state, theorists almost invariably rely on some form of voluntarism. Appeal is made to consent, contract, agreement, commitment or promises, or, more broadly, to the voluntary actions of individuals that, it is held, give rise to political obligation. That is to say, political theorists usually assume that political obligation is a form of self-assumed obligation, or a moral commitment freely entered into by individuals and freely taken upon themselves by their own actions. Underlying this assumption is a view of liberal democracy as a certain kind of society, with a specific kind of inhabitant, a view that has been nicely summed up by Rawls, who writes that liberal democracy comes 'as close as a society can to being a voluntary scheme . . . its members are autonomous and the obligations they recognize self-imposed.'[2] However, a striking feature of contemporary discussions of political obligation is that the question is rarely asked of exactly *why* voluntarism, or the ideas of consent, agreement and promising, are so important; why must obligations be self-assumed or self-imposed? An answer to this question is required if the magnitude of the problem of justifying political obligation in the liberal-democratic state is to be appreciated.

Political theories in which consent and the associated idea of the social contract were central and fundamental became prominent, as everyone knows, in the seventeenth and eighteenth centuries. Nor is this surprising. Political ideas and concepts, notwithstanding the way in which they are treated by so many political theorists, do not exist in a separate, timeless world of their own, but help to constitute specific forms of social life. Social contract and consent theories were formulated at a time of great socio-economic development and change, at a time when the capitalist market economy and the liberal constitutional state were beginning to emerge. As part of these developments, individuals and their relationships began to be seen in a new and revolutionary way. The contract theorists began their arguments from the premise that individuals are 'born free and equal' or are 'naturally' free and equal to each other. Such a conception was in complete contrast to the long-prevailing view that people were born in a God-created and 'natural' hierarchy of inequality and subordination. Within this traditional perspective, although disputes could frequently arise about the scope of specific rulers' right of command, there was scarcely room for general doubts about political obedience; rulers and political obedience were part of God's way with the world. But once the idea gained currency that individuals were born free and equal or were 'naturally' so (and how were they freely to enter contracts and make equal exchanges in the market, and pursue their interests as they saw fit, if they were not?) then a very large question was also raised about political authority and political obedience.

The social contract theorists were very well aware of the problem that liberal individualism brought with it; namely, how and why any free and equal individual could legitimately be governed by anyone else at all. The full implications of this subversive query have not, even today, fully worked themselves out; consider, for example, the argument of the feminists that there is no good reason for the widely held belief that a free and equal individual woman should be subject to the authority of the man whom she marries. Moreover, the emergence of this basic question means that the security in which political authority and political obedience were wrapped for so long can never return. To avoid misunderstanding I should note here that I am not, like the philosophical anarchists, arguing that a completely unbridgeable gulf exists between political authority and individual autonomy, or between individual freedom and equality.[3] I am not claiming that an acceptable answer to this fundamental question of government is impossible and that political obligation is an irrelevant concept. Rather, I am arguing that political obligation can be justified – and that it always requires justification – but that the only acceptable justification has implications that most writers on the subject neglect to investigate.

Given the initial postulate of individual freedom and equality, there is only *one* rational and acceptable justification for political obligation and political authority. Individuals must themselves consent, contract, agree, choose or promise to enter such a relationship. Political authority must have its basis in individuals' own voluntary actions, or, to put this the other way round, they must freely assume their political obligation for themselves. With the development of liberal individualism the relationship between individual and government has to be transformed from one of mere *obedience*, however engendered, into one of *obligation*, into a relationship in which individuals are bound by their own free acts. But political obligation then becomes a general problem; it can never be taken for granted, and a very specific justification is always required. The frequency with which voluntarist justifications are encountered in discussions of political obligation illustrates how reluctant theorists are to give up the liberal heritage bequeathed by the contract theorists. It also illustrates the widely held assumption that political obligation in the liberal-democratic state can quite easily be justified in the appropriate manner. However, most theorists display an extremely ambiguous attitude to the voluntarist justification of political obligation, although the ambiguity is not usually acknowledged.

It is frequently argued that whether or not individuals have agreed, consented or promised, they do nevertheless have a justified political obligation in the liberal-democratic state. This claim both upholds the assumption that political obligation in a liberal democracy is unproblematic and avoids the notorious difficulties of specifying who performed these actions, when, and how. An especially memorable instance of this line of argument can be found in Tussman's *Obligation and the Body Politic*. He argues that the liberal-democratic state should be seen as a voluntary association in which membership is based on consent. But he also states that not all citizens consent; some (the majority?) are 'child-bride citizens' who, like minors, are governed without their own consent. Yet these citizens too have a justified political obligation, although Tussman does not inform us as to its basis. It appears, then, that despite the apparent importance of consent, voluntarism is of only limited relevance to political life – and that political 'obligation' does not seem to be the appropriate characterization of the relation between all citizens and the state.

In our everyday lives the paradigmatic way in which we assume an obligation is by making a promise. When an individual says 'I promise . . .', he or she has assumed an obligation and has committed himself or herself to perform (or refrain from) certain actions. Political theorists have often suggested that political obligation is like, or rests upon or is a special kind of, a promise. But this is to assume once more that the relationship between citizens and the liberal-democratic state is indeed a form of self-assumed obligation. The comparison between political obligation and the social practice of promising is usually drawn in very general terms, and is rarely pursued. Yet it is precisely through a consideration of this comparison that the full extent of the problem of political obligation in the liberal-democratic state is revealed. In recent years moral philosophers have paid a good deal of attention to promising. I can mention here only some aspects of promising that are of particular importance for the present argument.[4]

Making promises is one of the most basic ways in which free and equal individuals can freely create their own social relationships. As part of their social and moral education, individuals learn how to take part in the social practice of promising and so develop as persons with certain kinds of capacities. These capacities include the ability to engage in the rational and reasoned deliberation required to decide whether, on this occasion, a promise ought to be made, and also the ability to look back and critically evaluate their own actions and relationships; sometimes a promise may justifiably be broken or altered or revised in some way. Now, if political obligation is like, or is a form of, promising there is an important question to be asked; namely, how can citizens assume their political, like their other, obligations for themselves; what form of political system would make this possible? In short, it must be asked what is the political counterpart of the social practice of promising.

In political life voting is the practice that enables individuals to engage in reasoned deliberation and decide for themselves how to order their political lives and environment. The result of a vote, like that of a promise, is a commitment or an obligation, although in the case of voting it will be a collective, not an individual, commitment. However, this abstract and conceptual connection between voting in general and political obligation does not tell us the specific form that voting must take if a political practice of self-assumed obligation is to exist. Political theorists frequently suggest that a liberal-democratic form of voting is required and I shall present some further objections to this suggestion later. At present it is sufficient to point out that, for the analogy with promising to hold, voting must enable individuals collectively to decide upon their political obligation for themselves. It is a direct or participatory democratic form of voting that allows them to do this. It is within a participatory form of democracy that individuals retain their political decision-making power as citizens. They exercise political authority over themselves in their private capacity as individuals (something which many people find an odd idea, so used are we to thinking of representatives exercising political authority over citizens), and they collectively commit themselves, or freely obligate themselves, to do whatever is necessary to implement their own decisions and to maintain their self-managed political association in being. It is also a participatory democratic form of voting that, like promising, enables citizens politically to exercise their capacity to reflect upon and evaluate their own actions and decisions and, if necessary, to change them. Thus, the liberal principle of individual freedom and equality and its corollary of self-assumed obligation lead towards and provide a justification for participatory, not liberal, democracy.

There are two further points that should be made here. The first, to which I shall return, is that political obligation, in a participatory democracy, is owed to fellow citizens and not to the state or its representatives. To whom else could it be owed? Second, it is important to emphasize that the question now being considered is *not* the question asked in recent discussions of political obligation. Theorists do not usually ask what are the political consequences of the ideal of self-assumed obligation – that would presuppose that there is a problem! Instead, following from their assumption that political obligation is justified in the liberal-democratic state, they (implicitly) ask: how is it that individuals voluntarily agree to their political obligation, or what are the voluntary actions that can reasonably be said to, or be inferred to, give rise to political obligation? Before looking at their answers to *this* question, I want to pause to say something about the relation of my argument, and recent discussions, to classic social contract theory, taking Locke's theory as my example.

The hypothesis of the contract is a way of showing how 'in the beginning' free and equal individuals can rationally agree to live under political authority. However, the *liberal* social contract has two stages and the significance of each stage is very different.[5] It is the first part of the contract story that shows how the 'dispersed' individuals form a new political community. This part of the social contract establishes an obligation between, and places authority in the hands of, the members of the community themselves. Thus the first stage of the contract, taken by itself, is related to the question about the comparison with promising. Locke treats the first part of the contract as necessary (a political community must be created) but as an unimportant preliminary. It is the second stage of the contract that is fundamental to liberal theory. The second stage embodies the assumption that it is necessary for the members of the new community to alienate their right to exercise political authority to a few representatives. The free agreement of the contract thus becomes an agreement that a few representatives shall decide upon the content of individuals' political obligation. Self-assumed obligation becomes an obligation to let others decide upon one's political obligation. The comparison with promising now begins to appear misplaced and, furthermore, political obligation is now owed to the state and its representatives, not by citizens to each other.

Locke could not complete his theory with the idea of the social contract. He had to meet the patriarchalists' objection that an agreement of the fathers could not bind sons, not if the latter were truly born free and equal. Locke had, therefore, to introduce the notion of consent into his theory.[6] The sons had, in their turn, voluntarily to consent or agree to the political arrangements made by their fathers. Locke had to answer the same problems as contemporary theorists: given a legitimate political system, how can individuals be said to consent to it? From what aspect of their actions can their political obligation be inferred?

In his discussion of consent, Locke remarks that no one doubts that express consent gives rise to political obligation and makes an individual the subject of government. The difficulty about consent arises 'where he has made no Expressions of it at all.' Locke solves this problem by his famous claim that the tacit consent of the members of the community can be inferred from their peaceful everyday interactions under the protection of government. But who gives express consent, and how? Locke's treatment of consent is hardly a model of clarity, but the most plausible answer to this question is that express consent is given by the individuals who inherit property, individuals who can also be called the politically relevant members of their society. Locke calls those who expressly consent 'perfect members' of society and indicates that they, unlike individuals who merely consent tacitly, have no right of emigration.[7] It therefore seems that Locke is implying that a differential political obligation exists: those who expressly consent have a greater obligation than the rest.

In this hint of a differential political obligation, as in his other arguments, Locke closely foreshadows more recent discussions of political obligation. But there is also a very important difference between Locke's social contract theory and contemporary arguments. In the seventeenth century Locke could not merely take it for granted that the political obligation of citizens of the liberal state was justified. He argued, in his conjectural history of the state of nature, that the socio-economic developments of his day had rendered unacceptable the claims for the divine right of kings and for patriarchy. Only a liberal, constitutional, representative state could protect individuals' property – and the social contract story provides the necessary voluntarist justification for the authority of such a state. It must be emphasized that it is quite clear that Locke's contract is an answer to a *problem* of political authority and political obligation, whereas in the most recent revival of contract theory, as in other present-day discussions of political obligation, no such problem is admitted. Rawls, in *A Theory of Justice*, assumes that the liberal-democratic state exercises a justified political authority over its citizens. His 'original position', and the choices of its 'parties', is a device to show why 'our' considered judgements about liberal democracy are rational and acceptable judgements. It shows us why we are right to regard the relationship of citizens and the state in the way that we do – as embodying a justified political obligation. Rawls's contract exhibits the rationality of the state; unlike classic social contract theory it neither begins from the position, nor admits, that the authority of the state poses a problem. In other words, the liberal-democratic state is today entirely taken for granted as if it were a natural feature of the world. This marks a most significant shift from the classic contract theorists' view that the state is conventional.

That political obligation is no longer seen as a problem means that consent is now treated explicitly 'as a constituent element of democratic ideology'.[8] Criticisms of the ideological character of much liberal-democratic theory are now familiar and I shall not pursue this here, but it is worth commenting on one ideological assumption and its relationship to social contract theory.[9] It is widely assumed by liberal-democratic theorists that liberal-democratic voting works in practice as it is held to in theory and, in particular, that voting protects and furthers the interests of all citizens. Locke was able to make his inference about tacit consent because, during the contract, individuals exchange their 'natural' freedom and equality for the civil freedom and legal equality of political subjects. The end of government is protection, and in their new status all citizens' 'property', in both of Locke's senses of the term, is protected (or they would not enter the contract), no matter what substantive social inequalities divide them. Hence, all can be said to continue to give their consent. Since Locke's day, the status of political subject has been transformed and institutionalized as the formally equal political status of liberal-democratic citizenship, which includes civil liberties and the right to exercise the franchise. Voting, it is claimed, protects the interest of all citizens, no matter how substantively unequal they are; and so all can be said to consent.

It is therefore not surprising that the most popular recent argument about consent is that it can be said to be given through, or even equated with the existence of, the liberal-democratic electoral mechanism. I have already challenged the assumption that the general conceptual connection between voting and political obligation is given actual expression through liberal-democratic voting (although the general connection helps to explain why this may appear 'obvious'). Even fairly cursory reflection on the empirical evidence about voting behaviour casts immediate doubt on the simple identification of consent with liberal-democratic voting. It is argued by Plamenatz, for example, that even electoral abstainers consent, and Gewirth states that the meaning of the electoral 'method of consent' is that 'one can participate if one chooses to do so' and, therefore, 'the individual is obligated . . . whether he personally utilizes his opportunity or not.'[10] The close relationship of this argument to conclusions drawn about political apathy by empirical theorists of democracy is obvious; and so are its defects. What is ignored, of course, is who abstains and why they do so. The empirical evidence shows that electoral abstainers tend to be drawn disproportionately from lower socio-economic groups and from the female sex. The evidence also suggests that they abstain because voting does not seem worthwhile; that is, they do not believe that voting achieves what it is claimed to in liberal-democratic theory. As Verba and Nie have shown, political participation, including voting, 'helps those who are already better off'.[11] It hardly makes sense to insist that individuals are consenting when they refrain from an activity which helps reinforce their disadvantaged position.

Yet, it might be argued, those who vote can surely be said to consent. The question of the 'meaning' of the vote is an extremely complex one and I can only briefly mention two of the major objections to this claim. The first objection concerns the votes of men and women. Political scientists often argue that men and women are doing something different when they vote; they argue that a female vote is 'qualitatively different' from a male vote. Men, acting like good liberals, vote from self-interest; women vote for moral reasons, out of 'a kind of bloodless love of the good'.[12] But, if that is so, then can women's votes 'mean' the same thing as men's votes, namely, consent? Either political theorists have to give up their male chauvinist prejudices or they have to construct a sex-differentiated argument about political obligation and voting.

The second objection centres on the requirements of a meaningful or genuine sense of 'consent'. When an individual makes a promise, he or she knows what they are committed to and can break or alter the obligation if this is necessary. An acceptable sense of 'consent' also implies that those consenting can have reasonable knowledge of the consequences of their action, or can refuse or withdraw their consent. There are some familiar features of liberal-democratic elections that illustrate how difficult it is for this requirement to be met. I shall leave aside the problems consequent upon attempts by representatives and officials to 'defactualize' the political world,[13] and from systematic lying on their part, and note, first, that parties and candidates are now 'sold' to the electorate through commercial advertising techniques and that citizens are urged to vote on the basis of 'images'; but in what sense can one consent to an image? Second, the crude equation of voting and consent ignores the arguments that liberal-democratic voting is no more than a ritual or, at least, contains large ritual elements. Certainly, many citizens see their vote as a 'duty' associated with citizenship and, again, the important question is how far, if at all, this leaves room for anything that could reasonably be called freely and deliberately given 'consent'.

Some theorists of political obligation have now ceased to make any reference to 'consent' at all. They offer a different form of voluntarist argument that, like Locke's doctrine of tacit consent, looks not to activities that are part of universal citizenship (which, of course, did not exist in Locke's day) but to everyday life. Such arguments typically appeal to individuals' acceptance of benefits from the state, or their participation in liberal-democratic institutions, as giving rise to obligations. This approach, like Locke's tacit consent, is neatly all-inclusive; indeed, it is a mere reinterpretation of 'tacit consent'. It is another way of inferring political obligation – yet apparently avoiding the difficulties associated with 'consent'. Locke's theory can be interpreted without reference to tacit consent and some commentators claim that this is the most appropriate reading.[14] Locke can be seen to argue that, having taken advantage of the social practice of inheritance, individuals (in fairness) have an obligation to play their part to keep the practice in being, or, having accepted the benefits of highways, they have an obligation to obey the government that builds and maintains them.

It is not clear [end of consent] constitute an argument at all. It looks su[...] extended collection of conceptual truis[...] or practice necessarily implies that ind[...] are participating or cooperating within it; they 'benefit' because all do their share ('recognize their obligation') to keep the institution going. However, the 'benefits' cannot be independently specified apart from the participation, and the latter *is*, or constitutes, the practice itself. But even if this form of voluntarism is treated as a genuine argument, there are some basic objections to it.

It is not, for example, obvious how the obligations (if, indeed, there are such) consequent upon participation in the multiplicity of liberal-democratic institutions are related to *political* obligation. The equation of voting and consent does have the advantage that it focuses on a political activity. Moreover, because these arguments look to everyday life, they are immediately open to the challenge that, if they show anything, it is that a differential political obligation exists. I have not found any attempts in the relevant literature to specify what counts as a 'benefit' but it seems clear that, taking liberal-democratic institutions in their entirety, some individuals 'benefit' a good deal more than others and the outcome of participation is very different for some individuals and groups than for others. This applies even if one takes the fundamental 'benefit' of liberal theory as an example; the protection of the property that individuals have in their persons. Empirical research shows that mortality rates differ between social classes;[15] that 'the poor do not receive the same treatment at the hands of the agents of law-enforcement as the well-to-do or middle class. This differential treatment is systematic and complete';[16] and that women are not afforded the same protection as men from sexual and other assaults by men[17] (and it can be added that men are widely believed to own the property that women have in their persons). Why, then, should most political theorists assume that the obligation held to be consequent upon participation in institutions, or acceptance of benefits, is an equal obligation for all citizens, whether rich or poor, working-class or middle-class, male of female?

Interestingly enough, Rawls concludes, on the basis of this form of voluntarist argument, that citizens are far from having an equal obligation – in fact, many citizens do not have a political *obligation* at all. It is only the 'better-placed members of society', who also take an active part in political life, who have a political obligation. The rest of the population have merely a *natural duty* to obey, which, 'requires no voluntary acts in order to apply'.[18] While Rawls has drawn a logical conclusion from arguments about participation and 'benefits', voluntarism and the ideal of social life as a 'voluntary scheme' have now been thrown aside for the bulk of the population.

This highlights the dilemmas facing theorists who wish to retain voluntarism and to treat political obligation in the liberal-democratic state as unproblematic. An all-inclusive obligation can be inferred ('tacit consent'), but at the price of reducing the idea of self-assumed obligation to meaninglessness. Yet to admit that some individuals may have a lesser obligation than others, or that some have only a 'natural duty' of obedience, is either to shake liberal-democratic theory to its foundations or to move well along the road to the abandonment of some basic liberal principles. And any attempt to give genuine content to the ideas of consent and self-assumed obligation immediately opens up all the critical questions about the liberal-democratic state that most contemporary theorists seem determined to avoid.

It is, perhaps, symptomatic of an unease about the present state of the argument about the relationship of the citizen to the liberal-democratic state that there is an increasing tendency for theorists to advance a rather startling argument. They argue that political obligation is owed primarily not to the state but to fellow citizens.[19] It must be added that they also assume that the state does have a justified claim on its citizens – but their own argument begins to cut the ground from under this assumption. The question cannot be avoided of why and on what grounds, if obligation is owed to fellow citizens, it must also be assumed that it is justifiably owed to the state.

It is not as surprising as it may appear at first sight that theorists have begun to argue in this way. The logic of the voluntarist arguments that look to everyday interactions of citizens, and to 'benefits' and 'participation', is that, if obligations are assumed in this way, they are owed to fellow members of institutions and fellow participants in social practices. I have already noted that this raises an important question about what counts as 'political' obligation. If 'political' obligation *is* owed to fellow citizens, then a sharp break must be made with liberal-democratic theory that insists that it is the state that is the locus of the political and the object of political obligation. The view of political obligation as owed to fellow citizens derives, as I have argued, from a perspective that takes seriously the idea of self-assumed obligation as a political ideal. This raises again the fundamental question of why, if self-assumed obligation is as important as 300 years of liberal argument assures us it is, we should not assume *all* of our obligations for ourselves and organize our political life on that basis.

Theorists of the liberal state have only one convincing answer to that question. They can argue that participatory democracy is not empirically feasible; the liberal-democratic state is the best that we can do. If that answer is given – and it is implicit in many discussions of political obligation – the consequences need to be spelled out. The answer implies that voluntarism is irrelevant to political life. Although we are capable of assuming obligations in our everyday life, the activity has no place outside the private sphere. It is, in short, to admit that the noble liberal ideal of individual freedom and equality and its corollaries of self-assumed obligation and the vision of social life as a 'voluntary scheme' can only be very partially realized.

Futhermore, if political theorists dismiss the possibility of participatory or self-managing democracy, they should stop pretending that the liberal-democratic state rests on a voluntarist basis of genuine commitments. That is, they should stop pretending that the freely created relationship of political *obligation* is involved, because this relationship is an integral part of a political ideal now admitted to be out of reach. Instead, they should argue directly that, given the empirical necessity of the liberal-democratic state and the advantages that it has over other existing forms of political system, there are good, but non-voluntarist, reasons for political *obedience*. Rawls's notion of a natural duty of political obedience, or a contemporary version of 'my political station and its duties', may commend themselves for this purpose. And there are, of course, political theorists who present a utilitarian account of the relationship between citizens and the liberal-democratic state. The reason why I have ignored this obvious competitor to voluntarism in my argument should now be clear. No matter how economical an argument utilitarianism can provide, or how appropriate it may appear, utilitarian arguments, despite the manner in which they are so often presented, are arguments for obedience, not obligation. However, theorists are unlikely to argue only in terms of 'obedience' instead of 'obligation', for this would strip the liberal-democratic state of a major portion of its ideological mantle. It would be to recognize that central liberal ideas, if taken seriously, lead beyond the liberal-democratic state.

NOTES

1 'Political Obligation and Conceptual Analysis', *Political Studies*, 21 (1973), pp. 199–218.

2 J. Rawls, *A Theory of Justice* (Oxford University Press, Oxford, 1972), p. 13.

3 A recent example of the philosophical anarchist argument can be found in P. Abbot, *The Shotgun behind the Door* (University of Georgia Press, Athens, GA, 1976). R. P. Wolff, *In Defense of Anarchism* (Harper & Row, New York, 1970) is equivocal about his philosophical anarchism. In the final section of the book he suggests that a solution to the problem of autonomy and authority can be found in institutions based on 'voluntary compliance'.

4 A detailed discussion of the social practice of promising and its relationship to political obligation and to contracts can be found in C. Pateman, *The Problem of Political Obligation: A Critical Analysis of Liberal Theory*, 2nd ed. (Polity Press, Cambridge, 1985; University of California Press, Berkeley, CA, 1985).

5 Rousseau's social contract theory provides a brilliant critique of, and non-liberal alternative to, liberal contract theory. His critique is usually ignored by writers on political obligation.

6 For the distinction between the contract and consent, usually treated as synonymous, see G. J. Schochet, *Patriarchalism in Political Thought* (Basil Blackwell, Oxford, 1975), pp. 9, 262.

7 J. Locke, 'Second Treatise of Government', in *Two Treatises of*

Goverment, ed. P. Laslett, 2nd ed., (Cambridge University Press, Cambridge, 1967), II, §116–22.

8   P. H. Partridge, *Consent and Consensus* (Macmillan, London, 1971), 23.

9   The continuing ideological importance of the legacy of liberal social contract theory is, rather curiously, overlooked by Marxist and neo-Marxist writers. C. B. Macpherson, in *The Political Theory of Possessive Individualism* (Oxford University Press, Oxford, 1962), ignores the contract in his interpretation of Hobbes and Locke, and argues that the liberal state was justified by the equal subordination of all individuals to the inevitable laws of the market. Similarly, J. Habermas, *Legitimation Crisis* (Heinemann, London, 1976), p. 22, argues that 'the bourgeois constitutional state finds its justification in the legitimate relations of production.' They thus neglect the directly *political* justification of the liberal state and the present ideological strength of the idea that all individuals have a common interest as citizens.

10   J. Plamenatz, *Man and Society* (Longmans, London, 1963), vol. 1, pp. 238–40; A. Gewirth, 'Political Justice', in *Social Justice* ed. R. B. Brandt (Prentice Hall, Englewood Cliffs, NJ, 1962), p. 138.

11   S. Verba and N. H. Nie, *Participation in America* (Harper & Row, New York, 1972), p. 338.

12   R. E. Lane, *Political Life* (Free Press, New York, 1959), p. 212.

13   The term is H. Arendt's in 'Lying in Politics', in *Crises of the Republic* (Penguin Books, Harmondsworth, Middlesex, 1973).

14   For a recent example of this interpretation, see A. J. Simmons, 'Tacit Consent and Political Obligation', *Philosophy and Public Affairs*, 5 (1976), pp. 274–91.

15   See, for example, A. Antonovsky, 'Class and the Chance for Life', in *Social Problems and Public Policy*, ed. L. Rainwater (Aldine, Chicago, IL, 1974).

16   W. J. Chambliss and R. B. Seidman, *Law Order, and Power* (Addison-Wesley, Boston, MA, 1971), pp. 475.

17   See, for example, E. Pizzey, *Scream Quietly or the Neighbours Will Hear* (Penguin Books, Harmondsworth, Middlesex, 1974); B. Toner, *The Facts of Rape* (Arrow Books, London, 1977). See also the judgement of the Court of Appeal in *R. v Holdsworth*, reported in *The Times*, 22 June 1977.

18   Rawls, *A Theory of Justice*, pp. 14, 116, 344.

19   See, for example, M. Walzer, *Obligations* (Simon & Schuster, New York, 1971); B. Zwiebach, *Civility and Disobedience* (Cambridge University Press, Cambridge, 1975); K. Johnson, 'Political Obligation and the Voluntary Association Model of the State', *Ethics*, 86 (1975), pp. 17–29; R. K. Dagger, 'What Is Political Obligation?', *American Political Science Review*, 71(1) (1977), pp. 86–94.

4

Women and Consent

The history of modern consent theory over the last three centuries largely consists of attempts by theorists to suppress the radical and subversive implications of their own arguments. More recently, writers on consent have been assisted in this endeavour by the contemporary consensus that women, and the relationship between the sexes, are of no special relevance to political theory. Yet an examination of the question of women and consent highlights all the problems that generations of consent theorists have tried to avoid.

Contemporary consent theory has no room for two fundamental questions: first, why consent is of central importance to liberal theory and practice; second, how far theory and practice coincide, and whether genuine consent is possible within the institutions of the liberal-democratic state. Consent is usually discussed only in a narrowly conceived political context in the course of arguments about political obligation. Most consent theorists are content to accept the verdict that

> the idea of 'consent' has survived as a constituent element of democratic ideology: as a specification of an essential characteristic of democratic regimes which distinguish them from the non-democratic.[1]

The straightforward assertion that liberal democracies *are* based on consent avoids the 'standard embarrassment' that occurs when theorists attempt to show how and when citizens perform this act.[2] This assertion also avoids the question of who consents, and therefore glosses over the ambiguity, inherent in consent theory from its beginnings, about which individuals or groups are capable of consenting and so count as full members of the political order. However, embarrassment is spared by reducing the concept of consent to meaninglessness. Consent as ideology cannot be distinguished from habitual acquiescence, assent, silent dissent, submission or even enforced submission. Unless refusal of consent or withdrawal of consent are real possibilities, we can no longer speak of 'consent' in any genuine sense.[3]

The relationship of consent in everyday life to the (postulated) consent of citizens to the liberal-democratic state remains unexplored. Consent theorists fail to consider those areas of social life where consent is of practical importance to individuals, but the problems involved form part of the general difficulties and evasions of consent theory. Women are thus easily ignored, because consent in everyday life particularly concerns them. The most intimate relations of women with men are held to be governed by consent; women consent to marriage, and sexual intercourse without a woman's consent constitutes the criminal offence of rape. To begin to examine the unwritten history of women and consent brings the suppressed problems of consent theory to the surface. Women exemplify the individuals whom consent theorists have declared to be incapable of consenting. Yet, simultaneously, women have been presented as always consenting, and their explicit non-consent has been treated as irrelevant or has been reinterpreted as 'consent'.

It might be objected that today women have been granted equal citizenship with men in the liberal democracies, so any major difficulties about their consent must lie in the past. To show why this appearance of equality between men and women is misleading, it is necessary to return to the origins of modern consent theory. Consent theorists in the seventeenth and eighteenth centuries were clear why consent was so important both in the state and in the relationship between the sexes. The starting point of early social contract and consent theory was a specific conception of individuals as 'naturally' free and equal, or as born free and equal to each other. The idea that individuals are 'naturally' free and equal raises a fundamental, and revolutionary, question about authority relationships of all kinds; how and why a free and equal individual can ever legitimately be governed by anyone else. Unlike philosophical anarchists, liberal and democratic theorists argue that this question can be satisfactorily answered. It is possible to find a justification for the exercise of authority, but there is only *one* acceptable justification: if their freedom and equality is to be preserved, free and equal individuals must voluntarily commit themselves – for example, by consenting – to enter into such a relationship. Consent theory is thus a specific example of a broader voluntarist theory of society which argues that relationships of authority and obligation must be grounded in the voluntary acts or commitments of individuals.

From the beginning, consent theorists have attempted to avoid the revolutionary implications of voluntarism. They have adopted two main strategies to neutralize the impact of their arguments: first, they have turned to hypothetical voluntarism;[4] second, they have excluded certain individuals and social relationships from the scope of consent. The most familiar example of hypothetical voluntarism is Locke's notorious 'tacit consent'. Not only did Locke argue from a hypothetical social contract, but his 'consent' is merely an inference from, or reinterpretation of, the existence of specific social practices and institutions. Most contemporary discussions of consent are little more than modernized versions of Locke's claim that the consent of future generations (to the social contract made by their forefathers) can always be said to be given if individuals are going peacefully about their daily lives, even though there are 'no Expressions of it at all'.[5] The reinterpretation of certain actions as 'consent' appears at its extreme in Hobbes's theory. His willingness to take individualism to its logical conclusion allowed him to argue that all authority relationships are based on consent, even between parent and infant. The parents' domination over a child derives not from procreation but from 'Consent, either expressed, or by other sufficient arguments declared'. For Hobbes, overwhelming power is sufficient argument, so that in the state of nature the infant's 'consent' to its mother's rule can be assumed.[6] Hobbes's concept of 'consent' merely reinterprets the fact of power and submission; it makes no difference whether submission is voluntary or obtained through threats, even the threat of death. Because Hobbes argues that fear and liberty are compatible, 'consent' has the same meaning whether it arises from submission in fear of a conqueror's sword or in fear of exposure by a parent, or whether it is a consequence of the (hypothetical) social contract.

Hypothetical voluntarism avoids the 'standard embarrassment' of arguing from actual consent, and the embarrassment is more securely circumvented if only some of the inhabitants of the state of nature or civil society are included in the category of 'free and equal individuals'. Voluntarism presupposes that individuals are rational, that they have, or are able to develop, the moral and intellectual capacities necessary to enable free commitment to be given. 'Free and equal individuals', to use Lockean terminology, own the property in their persons and their attributes, including their capacity to give consent. The individual is the 'guardian of his own consent'.[7] However, the latter formulation should be read literally; the consent is *his* consent. Neither the classic contract theorists nor their successors incorporated women into their arguments on the same footing as men. Contract and consent theory developed partly as an attack on patriarchal theory, but it is necessary to emphasize the limited character of the attack on patriarchal claims that political authority had a 'natural' basis in a father's procreative powers and that sons were 'naturally' in subjection to their fathers. Contract theorists did not extend their criticism to the relationship between men and women, or more specifically, husbands and wives (who are also fathers and mothers).

The state of nature is usually pictured as inhabited by patriarchal families.[8] It was also widely argued that fathers of families entered the social contract, wives being 'concluded by their Husbands'.[9] In Locke's conjectural history of the state of nature, fathers become monarchs with the 'scarce avoidable' and tacit consent of their adult sons. Locke does not mention mothers in this context, but his unspoken assumption is that the wife and mother also gives her 'consent' to this transformation of her husband. Indeed, such 'consent' is part of the marriage contract, for Locke agreed with Filmer that a wife's subjection to her husband had 'a Foundation in Nature', and that the will of a husband should 'take place before that of his wife in all things of their common Concernment'.[10] However, this means that women are excluded from the status of 'individual' that is basic to consent theory; if a wife's subjection to her husband has a 'natural' foundation, she *cannot* also be seen as a 'naturally' free and equal individual. Only if women are seen as 'free and equal individuals' is their consent relevant at all.

Even in the seventeenth century, marriage was seen as a contractual relationship.[11] Today, a husband's authority is not merely taken for granted as 'natural', but is said to be based on the consent of his wife; therefore, it can be objected, women are seen as capable of consent in everyday life at least. This appearance of consent, whether three centuries ago or today, should not be taken at face value. It obscures a fundamentally important question: Why should a free and equal female individual enter a contract that *always* places her in subjection and subordination to a male individual? Logically, two free and equal individuals should be expected to govern their families jointly. The past and present *content* of the marriage contract reveals the underlying assumption that women are *not* free and equal. Women are not 'individuals' who own the property they have in their persons and capacities, so the question of their 'consent' to the authority of men never actually arises. Rather, their apparent 'consent' to the authority of their husbands is only a formal recognition of their 'natural' subordination. Having been under the authority of their father, they do not, like sons, enter a new status on maturity, but are 'given away' by their father to another man to continue in their 'natural' state of dependence and subjection.

The implications of the convention that a wife must bow to the authority of and be economically dependent upon her husband, who is 'head of the household', are obscured more thoroughly in the late twentieth century than in earlier times, because it is now firmly held that marriage can properly be based only on the consent of two individuals. But this appearance of equality between two individuals cloaks the unequal status of husband and wife created through the marriage contract. In the 1980s, the authority of husbands can be explained only because the apparent 'consent' of one 'individual' is not consent at all. The contemporary significance of the contract theorists' reconciliation with patriarchalism has been hidden behind the liberal conviction that marriage is a matter of 'individual' choice.

Ironically, Rousseau, the only contract theorist who pursued the radical implications of the doctrine, is the most explicit about the reasons why women must be excluded from its scope. Rousseau accepted the patriarchal assertion that women were 'naturally' subordinate to men. He gives a full account of the contrasting 'natural' characters of the sexes, a contrast which, he argues, must be given expression in the sexual double standard.[12] Rousseau provides a clear statement of the claim that women are incapable of consent, but, at the same time, he also denies this and reinterprets explicit non-consent as its opposite. Rousseau attacked the hypothetical voluntarism of Hobbes's and Locke's versions of the contract argument as a fraud which was tantamount to a contract of slavery, but he advocated precisely such a contract as the basis of the relationship between the sexes. In Rousseau's participatory, voluntarist political order, women must remain excluded because of their 'natural' moral characters and their deleterious influence upon the morals and civic virtue of men. In time-honoured tradition, Rousseau divides women into the good and the dissolute, or whores. Women can remain good only if they stay within the shelter of domestic life. Geneva, following the ancient world, provided an example of civic virtue because its *circles*, social and political clubs, were sexually segregated. The sexes were allowed to come together only where it was proper for them to do so; this is 'the plan of nature, which gives different tastes to the two sexes, so that they live apart each in his [sic] way.' In the *circles*, men are able to educate themselves for civil life. They 'can devote themselves to grave and serious discourse without fear of ridicule' from women, and without fear of becoming 'feminized' and so weakened as citizens.[13]

The successive transformations of human consciousness or 'nature' that Rousseau charts in the *Discourse on Inequality* and the *Social Contract* are actually transformations of male consciousness.[14] Emile alone can be educated in the independence and judgement necessary in a citizen who gives consent and is capable of further education through political participation. Sophie's education fosters the characteristics – a concern with reputation, dependence and deceitfulness, for example – that Rousseau condemns as 'vices' in men. She is educated to serve and obey Emile. Women, Rousseau declares, 'must be trained to bear the yoke from the first . . . and to submit themselves to the will of others',[15] that is, the will of men. The influence of women, even good women, always corrupts men, because women are 'naturally' incapable of attaining the status of free and equal individuals, or citizens, and incapable of developing the capacities required to give consent.

Yet, at the same time, in sexual relationships, the 'consent' of women is all-important. Moreover, their consent can always be assumed to be given – even though apparently it is being refused. According to Rousseau, men are the 'natural' sexual aggressors; women are 'destined to resist'. Rousseau asks 'what would become of the human species if the order of attack and defense were changed?'[16] Modesty and chasteness are the pre-eminent female virtues, but because women are also creatures of passion, they must use their natural skills of duplicity and dissemblance to maintain their modesty. In particular, *they must always say 'no' even when they desire to say 'yes'*. And here Rousseau reveals the heart of the problem of women and consent. Apparent refusal of consent can *never*, in a woman, be taken at face value:

> Why do you consult their words when it is not their mouths that speak? . . . The lips always say 'No,' and rightly so; but the tone is not always the same, and that cannot lie. . . . Must her modesty condemn her to misery? Does she not require a means of indicating her inclinations without open expression?[17]

A man must learn to interpret a woman's 'consent' when, as in Locke's civil society, there are no obvious expressions of it at all.

> To win this silent consent is to make use of all the violence permitted in love. To read it in the eyes, to see it in the ways in spite of the mouth's denial. . . . If he then completes his happiness, he is not brutal, he is decent. He does not insult chasteness; he respects it; he serves it. He leaves it the honor of still defending what it would have perhaps abandoned.[18]

Rousseau's view of the relationship between husbands and wives also shows that the contradiction between the appearance of consent in the marriage contract and the reality of its content goes far deeper than I indicated in my earlier remarks. Rousseau, for example, argues that when married to Emile, Sophie can rule by love 'if you make your favours scarce and precious'. Her refusal must not be capricious, but reflect her modesty, so that Emile can 'honour his wife's chastity, without having to complain of her coldness'.[19] But whatever the intrinsic merits of this advice, a wife is unlikely to be able to carry it out. The consequence of entering into the marriage contract is that the subsequent 'consent' of the woman to her husband's sexual demands is legally and socially presupposed. The legal basis for the belief that the initial 'consent' of the woman in the marriage contract can never be retracted remains unexamined.[20] This fact, together with the difficulties encountered in attempts at reforming rape law to extend its provisions to women within marriage (success to some degree has been achieved only in Sweden and South Australia and in some states of the United States) testifies to the tenacity with which popular and legal opinion clings to the conviction that rape is impossible within marriage.

Legal writers in the period of classic contract theory left no doubt about the status of wives and their 'consent'. A wife, as Blackstone wrote in his famous *Commentaries on the Laws of England*, was a legal non-person; 'by marriage, the husband and wife are one person in law; . . . the very being or legal existence of the woman is suspended. . . .'[21] In what is 'still the most quoted authority on the British law of rape',[22] Hale's *History of the Pleas of the Crown*, it is stated that 'the husband cannot be guilty of a rape committed by himself upon his lawful wife, for by their mutual matrimonial consent and contract the wife hath given up herself in this kind unto her husband, which she cannot retract.'[23] It is hardly surprising that feminists in the mid-nineteenth century so frequently compared wives to the slaves of the West Indies and the American South, for legally and socially a wife was seen as the property of her husband; she could be legally imprisoned in the matrimonial house and could be beaten. John Stuart Mill was moved to comment that although he was

> far from pretending that wives are in general no better treated than slaves . . . no slave is a slave to the same lengths, and in so full a sense of the word as a wife is. . . . [A husband] can claim from her and enforce the lowest degradation of a human being, that of being made the instrument of an animal function contrary to her inclinations.[24]

A century later, a separate legal personality has been granted to women, but their formal legal status is contradicted by social beliefs and practices.

In certain areas of the law where 'consent' is central, notably in the law concerning rape, social reluctance to recognize women as 'free and equal individuals' denies in practice what the law proclaims in principle. Rape is central to the problem of women and consent in everyday life. Rape is widespread, both in and out of marriage, but although women of all ages and classes are attacked, the majority of rapes are not reported.[25] Here I shall concentrate on the implementation of the criminal law in the courts, because evidence is available, and because it reveals in a dramatic fashion how contradictory beliefs about women and consent are embedded in liberal-democratic social institutions.

Rape law has recently been described as a 'parody of justice'.[26] Of the many reasons for this, the most fundamental is the manner in which the 'consent' of the victim is interpreted – or ignored. In this matter, popular opinion and the courts are Hobbesian; they identify submission, including enforced submission, with consent. Accused rapists almost invariably offer the defence that the woman actually consented, or that they believed she did (and I shall return to the question of belief in a moment). One reason why this defence is so successful, and why such a small proportion of cases of rape are ever reported, is that a woman is unlikely to convince either the public, the police or a judge and jury that she did not consent to sexual intercourse[27] unless she is badly physically injured or unless she can prove that she resisted. However, the criterion for resistance, too, tends to be physical injury. To prove non-consent, 'the showing of physical damage beyond the simple evidence of penetration has, almost, the status of a legal standard'.[28]

The identification of submission with consent, unless resistance can be proved, is bound up historically with a legal distinction (that obtained before the Criminal Law Amendment Act of 1885) between acts 'against the will' of a woman, which were performed by force in the face of her resistance, and acts which were 'without her consent'. This distinction was crucial in cases where intercourse was obtained through impersonation or subterfuge. Such cases have fascinated legal writers on consent and rape, and one commentator has stated that 'since 1925 the sparse legal discussion . . . has remained focused on cases of intercourse induced by fraud' – not perpetrated by force.[29] For example, in cases where a husband, to whom the woman would have consented, was impersonated and no force was used, it was generally held that the act was not 'against her will' and so was not rape.[30] Legal opinion wrestled for many years with the problem of whether fraud vitiated consent, and the issue is still not fully resolved. The Sexual Offences Act 1956 (UK) makes it an offence to obtain intercourse through the impersonation of a husband, but remains silent about the impersonation of other men.[31] Moreover, there is still a large area of legal uncertainty about the acts that constitute an instance of 'force' or 'threat' that separate forced 'submission' from voluntary 'consent'.

In a rape case in Britain in 1975, the judge stated of the accused: 'I have no doubt you instilled terror into this woman when you went into that room and made your intentions quite clear'[32] – yet the accused was found not guilty of rape. Although the law holds that submission gained under threat of death or severe bodily harm is not 'consent', in practice, threats that 'instill terror', or lesser threats, may not be held by the courts to show non-consent. The Maryland Court of Appeals recently overturned a conviction for rape 'on the grounds that the victim did not have sufficient cause to think she was in danger', although she had unwillingly entered a house and was 'lightly choked'. The court held that the circumstances did not give grounds for 'reasonable fear' that harm would result if she resisted.[33] There is also considerable legal doubt about 'consent' and threats by persons other than the rapist, or threats to persons other than the victim, for example, her children or relatives.[34] The law provides that a contract entered into under 'threat' or 'duress' is voidable, and a person can offer as a defence to a criminal charge that an offence was committed only under threat of severe bodily harm or death. But although, historically, contracts in economic life and consent in sexual relations derive their importance from the same complex of social and theoretical developments, it is significant that legal interpretation of 'duress' in (non-criminal) contract law is much wider than the interpretation of 'threat' in rape cases. The standard of 'consent' in rape has been formulated within the same narrow boundaries as 'duress' in the performance of criminal acts.[35]

The legal failure to distinguish between 'acts of sexual assault and consenting sexual relations among adults',[36] or between enforced submission and consent, is grounded in a complex of beliefs about the 'natural' characters of the sexes. Eminent lawyers as well as the public are convinced that the 'naturally' sexually aggressive male must disregard a woman's refusal as merely a token gesture that hides her true desires.[37] Rape victims are divided into 'good' and 'bad' women, and even where violence has unquestionably been used, 'consent' can be held to have been given if the victim can be said to be of 'doubtful reputation' or have 'poor' sexual morals.[38] It is also very difficult for a woman to convince a court that she did not consent when standard works on evidence reinforce the view that women, especially 'unchaste' women, are 'naturally' deceitful and prone to make false statements, including false accusations of rape.[39] Hale's words have been regularly cited in courtrooms for three centuries: 'rape . . . is an accusation easily to be made and hard to be proved, and harder to be defended by the party accused, tho never so innocent.'[40] Yet a high proportion of rapes that are actually reported are rejected by the police as 'unfounded'.[41] Even allowing for problems of evidence, it is hard to account for these practices except as a direct outcome of an extraordinary perception of women's 'natural' characters. The same perception underlies the conventional requirement that the rape victim's evidence must be corroborated; it is 'only rape complainants, along with children, accomplices and witnesses in treason trials who are [treated as] notoriously unreliable witnesses.'[42]

Because so few cases of rape are reported, and because so many of these are rejected, the offences that come before the courts are usually only the most vicious and brutal. It has recently been claimed that 'the facts about rape are even more elusive than most',[43] but there is rarely much that is very elusive if a case is prosecuted – at least, not if 'consent' has any meaning. Ambiguous cases that involve complex matters of social convention and expectation do not usually reach the courts. For example, the courts are not usually judging cases where a woman unwillingly submits to a man who has taken her out for the evening, because it is 'expected' that she should 'pay' for her supper, or where she submits to an employer or foreman to retain employment. In cases where an accused comes to trial, 'consent' in any genuine sense of the concept is not usually at issue.[44] This does *not* mean, however, that the victim's non-consent is therefore taken seriously. Instead, the beliefs of the accused about a woman's consent, even his unreasonable beliefs, are often taken to be the most relevant 'fact about rape' for the verdict of the court.

The beliefs and intentions of accused persons are a central criterion for establishing criminal responsibility. A mental or subjective element, *mens rea*, must be shown to be present for guilt to be proved. It must be shown that an accused intended to commit a criminal act; 'intention to do the act forbidden by law, or something like it, is . . . generally *necessary* for serious crime. . . .'[45] The problem in rape cases is not this criterion as such but the manner in which it has been interpreted, in particular in the Morgan case in Britain and in the Mayberry case in the state of California.[46] These cases created 'a totally new defense to the crime' of rape, the defence of a mistake-of-fact as to consent.[47] It was ruled in Morgan that a man's belief in a woman's consent did not have to be a reasonable belief, and in Mayberry that a jury must specifically reject a defence of reasonable but mistaken belief in consent. The impact of this defence can be illustrated by the case referred to earlier, in which the man had 'instilled terror' into the victim. The defence was successfully presented that – although the accused had broken into the woman's flat – he genuinely believed she consented. In another case, the bizarre results of the Morgan ruling, and also the peculiar legal view of the relations between husbands and wives, were further reinforced. It is impossible for a husband to be prosecuted for the rape of his wife in Britain. However, in common law, he can be prosecuted for aiding another man to do so. In *R. v. Cogan* and *R. v. Leak* (1976), a drunken man punished his wife by forcing her to have intercourse with his drunken friend, and he was found guilty of aiding and abetting the rape of his wife – but the friend was found not guilty of rape. The defence was that the latter believed the wife to consent, even though there were no reasonable grounds for the belief and an appeal judge stated that intercourse took place 'without her consent'.[48]

One writer on rape has argued that the legal reasoning in Morgan is 'clearly correct if the rights of the man accused of rape [are] to be maintained.'[49] But it is far from obvious that it is 'clearly correct' (even if it is held that the belief must be 'reasonable'). In Morgan, a judge argued that if a sexual act took place because a man had falsely believed that the woman consented, then it would generally be held that, although the man might be careless, he did not commit rape.[50] But would it so be held? And should it? Certainly, many lawyers seem to think so. The Morgan decision has been defended on the grounds that

> the opposing view was that a man could be convicted of rape . . . if he was stupid (unreasonable) in forming that belief. To convict the stupid man would be to convict him of . . . inadvertent negligence – honest conduct which may be the best this man can do but that does not come up to the standard of the so-called reasonable man . . . it would be wrong to have a law of negligent rape.[51]

Such legal opinions imply that many, perhaps most, rapists are not criminal or vicious men, or men clearly deficient in concern for the well-being, integrity and respect of other persons, but merely stupid or careless. This ignores the empirical evidence about rape. As many as 70 per cent of rapes are planned in advance,[52] a high proportion involve two or more men in an attack upon one woman,[53] and there are 'documented incidences of organized rape as a social institution'.[54]

Furthermore, such arguments about 'carelessness' and 'stupidity' pay no attention to the manner in which the belief is formed. If a man's defence is that he believed the woman to consent, 'then we must assume that he considered the possibility that she was not consenting, and rejected it'.[55] The circumstances in which a man might so deliberate, and come to an honest, but mistaken, belief about consent, are unlikely to be straightforward or simple – and surely would preclude explicit, prolonged manifestations of refusal by the woman and threatened or actual physical violence by the man. The mistake-of-fact defence is based upon 'the objective reasonableness' of the mistake; it 'must be one that you or I or anyone could reasonably have made under the circumstances'.[56] This defence is already recognized in cases of carnal knowledge (statutory rape). Most people would agree that a genuine mistake is possible today about the age of a boy or girl (and objective evidence of date of birth can be produced). But how could 'you or I' make such a mistake about a woman's consent? And is it the kind of slip that results from ordinary human failings? How often is it a 'mistake' at all? The circumstances that lead to most prosecutions for rape, and the very high incidence of planned rape, suggest that usually, far from a minor mistake being made, the very assumption that a woman's consent has been considered at all is misplaced. Most rapes occur not because a stupid or careless man has engaged in faulty reasoning about a woman's consent, but as a result of a deliberate attack.

However, in this matter, it is not sufficient to state what might seem an obvious point. There is an additional, fundamentally important problem with 'reasonable mistakes' about consent. Curley has pointed out that in rape cases, 'the imposition of objective standards of liability does not always represent the triumph of utility over justice'.[57] But it is not possible, in the present state of sexual relationships between men and women, to arrive at an 'objective standard' of 'reasonable' conduct.

At present it is widely believed that a woman's 'no' does *not* constitute a refusal, that it *is* 'reasonable' for men to put a lesser or greater degree of pressure on unwilling women in sexual matters, and that it *is* 'reasonable' for consent to be inferred from enforced submission. In short, unless accompanied by visible signs of severe physical violence, rape is not actually seen as a serious crime – or even a crime at all – despite its formal legal status. If this seems a doubtful argument, reflect for a moment on all the 'jokes' about rape in popular variety and comedy programmes, on the sexual activities of heroes of films and novels, and on legal judgements such as that in the Appeal in *R. v. Holdsworth* where a man's sentence for a sexual attack, causing most serious injury, was set aside on the grounds that it would harm his career.[58] Rape is conventionally presented as a unique act that stands in complete opposition to the consensual relations that ordinarily obtain between the sexes. The most tragic aspect of even a brief consideration of the problem of women, rape and consent is that rape is revealed as the extreme expression, or an extension of, the accepted and 'natural' relation between men and women.[59]

The problem of 'objective standards' and 'reasonable mistakes' in rape highlights the extent to which 'consent' and 'non consent' have been emptied of meaning. That this fact appears unremarkable is tribute to the success of three centuries of mutual accommodation between liberalism and patriarchalism, which reinforced the contradictory perception of women and their consent and resulted in their present highly uncertain and ambiguous status as 'individuals'. Despite the apparent importance of women's consent, it is legally and socially declared irrelevant within marriage, and a woman's explicit 'no' can all too frequently be disregarded or reinterpreted as 'consent'. However, if 'no', when uttered by a woman, is to be reinterpreted as 'yes', then all the comfortable assumptions about her 'consent' are also thrown into disarray. Why should a woman's 'yes' be more privileged, be any the less open to invalidation, than her 'no'?

There can be no answer to this question until women are admitted unequivocally as 'free and equal individuals', guardians of their own consent. At present, notwithstanding their formal civic status, women are regarded as men's 'natural' subordinates, and hence as incapable of consent. In the light of the character of existing relations between the sexes, it is therefore not surprising that in matters of women's consent in our everyday lives, so wide a gulf exists between appearance and reality. Moreover, the problem extends further than our everyday lives. If the problem of women and consent is to be resolved, some radical changes are required, reaching much further than necessary reform of rape law into the heart of the theory and practice of the liberal democratic state. The consent of women, and the example of rape, is only one dimension of the problem of consent – of men and women – which itself is part of the more fundamental problem of whether the ideal of free commitment, or voluntarism, is to be taken seriously in liberal democratic theory and practice.

Consent is central to liberal democracy, because it is essential to maintain individual freedom and equality; but it is a problem for liberal democracy, because individual freedom and equality is also a precondition for the practice of consent. The identification of enforced submission with consent in rape is a stark example of the wider failure in liberal-democratic theory and practice to distinguish free commitment and agreement by equals from domination, subordination and inequality. Writers on consent link 'consent', 'freedom' and 'equality', but the realities of power and domination in our sexual and political lives are ignored. Contemporary consent theory presents our institutions as if they were actually as consent demands, as if they were actually constituted through the free agreement of equal persons. The reduction of 'consent' to a mere 'constituent' of liberal-democratic ideology leaves consent theorists unable to ask many vital questions. This includes the question whether the character of our socio-political institutions is such that consent ought to be given to (all or some of) them, by men or women. Most liberal theorists would wish to argue that there is one relationship, at least, to which consent ought not to be given. A person ought never to consent to be a slave, because this totally negates the individual's freedom and equality and hence, in a self contradiction, denies that the individual is capable of consent.[60] However, if this argument is accepted, then should not consent theorists look searchingly at existing institutions, as J. S. Mill examined marriage in his own day, to ensure that there is no denial, or tendency to deny, the very status of individuals that is claimed to be upheld? The problem with this suggestion is that it requires that three centuries of argument about consent be overthrown and that theorists formulate a *critical* theory of voluntarism including both men and women.

At present, consent theorists have failed to recognize even the obvious problems posed for arguments about political obligation by popular belief and the ambiguous status of women as 'individuals'. Furthermore, if the subordination of women to men is not considered, neither is the class structure of the liberal-democratic state. If consent theorists do not discuss the marriage contract, neither do they discuss the employment contract or the 'despotic organization'[61] of capitalist production. The consent of women is treated as irrelevant, and the consent of men is assumed to be given in political and everyday life when there are 'no expressions of it at all'. Walzer is the only theorist who has treated consent, or its absence, as a genuine moral and political problem, and he has concluded that the facts of liberal-democratic citizenship are 'a reflection on the moral quality of the modern state. They may well constitute an entirely sufficient argument for its radical reconstruction.'[62] But Walzer, too, fails to consider the special problem of women and consent. When that is also taken into account, we have an entirely sufficient argument, not only for the democratic reconstruction of the liberal state, but for a simultaneous reconstruction of our sexual lives. Indeed, these two dimensions are inseparable if there is to be a democratic transformation of our social life.

To work toward such a reconstruction is also to begin to transform the legacy of the early contract theorists. The importance of consent in liberal-democratic theory can be fully understood only in the light of the arguments of the originators of modern theory three centuries ago. However, part of their heritage is the assumption that 'consent' and 'consent theory' are coextensive with voluntarist political theory, an assumption that prevents a proper understanding of the real character of the liberal-democratic state. Consenting is only one way, and not the most important way, in which free and equal individuals can mutually commit themselves or assume obligations. I have explored the wider relationship between consent and voluntarism, and some of its implications for democracy, in *The Problem of Political Obligation*, but one final point about women and consent must be made here. The conventional use of 'consent' helps to reinforce the beliefs about the 'natural' characters of the sexes and the sexual double standard discussed in this essay. Consent must always be given *to* something; in the relationship between the sexes, it is always women who are held to consent to men. The 'naturally' superior, active and sexually aggressive male makes an initiative, or offers a contract, to which a 'naturally' subordinate, passive woman 'consents'. An egalitarian sexual relationship cannot rest on this basis; it cannot be grounded in 'consent'. Perhaps the most telling aspect of the problem of women and consent is that we lack a language through which to help constitute a form of personal life in which two equals freely agree to create a lasting association together.

NOTES

1 P. H. Partridge, *Consent and Consensus* (Macmillan, London, 1971), p. 23. Michael Walzer's *Obligations: Essays on Disobedience, War and Citizenship* (Simon & Schuster, New York, 1971) is an exception to this complacency. Walzer writes that he will not assume consent exists 'without looking for evidence that it has actually been given' (p. viii).

2 R. E. Flathman, *Political Obligation* (Atheneum, New York, 1972), p. 209.

3 A detailed discussion of these aspects of consent theory and arguments about political obligation, including the claim that consent is given through voting, can be found in C. Pateman, *The Problem of Political Obligation* (Polity Press, Cambridge, 1985; University of California Press, Berkeley, CA, 1985). For empirical evidence of the contradiction between women's status as citizens and popular beliefs about their 'proper' place, see M. M. Lee, 'Why So Few Women Hold Public Office: Democracy and Sexual Roles', *Political Science Quarterly*, 91 (1976), pp. 297–314.

4 I have explored this concept at length and discussed its importance for classical contract theorists and their successors in *The Problem of Political Obligation*.

5 J. Locke, *Two Treatises of Government*, ed. P. Laslett, 2nd ed. (Cambridge University Press, Cambridge, 1967) II, §119.

6 T. Hobbes, *Leviathan*, ed C. B. Macpherson (Penguin Books, Harmondsworth, Middlesex, 1968), pp. 253–4.

7 Flathman, *Political Obligation*, p. 230.

8 Hobbes is a notable exception to this generalization. He was consistent enough in his individualism to argue for the freedom and equality of all individuals in the natural state, irrespective of sex. There is no assumption that a female will always 'consent' to (submit to) the authority (protection) of a male. On this point, and for a more detailed account of the arguments of Hobbes and Locke on the relation of husbands and wives in the state of nature and civil society, see T. Brennan and C. Pateman, ' "Mere Auxiliaries to the Commonwealth": Women and the Origins of Liberalism', *Political Studies*, 27(2) (1979), pp. 183–200.

9 The words are those of Locke's friend, Tyrrell; cited in G. J. Schochet *Patriarchalism in Political Thought* (Basil Blackwell, Oxford, 1975), p. 202.

10 Locke, *Two Treatises*, II, §75, 76; I, §47–80.

11 The analogy between the marriage contract and the contract of government was much discussed at the time; see M. L. Shanley, 'Marriage Contract and Social Contract in Seventeenth Century English Political Thought', *Western Political Quarterly*, 32(1979), pp. 79–91.

12 For an excellent discussion of the sexual double standard – which is

'the reflection of the view that men have property in women' – see K. Thomas, 'The Double Standard', *Journal of History of Ideas*, 20 (1959), pp. 195–216.

13 J.-J. Rousseau, *Politics and the Arts*, tr. A. Bloom (Cornell University Press, Ithaca, NY, 1968), pp. 107, 105.

14 In Rousseau's 'true' state of nature, the sexes are equal in their ability to protect themselves. In his conjectural history of the state of nature, Rousseau suddenly asserts that, in the 'happy epoch', the 'first difference was established in the way of life of the two sexes', a difference that demands the future subordination of women. J.-J. Rousseau, 'Discourse on the Origin and Foundations of Inequality', in *The First and Second Discourses*, ed. R. D. Masters (St Martin's Press, New York, 1964), p. 147. The reason why Rousseau sees women's 'natures' as necessarily subversive of men's civic virtue is discussed in chap. 1. His general arguments about women are discussed in detail in S. M. Okin, *Women in Western Political Thought* (Princeton University Press, Princeton, NJ, 1979).

15 J.-J. Rousseau, *Emile*, tr. B. Foxley (Dent, London, 1911), p. 332.

16 Rousseau, *Politics and the Arts*, p. 84.

17 Rousseau, *Emile*, p. 348.

18 Rousseau, *Politics and the Arts*, p. 85.

19 Rousseau, *Emile*, p. 443.

20 J. A. Scutt, 'Consent in Rape: The Problem of the Marriage Contract', *Monash University Law Review*, 3 (1977), pp. 255–88, argues that this belief can be challenged from the judgements in leading cases. The Victorian claim that women lacked sexual passion and were more 'moral' than men should also be considered in the context of the belief that married women could not withdraw their initial 'consent'. See the excellent discussion by N. F. Cott, 'Passionlessness: An Interpretation of Victorian Sexual Ideology, 1790–1850', *Signs*, 4(2) (1978), pp. 219–36, especially p. 234.

21 Sir W. Blackstone, *Commentaries on the Laws of England* (Sweet, Maxwell, London, 1844), p. 442.

22 B. Toner, *The Facts of Rape* (Arrow Books, London, 1977), p. 95.

23 Sir M. Hale, *The History of the Pleas of the Crown* (Emlyn, London, 1778), vol. I, p. 629.

24 J. S. Mill, 'The Subjection of Women' in *Essays on Sex Equality*, ed. A. S. Rossi (University of Chicago Press, Chicago, IL, 1970), pp. 159–60.

25 Both rape and unreported rape have only recently begun to receive attention. Reasonable estimates suggest that no more than a third of (extramatrimonial) rapes are reported, and rates of reported rape appear to have increased in the Anglo-Saxon countries in the last twenty years: see figures in E. Shorter, 'On Writing the History of Rape', *Signs*, 3(2) (1977), p. 480. P. R. Wilson, *The Other Side of Rape* (University of Queensland Press, Brisbane, 1978) investigates unreported rapes. The realities of rape are hidden by deeply

entrenched cultural myths and stereotypes. One of the most common is that rape is an act perpetrated by a stranger on a woman who probably 'precipitated' the attack. In fact, no woman is immune, whether she is 70 or older, a very small girl or heavily pregnant, whatever her appearance, and whether or not she is within the shelter of her home. About half of all reported rapes are committed by men known to their victim, including relatives – see summaries of evidence in B. Smart and C. Smart, 'Accounting for Rape: Reality and Myth in Press Reporting', in *Women, Sexuality and Social Control*, B. Smart and C. Smart (Routledge, London, 1978); L. R. Harris, 'Towards a Consent Standard in the Law of Rape', *University of Chicago Law Review* 43 (1975), pp. 613–45; C. Le Grand, 'Rape and Rape Laws: Sexism in Society and Law', *California Law Review*, 61 (1973), pp. 919–41; S. Brownmiller, *Against Our Will: Men, Women and Rape* (Penguin Books, Harmondsworth, Middlesex, 1976). Women are also raped by the police who are to apprehend rapists; in Paris, for example, in 1979, three Guardiens de la Paix were convicted of raping a 13-year-old girl, and two police patrolmen were convicted of raping a German tourist in their car 'because they were bored'. (Report in *Guardian Weekly*, 21 October, 1979.)

26 L. Bienen, 'Mistakes', *Philosophy and Public Affairs*, 7(3) (1978), p. 229. Rape is an offence where the victim, rather than the offender, is socially stigmatized. Rape victims are frequently held to 'have brought it upon themselves' (and psychologists have helped foster the belief that it is women, not men, who are really to blame; on this point, see R. S. Albin, 'Psychological Studies of Rape', *Signs*, 3(2) (1977), pp. 423–35). More generally, on police and court procedures and attitudes to rape victims, see, for example, Toner, *The Facts of Rape*, chaps 7–10, and on press reporting of rape, see Smart and Smart, *Women, Sexuality*, 1978.

27 Although rape is conventionally defined as penetration of the vagina by the penis, it frequently involves foreign objects and other acts, usually degrading and humiliating to the victim.

28 J. A. Scutt, 'The Standard of Consent in Rape', *New Zealand Law Journal*, November (1976), p. 466.

29 Harris, 'Towards a Consent Standard', p. 632.

30 See K. L. Koh, 'Consent and Responsibility in Sexual Offences', *The Criminal Law Review*, (1968) pp. 81–97, 150–62, and J. A. Scutt, 'Fraudulent Impersonation and Consent in Rape', *The University of Queensland Law Review*, 9(1) (1975), pp. 59–65.

31 Scutt, 'Fraudulent Impersonation', pp. 64–5.

32 Toner, *The Facts of Rape*, p. 9.

33 Report in *Guardian Weekly*, 4 November, 1979, p. 17.

34 See the discussion by J.A. Scutt, 'Consent versus Submission: Threats and the Element of Fear in Rape', *University of Western Australia Law Review*, 13(1) (1977), pp. 52–76, and Harris, 'Towards a Consent Standard', pp. 644–5.

35 Scutt, 'Consent v. Submission', p. 61; Harris, 'Towards a Consent Standard', p. 642–3.
36 Bienen, 'Mistakes', p. 245.
37 See Toner, 'The Facts of Rape', p. 104.
38 See cases cited by P. C. Wood, 'The Victim in a Forcible Rape Case: A Feminist View', *The American Criminal Law Review*, 11 (1973), pp. 344–5. Advocates of legal reform have drawn attention to the common use of evidence about the complainant's prior sexual history, mode of dress, general reputation and so on in rape cases. Harris, 'Towards a Consent Standard', p. 617, notes that because the defence of consent admits essential facts, defence lawyers almost invariably attempt to show that the woman is the 'type' who must have consented.
39 See Bienen, 'Mistakes', p. 237, and Harris, 'Towards a Consent Standard', p. 626.
40 Hale *History of the Pleas*, p. 635.
41 In Victoria in 1974–5 in four police districts, only 50 per cent of rape complaints were accepted as 'founded'; evidence in *Royal Commission on Human Relationships* (Australian Government Publishing Service, Canberra, 1977), vol. 5, pt 7, p. 178.
42 Toner, *The Facts of Rape*, p. 112.
43 T. C. M. Gibbens, 'More Facts About Rape', *New Society*, 10 February 1977, p. 276.
44 See Bienen, 'Mistakes', pp. 242, 244.
45 H. L. A. Hart, *Punishment and Responsibility: Essays in the Philosophy of Law* (Oxford University Press, Oxford, 1968), p. 115. The other element necessay for *mens rea* is that the act was voluntarily performed (Hart, p. 90). Popular views about rape and the 'natural' sexual characters of men would suggest that few men accused of rape are responsible for their actions. It is widely believed that rape is the result of a man being gripped by an 'ungovernable passion' or an 'uncontrollable urge', and so not acting truly voluntarily. This myth contrasts sharply with empirical evidence about rape.
46 *DPP* v. *Morgan*, 1975, and the legal precedents on which the verdict was based are discussed in detail in E. M. Curley, 'Excusing Rape', *Philosophy and Public Affairs*, 5(4) (1976), pp. 325–60. *People* v. *Mayberry*, 1975, is examined by Bienen, 'Mistakes'. Both are excellent analyses. Bienen (pp. 238–9) argues that one result of Mayberry is that accused rapists in California will not need to take the stand to present a mistake-of-fact defence. The impact of Morgan was somewhat limited by the Sexual Offences (Amendment) Act of 1975.
47 Bienen, 'Mistakes', p. 230.
48 See Curley, 'Excusing Rape', p. 342; Scutt, 'Consent in Rape', pp. 259–60.
49 Toner, *The Facts of Rape*, p. 107.
50 See Curley, 'Excusing Rape', p. 341.
51 Cited in Toner, *The Facts of Rape*, pp. 106–7.

52 Le Grand, 'Rape and Rape Laws', p. 923.

53 Brownmiller, *Against Our Will*, p. 187.

54 Wilson, *Other Side of Rape*, p. 112. One example is found in the country town of Ingham, in Queensland. Since 1972, group rape 'as a social activity' has been organized in the town. A woman is chosen and the intention signalled between the group of men (which may be thirty strong) in the hotels (pubs). The history and sociology of organized rape in Ingham is discussed by Schultz in Wilson, *Other Side of Rape*, pp. 112–25. It should be noted that an attack by several assailants is not, in itself, necessarily sufficient to uphold a woman's claim that she did not consent. A Solicitor-General of New South Wales has written that, if pack-rape is to be 'rape', the victim 'unless virtually insensible or completely overcome by terror or fatigue, ought, so long as she is able, to manifest as to each act some objection even if slight'; H. A. Snelling, 'What is Non-Consent in Rape?', *The Australian Journal of Forensic Science*, March (1970), p. 106. More recently, a judge in Connecticut acquitted one defendant in a pack-rape case who pleaded 'impotence' with the comment, 'you can't blame somebody for trying', cited in *Ms.* November 1978, p. 20.

55 Curley, 'Excusing Rape', p. 348.

56 Bienen, 'Mistakes', p. 241.

57 Curley, 'Excusing Rape', p. 355.

58 Report in *The Times*, 22 June, 1977.

59 See P. Foa, 'What's Wrong with Rape', in *Feminism and Philosophy*, ed. M. Vetterling-Braggin, F. A. Elliston and J. English (Littlefield, Adams, Totowa, NJ, 1977).

60 Some further comments on this aspect of the problem of consent with particular reference to promising to obey, can be found in C. Pateman, *The Problem of Political Obligation*, pp. 19–20, 169–171.

61 The characterization is that of B. Clark and H. L. Gintis, 'Rawlsian Justice and Economic Systems', *Philosophy and Public Affairs*, 7 (1978), pp. 302–25. It should also be noted that another aspect of the 'consent' of the wife in the marriage contract is to the exchange of (unpaid) work in the home for subsistence from her husband. For analyses of the history and content of the marriage contract, see C. Delphy, 'Continuities and Discontinuities in Marriage and Divorce', in *Sexual Divisions and Society: Process and Change*, ed D. L. Barker and S. Allen (Tavistock, London, 1976) and D. L. Barker, 'The Regulation of Marriage: Repressive Benevolence', in *Power and the State*, ed. G. Littlejohn, B. Smart, J. Wakeford and N. Yuval-Davis (Croom Helm, London, 1978).

62 Walzer, *Obligations*, pp. 186–7.

5

Sublimation and Reification: Locke, Wolin and the Liberal-Democratic Conception of the Political

A fundamental question for any study of political life is that of the proper conceptualization of the 'political' itself. Very different conclusions will be drawn, for example, about the ends to which political life should be directed; exactly who should participate, and how, in political life; the principles on which political life should be based and the organizational forms that best give expression to those principles, from differing theoretical conceptions of the political and differing views on what, empirically, the political sphere of life does and should comprise.

Most recent English-language political theory has been the political theory of the existing liberal-democratic system and it has usually taken a particular conception of the political very much for granted. Some of the radical critics of liberal democracy and its theorists, especially in the women's liberation movement, have now raised a challenge to this conception – a challenge neatly summed up in the slogan 'the personal is the political'. This idea runs completely counter to the 'commonsense' view of the political seen in terms of the modern state, the liberal-democratic version of which developed from the liberal notion of limited, constitutional, representative government. The liberal-democratic conception of the political is based on the division of life into two separate spheres: that of private life (or, more narrowly, the personal) where individuals go about their everyday lives having, and needing, no more than a passing interest in political life; and the political sphere, or the state, where specially chosen representatives act to protect the life of the private sphere, and arbitrate between its conflicting interests, making political decisions aimed at the benefit of the community as a whole, or the public interest.

My argument in this chapter has as its starting point the existence of two completely opposed arguments – the sublimation and reification arguments – about the appropriate characterization of the liberal-democratic conception of the political; arguments that also involve conflicting interpretations of the development of one aspect of the modern, Western capitalist, liberal socio-political system. One of these arguments can be found in Sheldon Wolin's *Politics and Vision*, which I discuss in the first section, where it is claimed that the development of liberalism saw the loss or sublimation of a distinctive conception of the political as a sphere concerned with what is common or general to a society.

A particular interpretation of Locke's political theory is central to Wolin's thesis, and in the second and third sections I shall present my own interpretation of Locke. This is an argument that Locke saw a limited, representative govenment, that is, an embryonic liberal-democratic state, as the only proper *political* government. If this, initially, sounds an odd claim, it is worth noting at this point that the idea did not die with Locke. Today, there are not only writers who insist that it is liberalism that has provided liberal-democratic theory with its specifically political element,[1] but, for example, Bernard Crick, in *In Defence of Politics*, goes so far as to argue that it is only a liberal-democratic conception that is really political at all. At least, this is the implicit argument of the book. Explicitly, Crick discusses an abstraction, 'politics', but his argument makes sense only in terms of liberal democracy, and his concrete references to what 'politics' involves clearly point to a liberal-democratic state – the conciliation of differing interests, representation, responsible party government and periodic elections.[2] Properly, according to Crick, 'politics' arises when traditional or arbitrary rule no longer suffices; it has specific origins in Western European experience and it is 'unknown in any but advanced and complex societies'.[3]

An appreciation of Locke's 'moderate and sensible'[4] theory is important for an understanding of the nature of the conception of the political presented by his liberal-democratic successors. I shall argue that in their theories, as in Locke's, a reified conception of the political is built upon what I shall call the fiction of citizenship. This second characterization of the liberal-democratic idea of the political was given its classic expression by Marx, who wrote that

> Where the political state has achieved its full development, man leads a double life, a heavenly and an earthly life, not only in thought or consciousness but in *actuality*. In the *political community* he regards himself as a *communal being*; but in *civil society* he is active as a *private individual*, treats other men as means, reduces himself to a means, and becomes the plaything of alien powers. The political state is as spiritual in relation to

civil society as heaven is in relation to earth. . . . The contradiction between
the religious and the political man is the same as that between *bourgeois* and
citoyen, between the member of civil society and his *political lion skin*.[5]

Liberal-democratic theory today, the theory of the fully developed
modern 'political state', continues to present the political as something
abstracted from, as autonomous or separate from, the social relationships
of everyday life. Standing over and above the inegalitarian relationships
and conflicting interests of the private sphere of social life, the state, and
its representatives, appear as the guardians of what is common to all
members of society. One aim of this chapter is to investigate in more
detail the liberal background of some aspects of this conception of the
political. It will be argued that far from being an obvious or commonsense
view, this conception rests on a central and unavoidable paradox and that
it serves to obscure the realities of the liberal-democratic socio-political
system and the nature of its citizenship.

In recent years political scientists have in fact put forward 'unorthodox'
definitions of the political and what it comprises; two of the best known
of these are Easton's study of the 'authoritative allocation of values for a
society';[6] and Dahl's 'a political system is any persistent pattern of human
relationships that involves, to a significant extent, power, rule, authority.'
Dahl comments that 'perhaps even families' could thus be seen as political
systems.[7] However, such definitions are rarely taken seriously, even by
their formulators, in discussions of political life. For substantive
questions to be asked about the significance for liberal democracy if
'private' associations and organizations are seen as political, requires a
more critical attitude than is taken by most political scientists. Indeed, a
thorough critique of liberal democracy demands precisely that such
questions are asked. All the time that the theory and institutions of the
liberal-democratic system are seen from within the perspective provided
by the liberal-democratic conception of the political itself, the whole
range of assumptions about political life, citizenship and democratic
values on which that conception rests are implicitly being accepted. If a
decisive move is to be made beyond liberalism to a non-liberal democratic
theory, then some beginning has to be made towards a reconceptualization
of the political; any non-liberal, participatory democratic political
practice requires the development of a non-liberal democratic theory –
and that must include an appropriate conception of the political. Hence
the attempt made to confront the complex, and, perhaps, seemingly
rather esoteric problems discussed here.

Wolin and the Sublimation of the Political

The general argument of *Politics and Vision* is that, in the modern period, a distinctive and autonomous conception of the political has been lost or sublimated: 'the main trends in political thought, irrespective of national or ideological variations, have worked towards the same end: the erosion of the distinctively political.'[8] Wolin sees Locke as a key figure in the development of this process.

I do not find Wolin's notion of the 'sublimation' of the political entirely clear – he also refers, as in the passage just cited, to the erosion of the political, and for example, to its loss, fragmentation, transference and absorption – but I hope that what follows, though brief, is a fair account of his argument. Wolin emphasizes that from ancient times the political has been seen as the sphere that concerns what is public, common and general to an entire community, and has been seen as standing in sharp contrast to, and as distinctive and autonomous from, the private sphere. Traditionally, the political has been seen as vital to the existence of society, and political participation and citizenship have been viewed as unique and self-fulfilling activities. In the modern period, with the development of liberal theory (particularly that of Locke), this traditional conception of the political began to be lost; lost because of the emergence of the conception of the realm of the 'social' as a virtually self-regulating sphere – as in Locke's state of nature. By the twentieth century the result of the 'glorification of society'[9] is, according to Wolin, 'to obscure the identity and depreciate the status of the political'.[10] The political has been left with only residual significance, citizenship has been deprived of meaning and political participation has been devalued to a defensive activity, and, instead of being a 'vital precondition' of society, the political has become a mere 'superstructure'.[11]

Wolin's use of the term 'sublimation' to characterize this process follows what I take to be the psycho-analytic connotation of the term (my dictionary says 'to direct unconsciously the sexual impulse into some non-sexual activity'). As 'sublimation' of an unreturned passion for a person in, say, hard work, may lead to apparently unrelated manifestations such as psychosomatic disorders, so the sublimation of a distinctive, autonomous conception of the political leads, in modern political theory, to its reappearance in, or, at least, the reapplication of the concept to, other social areas previously seen as private or non-political. Wolin sees all modern theorists as seeking 'substitute love-objects for the political'.[12] Some of them, for example, are led to treat industry as political, thus leading, Wolin argues, to 'a series of dead ends' and the 'chopping up' of political man. Society becomes seen as a 'series of tight little islands . . .

each without any natural affiliations with a more comprehensive unity'.[13]

Locke's theory forms a crucial step in the process of the sublimation of the political because, on Wolin's interpretation of his theory, Locke obscures the distinctive political status of civil society by postulating a state of nature that is not only social but also political. Wolin argues that Locke's state of nature is an 'ideal' political society where political power is 'dispersed among all the members'.[14] In answer to the two puzzles of why, given this 'ideal' state, Locke's individuals should leave the state of nature; and why, given his reference to a state of war, Locke is able to avoid Hobbesian conclusions, Wolin argues that Locke interjected a 'third condition' into his state of nature. This forms the basis for civil society and Wolin calls it the 'fallen state of nature'. It is this condition that is full of 'inconveniences' and these, and the remedies for them, Wolin argues, are 'cognizable only in the light of the norms embodied in the ideal state'. Hence the only really 'new' political elements in Locke's civil society are the express agreement to accept a set of common rules and the acceptance of majority decision-making.[15] The political order becomes 'something like a better set of accommodations for those who already were home-owners, rather than a shelter erected in desperation by the shelterless'.[16]

Locke's theory on this interpretation could not be seen as a forerunner of liberal-democratic theory – as I have briefly characterized it. But, then, Wolin would presumably also give a different account of liberal-democratic theory (although he does not specifically discuss it) since he insists that the sublimation of the political is a major feature of *all* political theory today. The end of the argument of *Politics and Vision* is a call for the 're-assertion of the general political dimension'.[17]

Locke's Conception of the Political

Locke's conception of the political has been less commented upon than other aspects of his theory; probably for the very reason that to twentieth-century liberal-democratic political philosophers it has seemed so straightforward and sensible, such a reasonable, embryonic statement of our own way of looking at the socio-political world. It is his emphasis on this aspect of Locke's theory that makes Wolin's discussion so illuminating in many ways, notwithstanding what I shall have to say in criticism in my own interpretation of Locke which follows.

In any discussion of Locke it is important to keep in mind, to use Wolin's words, 'that Lockeian liberalism was fully as much a defense against radical democracy as an attack on traditionalism'.[18] One aspect of this defence that is particularly relevant to Locke's conception of the political is that from his earliest writing (and despite his reference to express consent) Locke's political theory is based on the premise that the political sphere is no place for the exercise of individual 'private judgement'. A second point of importance is that Locke's arguments about the legitimate form of government are based on an assessment of historical socio-economic development. Many of the misunderstandings of Locke's state of nature have arisen because of a failure to realize that Locke's account is two-sided. His discussion, as Ashcraft has pointed out, contains an argument about 'the moral state of man' and also a conjectural account of 'the historical state of man',[19] including the origins and defects of pre-political forms of government.

Locke's description of the moral state of man is Wolin's 'ideal state of nature', and it is a purely formal description, set in the context of God's purpose for human beings. This last point is crucial, for it means that Locke's theory is based on the assumption that individual private judgement is never completely unconstrained. Each individual's judgement is morally circumscribed and limited by the God-given law of nature. This ensures that all individuals, all equal before the law of nature, have an equal freedom. Without law there can only be licence, the arbitrary and unconstrained action of all against all, which (as Hobbes showed so well) is no freedom at all. Locke's individuals are thus bound by the law of nature into a system of reciprocal relationships, into a 'society'. As Ashcraft has argued, Locke's arguments are 'grounded in the theological conviction that God cannot have issued rules for men to obey and then have created beings who, in their most natural state, are necessarily unable to follow those rules'.[20]

The law of nature may circumscribe individual judgement but the root of the problems of Locke's state of nature is that there is no way of 'consulting', interpreting and enforcing the law of nature except through the judgement – and action – of each individual. Hence, Locke's 'strange doctrine' of each individual's natural power to execute the law of nature. The state of nature, Locke tells us, is 'Men living together according to reason, without a common Superior on Earth, with Authority to judge between them' (§19.)[21] Because private judgement cannot be avoided in the state of nature, the possibility is always open that some individuals may fail in their duty to consult the law of nature, or may not interpret or execute it properly. This does not necessarily imply individual wickedness; rather it arises from the 'natural' moral failings of laziness and weakness of will and, especially, the partiality of individuals in their own case. Locke notes that his 'strange doctrine' will be objected to for just this reason (§13).

The 'inconveniences' of the state of nature thus arise from the fallibility of individual judgement. But it is important to emphasize that these inconveniences are not the same as the state of war. The latter exists whenever 'force, or a declared design of force upon the Person of another' exists, and force, according to Locke, is a 'sedate settled Design, upon another Mans Life'; it is not 'a passionate and hasty' word or action, i.e. it is not the kind of 'inconvenience' that can arise 'naturally' from ordinary moral lapses (§16, 19). Far from being a moral weakness, to set out deliberately to use force is to *deny* one's moral nature, whether the offender is a private individual or a ruler. Locke states that a 'great' reason for establishing civil society is to escape the state of war. But why is the state of nature not merely a state of 'inconveniences' – which, after all, might be thought tolerable – but also a state of war? Postulating a 'fallen state of nature', as Wolin does, merely rephrases the problem, for the question then arises of why the 'fall' occurred. To answer this puzzle it is necessary to turn to Locke's conjectural history of the state of nature. Locke's discussion is complex, and in order to consider his conception of the political it is necessary to look at two aspects; at his theory of property, and at his theory of the origins of government.

Locke's justification of private property falls into two stages. In the early stage of historical development, individual appropriation on the basis of the 'mixing of labour' results in a situation of broad equality; no one is entitled, according to the law of nature, to appropriate more property than can be made use of without spoiling or wasting what God has provided for everyone. At this stage, too, individuals' desires will be simple and easily satisfied; 'The equality of a simple poor way of liveing confineing their desires within the narrow bounds of each mans smal propertie made few controversies' (§107); there could be 'no doubt of Right, no room for quarrel' (§39, also §31, §51). The invention that led to the end of this 'golden age' (§111) and to the second stage of the state of nature is money.[22] Money does not spoil or waste and can be hoarded up. It allows property holdings to be expanded beyond what is essential for the individual's own use, with no infringement of the law of nature. Locke also links the invention of money to the expansion of desires: 'Find out something that hath the Use and Value of money amongst his Neighbours, you shall see the same Man will begin presently to enlarge his possessions.' (§49; also §48).

Locke argues that in tacitly agreeing to the introduction of money, 'it is plain, that Men have agreed to disproportionate and unequal Possession of the Earth.' (§50) In the second stage of historical development, where individuals can legitimately accumulate very unequal property holdings (i.e. without infringing the law of nature), it seems plausible, although Locke leaves this largely implicit in his account, that disputes would become more frequent, moral lapses and partiality would increase and there would be more incentive for transgressors against the law of nature to try to avoid the penalties. 'Inconveniences', especially for those with large amounts of property, would become pressing, and with a rapid expansion of desires and increase in ambition, some individuals might begin to use force to get what they desire. The state of war would enter the state of nature (which is not a 'third description' of the state of nature, but rather a stage in its historical development). There would be no Hobbesian state of war but there would be enough individuals prepared to 'design' to use force for the security of wealth and property to be jeopardised.[23] Thus Locke has a justification for the establishment of civil – or political – society.

The other aspect of Locke's conjectural history that needs consideration is his account of the origins of government. To speak of 'the origins of government' immediately suggests that Locke really meant the state of nature to be a political state, and it has seemed odd to Locke's commentators that a developed commercial economy could exist in a non-political situation. However, this is not to say that there is no government. Locke regards the state of nature as a non-political state, but not lacking a government; he does not treat 'government' and 'political' as synonymous. Locke is not entirely consistent in his use of terms such as 'society', 'civil society', 'political society' and 'government'. At one point, for example, he contrasts the state of nature and government (§101), but he is, however, quite consistent in his general arguments about a properly political society.

Locke's conjectures about the origins of government are part of his attack on Filmer, and one of the central arguments of *The Second Treatise* is concerned with the distinction between parental and political authority.[24] Indeed, this distinction follows from Locke's definition of the natural state of human beings as rational, free, moral equals; children have yet to reach maturity and hence the rationality and moral equality that comes with adulthood. Parents legitimately exercise a natural authority over children – while they are children. Governmental or political authority exercised over adults can only, legitimately, be with their consent (§104, 112, 119). But Locke also argues that government is 'appointed' by God (§13), and so must be 'natural' too. This helps to explain why Locke argues that the authority of government originated in the authority of the father over the children.

The first governments were the rule of one man, or monarchical. Locke suggests that this was because the authority of the father had accustomed children 'to the Rule of One Man, and taught them that where it was exercised with Care and Skill, with Affection and Love to those under it, it was sufficient to procure and to preserve to Men all the Political

Happiness they sought for, in Society' (§107). Locke, however, goes further and also argues that fathers 'by an insensible change' (§76) actually become rulers. This happens when children reach maturity. Locke argues that, once adults are involved, 'without some Government it would be hard for them to live together.' So what is more natural than that the (now mature) children should allow the father to exercise the right that belongs to every individual in the state of nature to execute the law of nature, and so give him a 'Monarchical Power'? That is to say, everyone tacitly assents to the natural authority of the father being transformed into the conventional authority of the ruler (§74–5, 105).

No explicit limitation was needed on these early rulers' powers; everyone understood that 'no body was ever intrusted with [authority] but for the publick Good and Safety', and, Locke adds, using the patriarchal metaphor, without such 'nursing Fathers tender and carefull of the publick weale' these early societies would not have survived (§110). These first subjects could rely on the 'Honesty and Prudence' of the man they consented to, just as children could rely on their father (§112).

However, the simplicity and the benefits of this form of government are eventually overtaken by historical developments; it is a form of government most suited to the first stage of the historical state of nature – the pre-monetary stage. It is in this 'innocent age' (§94) that the 'honesty and prudence' of the rulers can be relied on. With the development of a monetary economy and large inequalities in property holdings, it gradually becomes impossible to trust the monarch to use his authority for the 'publick good'. Rulers as well as private individuals become affected by the expansion of desires, by 'Ambition and Luxury', which is, in the case of the ruler, 'aided by Flattery'. Monarchs develop 'distinct and separate Interests from their People', and in Locke's own age things have gone so far that it is being claimed that monarchs rule by divine right (§111–12). So, in the face of theories like Filmer's, it has become necessary to examine the origins of government again, although Locke is very careful to add 'at best an Argument from what has been, to what should of right be, has no great force.' (§103)

However, while Locke may argue that few conclusions can be drawn from conjectures about the origins of government, this is not to say that the account of the historical development of the state of nature is either 'a descriptive or morally neutral anthropology',[25] or merely 'expository and polemical' rather than 'logically essential' to Locke's argument.[26] Together with the formal account of the moral state of man, the historical account is essential for Locke's moral and political argument that, given the character of his own society, i.e. given the social relationships of an embryonic capitalist market economy, there is only one legitimate form of government – and that is a civil or *political* form. Locke's conjectural history is a central part of his justification of a particular form of government.[27]

The rule of one man is a form of government that could never, Locke argues, be political or civil government. Absolute monarchy 'is indeed inconsistent with Civil Society, and so can be no form of Civil Government at all.' (§90) It is inconsistent because it can never overcome the fundamental 'inconvenience' of the state of nature, namely the reliance on individual judgement. In the non-political state of nature, 'one Man commanding a Multitude, has the Liberty to be Judge in his own Case.' (§13) Even in the case of those first father-rulers, whose honesty and prudence could be relied upon, and whom Locke refers to as fit 'umpires', the law of nature is still being interpreted by the morally fallible private judgement of one individual, and this is no secure foundation for social order, even if it did suffice during a certain 'innocent' historical epoch.

In a situation of inequalities of wealth and property, of a diversity of beliefs and interests, only a political form of government, i.e. one which excluded individual private judgement, was both legitimate and effective. The people, Locke states, could never 'think themselves in Civil Society, till the Legislature was placed in collective Bodies of Men, call them Senate, Parliament, or what you please.' (§94) At the formation of a civil or political society, at the time of the social contract, each individual gives up the right of interpretation and execution of the law of nature and passes it to the community. The community then passes it on to its representatives, who are themselves then bound by the laws that they make (and everyone is still bound by the laws of nature): '*thus all private judgement of every particular Member being excluded*, the Community comes to be Umpire, by settled standing Rules, indifferent, and the same to all Parties; and by Men having Authority from the Community, for the execution of those Rules . . .' (§87, my emphasis).

More accurately, it is the representatives who are 'umpire' on behalf of the community and they exercise not their own private judgement but political judgement. Locke goes on to argue for the empirical necessity of decision-making by majority vote and thus completes his justification of an embryonic liberal-democratic state as the only proper political government – and a justification of this conception of the political as that fitted to an embryonic capitalist socio-economic system. Rather than 'obscuring' the political nature of civil society, as Wolin argues, Locke was perfectly explicit about the crucially important 'new elements' that entitled it, and only it, to be called a 'civil' or 'political' society.

Reification and the Paradox of the Political

Locke's argument that it is only civil government that is properly a political government suffers from one insuperable difficulty: his state of nature, as Wolin argues, must be a political state. Indeed this follows from Locke's formal account of the state of nature. It is not the political nature, as such, of civil government that is its distinguishing feature, but, rather, the fact that it embodies a specific conception of the political; a conception that, I will argue, is a reified one.

According to Locke, all legitimate governments in the state of nature arise because individuals give up their natural right to interpret and execute the law of nature, and consent to a ruler exercising it on behalf of everyone. All individuals, therefore, must have a natural, *political* right along with their other natural rights. From a situation of moral equality there is no other way in which this 'new' political authority of the ruler over the ruled can originate; either it appears magically, or individuals have it to give up. If individuals did not have this natural political authority, if this aspect of their moral selves was not also given by God, then there could, for Locke, be no question of any such thing as political authority arising at all. In fact, Locke does at one point explicitly say that 'Political Power is that Power which every Man, having in the state of Nature, has given up into the hands of the [civil] Society, and therein to the Governours, whom the Society hath set over it self,' (§171; see also §9); and the power that is given up is also the power or right of the 'strange doctrine'.

Why is this a political right? In Locke's formal account of the state of nature, the 'law of nature' can be seen as a statement of the basic, minimal social rules of mutual aid and mutual forbearance required if a 'society' is to exist at all. However, in the state of nature there are only individuals, singularly, to interpret and enforce the laws of nature. That is to say, each individual has to perform the task that, historically, has been performed by a monarch or, in civil society, by a representative government, of 'deciding', interpreting and enforcing the rules necessary if social life is to be carried on in an ordered and peaceful fashion. Locke says of this natural right that it refers to the individual's right of 'Preserving all Mankind, and doing all reasonable things . . . in order to that end' (§11); i.e. it refers not to the individual's preservation *qua* individual, but to the preservation of the individual along with others, seen as a member of society. The exercise of the natural political right requires that each individual judges 'directly' what is the right and good thing to be done to preserve communal life,[28] and then acts on that judgement. Each individual has to ask 'direct' political questions within the framework provided by the laws of nature, but the oddity of that framework is that it is nowhere publicly known or displayed but depends entirely on the 'private judgement' of individuals – hence the 'inconveniences' of the natural state.

It is important to stress that the natural political right forms part of the formal description of the state of nature. Looked at in the light of the conjectural history the political right 'disappears'. Government, too, is 'natural' and as soon as the 'first' generation of children reach maturity they and their parents form a political society. The natural political right is *given up* to the father, who becomes the first ruler and exercises the right on behalf of them all – and only he exercises it. Thus, in Locke's political theory, and in the liberal-democratic theory developed subsequently, there is an essential paradox about the political. The paradox is that the political right of the individual, a 'natural' right along with the other natural rights of life, liberty and estates, is, unlike those other rights, *always given up*.

This paradox has some significant implications. The most important of these is the separation of social life into two separate, or autonomous, spheres – the private and the political sphere – in order to encompass the retention by individuals of their natural rights other than the political right, and the giving up the latter. The paradox is also fundamental to the reification of the political in Locke's, and later, liberal-democratic theory, and is central to the liberal and liberal-democratic defence against 'radical democracy'.

The obvious question at this point is, why must the natural political right always be given up? In part, the answer has already been given; Locke argues that government is given by God, and government is the exercise of the right by one, or a few, men on behalf of everyone else. The other part of the answer is more complicated. The development of the second historical stage of the state of nature, i.e. the development of a modern, liberal, market society, also involves the emergence of liberal individualism, that is to say, a certain conception of 'individuals' and their social relationships.[29] No longer bound into the pre-modern, God-given hierarchical social order, individuals are now seen as free to decide, conscientiously, for themselves, to exercise their own private judgement in all areas of their life, including their religion. Locke makes this abundantly clear in his *Letter On Toleration*, arguing that in religion, just as in the management of estates and domestic affairs, 'every man is entitled to consider what suits his own convenience, and follow whatever course he judges best'[30] with no interference from state or church.

In the pre-modern world, individuals and their consciences were constrained within a society ordered by common principles derived from a common belief in God's design for the world. In the modern, liberal world no such common belief or principles any longer existed; they were replaced by each individual's own private judgement of the social world and their own 'interests' in it. The individual's view of the world, in all its aspects, become privatized or internalized, and this development involved a transformation or inclusion of the idea of the individual conscience, which, in its modern form, emerged with the Reformation, into that of 'interest'. As Wolin argues, 'under the auspices of liberalism, the great transformation was effected whereby "individual interest" was substituted for individual conscience. Interest gradually came to play the same role in political and social thought that conscience had played in relation.'[31]

Individuals' judgements and interests were likly to conflict in a situation where desires were expanding and there were large inequalities of property. The liberal answer to the problem of social order inherent in such a society was to divide social life into two spheres and to substitute for shared principles a 'political method'[32] or procedure for arbitrating between conflicting individual interests and deciding on the 'public interest'. In the private sphere of social life individuals' non-political natural rights are given expression: this is the proper sphere for individuals to exercise their private judgement and pursue their interests. In the political sphere individual private judgement is excluded, the natural political right is given up and decisions are made on behalf of individuals by specially chosen representatives.

To talk of the 'giving up' of the natural political right is, in one sense, rather misleading, since there is an implication that individuals actually have it to give up, just as they have other natural rights which it is their prerogative to exercise. It is quite otherwise with the natural political right. In order for Locke to justify political authority, he has to allow that individuals do have a natural political aspect to their selves. However, as I have already emphasized, this is a purely formal statement (which is, perhaps, partly why Locke called his doctrine 'strange'). This means that the political right of the individual is *a fiction*, posited only to justify a certain kind of political authority in a specific manner. The individual's political right has no *actual* expression either in the (conjectural history of) the state of nature or in civil society. It is a conceptual hypothesis that serves to justify the exercise of political authority by one man, or a few representatives, given the liberal starting point of the 'natural' freedom and equality of all individuals.

It might be argued at this point that even if the right that is given up is a fiction, nevertheless something concrete is received in exchange, namely protection and security of property (in Locke's wide sense of the term). This is precisely why consent can rightfully be given to civil government at a certain stage of historical development, precisely why individuals should enter into civil society through the medium of the social contract.

The contract is necessary not to justify the giving up of the individual's right of political judgement as such, which was given up in the state of nature, but to justify giving it up to a particular form of government that can effectively protect (unequal) property rights. The introduction of the social contract is, however, to add fiction to fiction, for no one suggests that it should or could be taken as an actual event. What, though, is the notion of the social contract a fiction about? The answer to this question is central to Locke and the liberal-democratic reification of the political. The social contract is a fiction about citizenship.

In Locke's theory, property is secured under a form of government where impartial laws are made publicly by representatives according to known procedures, and are impartially and effectively enforced. Everyone (including representatives) is formally equal under the law, the pauper and the owner of thousands of acres of the English countryside; each receives equal protection for his unequal 'interests'. And, it might be suggested by a critic of my argument at this point, something else is received through the contract in exchange for the fictional right that is given up – in fact, something which illustrates that the right is not, or, at least, today is not, a complete fiction. Together with the formal legal equality, a formal, equal political status of citizenship is also established. It is an equality that extends beyond the receipt of protection. Political equality theoretically involves individuals in some activity; activity in a political capacity, i.e. as *citizens*, not as private individuals. This activity is in order to 'protect their protection'.[33] That is, they are able as citizens to vote for the appropriate representatives to ensure protection. Again, this appears only in embryonic form in Locke's theory. A formal equality of citizenship, a formal political equality of everyone (all adults) as voters, over and above their substantive inequalities as individuals, is only established once the liberal theory of representative government becomes liberal democratic with the introduction of universal suffrage.

However, this apparent return of the individual's political right *is* only apparent. Citizenship remains a fiction. The first thing to note is that the paradox of the political immediately re-enters at this point. Citizens vote for representatives, but they do so precisely so that representatives can make political decisions on their behalf; once again the right of political judgement is being given up. The representatives now become, as it were, the embodiment of the political selves, the citizens selves, of the members of the community.[34] These selves can then be 'viewed' by those members in a separate, autonomous sphere, the political sphere. The task of the representatives is precisely to represent the interests of all citizens, i.e. to represent the political or public interest, not the separate, conflicting interests of individuals. This means that representatives, on entering the political sphere, put on their own version of the 'political lion skin'. As

Locke stresses, private judgement is now excluded; representatives do not judge privately but politically. They make political decisions which are not so much matters of principle as of procedure or technical expertise, that of the umpire of the conflicting interests in the game of the market.[35] But what is the collective, political interest of citizens who are bound together by only a formal status? This is difficult, if not impossible, to answer.

The giving up of the fictional political right by private individuals leaves the political sphere with no concrete or actual embodiment in the community. Individuals have nothing in common to bind them together, so what is 'common' to society, i.e. Wolin's 'traditional' conception of the political, can only be seen as something over and above society, something abstracted from the actual social relationships of private individuals, an 'autonomous' and external embodiment of a common fictional status.[36] Citizens can only look at such a political sphere and not act in it. In other words, the conception of the political in Locke's and liberal-democratic theory is a reified one. The political sphere appears as a 'thing' – 'the state' – objectified and external to the members of society.

Nor is there any way in which the liberal-democratic political sphere can be seen as other than a reified abstration, and the separation of the private and the political spheres can be bridged. The political sphere is bound to remain a reified entity, always out of the reach of citizens. This is because although, formally, citizenship is a political status and citizens vote as political actors, so that, theoretically, the two spheres are brought together during the exercise of the democratic franchise, actually this never happens, and cannot happen.[37] The liberal-democratic citizen does not vote as a political actor, but in defence of private interest, which is one of Wolin's criticisms of liberalism.

Citizenship is a 'political lion skin' which covers, temporarily, an individual whose natural habitat is private life. As Dahl has so graphically said of *Homo civicus*, today's equivalent of Locke's individual who consented to enter political society, he 'is not by nature a political animal'.[38] He is that paradoxical creature, a 'private citizen', and this reveals yet a further paradox. Instead of private judgement being excluded when the liberal-democratic 'political state' is fully developed and universal suffrage is introduced, it is exactly private judgement that re-enters. The private citizen can vote only on the basis of private interests underneath the lion's skin that covers the symbolic giving up of the fictional political right. If citizens actually acted in the way in which the formal political status suggests they should, one of the cornerstones of liberal democracy's defence against 'radical democracy' would be dismantled; the assumption that whereas individuals can and should judge for themselves in all matters in private life, this is not possible in political life. In a properly political society political decisions must be made by periodically elected representatives.

Concepts and Political Life

Some further discussion is necessary to put two such different intepretations of Locke's and subsequent liberal-democratic theory into perspective. First, I want to look at Wolin's interpretation of Locke from a different viewpoint.

If Locke is at fault for postulating a political state of nature, the problem arises of how, from a non-political natural state, a political sphere emerges. If it is a 'vital precondition' of a society, where, as it were, does it come from? Is it imposed (by whom? how?) as an external sphere on a non-political social order? Moreover, if the absence of a political order leaves individuals, in Wolin's graphic phrase, in desperate homelessness, can we even talk of a 'social order' at all? If we are to start the argument by postulating merely a collection of unrelated, abstract, atomized 'individuals', then problems arise of how 'society', let alone a 'political society', can be conceived – as Hobbes's theory illustrates.[39] Locke's formal account of the 'moral state of man' can be seen as a version of what I have elsewhere called the conceptual argument;[40] namely, the argument that a coherent conception of a 'society' presupposes concepts such as 'rights', 'obligation', 'rules' and 'authority', concepts which are summed up in Locke's 'law of nature'. And if 'authority' is an integral part of 'society', then, at least according to some definitions of the political (cf. Dahl, cited at the beginning of the chapter) all societies are political societies. This only appears odd if the political is seen in terms of the modern state, as an autonomous sphere, separate from the rest of social life.[41] In that case Locke's civil government does appear less distinctive than it might, being anticipated by a political state of nature.

Locke's account of the state of nature, though, is two-sided. The contrast that is relevant for his conception of the political is not between civil government and the formal account – the conceptual argument – of the state of nature (Wolin's 'ideal' state of nature), but between the actual social relationships of the private sphere and the liberal state that is superimposed upon them. This is not to say that the state of nature is irrelevant. Far from it. These social relations, too, have been foreshadowed in the conjectural history of the state of nature, in which Locke advances some empirical hypotheses about individual's natures: for example, they are such that desires expand (infinitely?) once money is introduced, and they are such that government is a natural necessity (i.e. the right of political judgement must 'naturally' be given up. Locke thus provides a justification for the social relations of the embryonic capitalist system of his own time (the private sphere), and for the – properly political – government that has developed into the liberal-democratic state of our own time.

None of this is surprising. Political theory is not, and cannot be, a purely conceptual matter. Concepts do not exist in a timeless void but are an integral part of social life, and cannot be treated in isolated abstraction from concrete forms of social relationships. It is, I would argue, an abstractly conceptual focus that underlies Wolin's arguments about the sublimation of the political. It is a focus that insists that it must be possible to reapply a general and a 'traditional', a timeless and abstract, conception of the political to the present-day realities of the liberal-democratic state, even though Wolin himself states early in the argument of *Politics and Vision* that 'the political' has always been a 'created' sphere.[42]

A puzzling feature of Wolin's arguments is what in real terms, in terms of actual institutions and relationships, a 're-assertion' of a common and general traditional conception of the political might mean. Wolin never really makes clear whether 'sublimation' has occurred in practice, or whether it is purely a matter of the political theorists' conception of the political, but the latter forms the major thrust of his argument. The question that has to be asked is what, empirically, Wolin's 'autonomous' political sphere comprises? The answer seems to be, the modern (liberal-democratic) state. His argument is opaque on this point but one explicit reference is his comment, in criticism of the theories of Marx and Durkheim, that 'to reject the state meant denying the central referent of the political.'[43] Ironically enough, Wolin's references to 'totalitarianism' in the final chapter of *Politics and Vision* suggest that it is specifically the liberal-democratic conception of the state that would meet his requirements. Liberal-democratic theory still provides (with no need for 're-assertion') the very 'autonomous' conception of the political that Wolin argues has been sublimated and lost from view.

That Wolin fails to consider this possibility is due, I would argue, to his misunderstanding of liberal-democratic theory from its beginnings. As his interpretation of Locke illustrates, he has already dismissed it, in its early form, as a 'sublimated' view of the political. Central to this misunderstanding is Wolin's view that the political sphere must appear *de nouveau* as autonomous; it cannot be rooted in 'natural' human relationships, for the latter are 'shelterless'. Thus Wolin continues to demand an 'autonomous' political sphere, or at least the conception of such, to provide the 'comprehensive unity' for society that he has argued is lacking in the modern world – or, at least, among modern political theorists. He overlooks both the possibility that the liberal-democratic state itself might be performing that task, albeit not in the 'traditional' manner, and the fact that liberal-democratic theory certainly presents the liberal-democratic state as doing so.

Wolin's failure either to consider the actual role and nature of the contemporary liberal state or the way in which it is presented in liberal-democratic theory means that the activities of contemporary political theorists who go grubbing around in 'private' areas like industry and calling them 'political' can only look peculiar. The perspective of *Politics and Vision* obscures the fact that what is at issue in the sublimation/reification problem is precisely how, right here and now in a liberal democracy, the political sphere should be characterized. Or, to put it another way, what is obscured is the important question of the significance for the 'political' sphere, and, more specifically, for democratic political theory and practice, of the vast historical transformation that has been taking place since Locke formulated his 'sensible' theory. The emergence of the market economy (or, alternatively, the rise of the 'social', which Crick argues was necessary for the development of, not the sublimation of, the 'political') and its subsequent transformation into state-managed capitalism is also the transformation of Locke's autonomous, representative, 'umpire' civil government. The umpire is one of the players. The liberal-democratic state now intervenes massively in all areas of social life, especially, of course, the economic, and – the other side of the same process – the economic and other areas of social life have become interwoven into a huge military-industrial-political-ideological complex of the state apparatus.[44]

Hannah Arendt's account of the development of the modern, capitalist world in *The Human Condition* provides an interesting comparison with Wolin's arguments. Arendt's discussion emphasizes how completely the ancient (the 'traditional') conceptions of, and antithesis between, the private and public or political spheres have been transformed. She states that 'the emergence of the social realm, . . . coincided with the emergence of the modern age and . . . found its political form in the nation state.'[45] In the modern world economic activity was freed from its ancient confines of the private household and attained 'public significance', thus changing the conception of political life and its relationship to the private sphere. Economic activity became the accumulation of capital based on labour power, and 'society' emerged as an organization of private property-owners and job-holders who demand protection from government. The contemporary result, Arendt argues, is that the political sphere now appears as an administrative organ for nation-wide 'housekeeping'.[46] Although Arendt does not suggest that a 'traditional' conception of the political can somehow be directly reasserted in the face of economic and political transformations of the modern, liberal world, she does argue that both the private and political spheres are being submerged in the social realm;[47] a claim that seems to parallel Wolin's claim about sublimation.

However, Arendt's argument is not a purely conceptual one. She refers in her work both to historical changes and to the possibility of further developments, drawing attention especially to a striking feature of revolutions over the past century, the emergence of self-managing councils, as significant for the future.[48] In the light of the contemporary role of the liberal-democratic state, the sublimation argument may appear more plausible when given an additional empirical gloss. Yet this plausibility still depends upon a conception of the political as an essentially autonomous sphere (a conception that Arendt endorses),[49] whose autonomy has, at the present time, been 'lost' or sublimated or submerged in social life. Without this starting point there is really no problem about 'sublimation'. Or, at least, there is not the problem that Wolin makes so much of; there are still plenty of problems left about the role of, nature of, and proper characterization of the political sphere in contemporary liberal democracies and their state-managed capitalism, and I have only begun to nibble at the edges of them.[50] Nor, in the absence of this specific conception of the political, are the political scientists' unorthodox definitions of the political, to which I referred at the beginning of the chapter, a 'series of dead ends'. Rather they can be seen as attempts to recognize the realities of the contemporary liberal-democratic state.

It may seem that the preceding paragraph runs against the earlier argument that the liberal-democratic conception of the political is of a reified and autonomous sphere, and that this is a more adequate characterization of the liberal-democratic state than the sublimation argument. Here, the interrelationship of concepts and socio-political life, and the complexity of that relationship, needs to be re-emphasized. To claim that the liberal-democratic state is not in fact 'autonomous' from the rest of social life, that in the form of Locke's and Wolin's 'superstructure' it was left behind long ago (if, indeed, it ever existed in that form) says nothing about the way in which the 'political' is presented in liberal-democratic theory. The insights of sociology and philosophy have taught us that political institutions are not independent of (or autonomous from) the social interactions of individuals, and it can be argued from liberal and liberal-democratic theory itself that the political right of individuals is a 'natural' right and that political relationships have a basis in 'natural' social relationships. Yet none of this is to say that those political institutions may not be presented as 'autonomous' by political theory, or that patterns of political interaction (political institutions) may not become so well established as to appear as, and in fact to be, external to, and out of the control of, citizens.

Liberal theory, as the discussion of Locke illustrates, is based on the paradox of a 'natural' political right that has no actual expression, and this forms the basis for the justification of an allegedly 'autonomous' political sphere, reified in Marx's 'heaven' of the liberal-democratic state. Thus, on the one hand, liberal-democratic theory mystifies the realities of political life. On the other hand, it also contains, buried within itself, an important truth about the liberal-democratic state and contemporary citizenship: namely, that the latter is a fiction and that the state is in fact external to and out of the control of its citizens. It is for this reason that Wolin's problems of the devaluation of political participation and the 'chopping up of political man', which he associates with the sublimation of the political, are problems that are integral to liberal-democratic theory and practice itself. A solution will hardly be found within the liberal-democratic state and within the liberal-democratic conception of the political.

Towards a Participatory Conception of the Political: Some Comments

The fiction of citizenship and the paradox of a 'natural' right that must always be given up are integral to the liberal-democratic conception of the political and to liberal democracy's 'defence against radical democracy'. If citizenship is to be more than a 'lion's skin', if it is to be the meaningful, self-fulfilling activity that Wolin wishes it to be, then the 'natural' political right of the individual that liberal theory admits (however obscurely that admission is made) has to be given an actual expression. This expression presupposes a non-liberal democratic theory and practice that looks beyond the liberal-democratic state. A political anthropologist recently remarked upon 'the spell that the state has long exerted on political theorists',[51] and it is only a few modern political theorists who have not been theorists of the state.[52] Liberal-democratic theory's main rival, Marxism, has seen the political in the same terms and, oddly enough, has also contributed to the identification of the liberal-democratic state of the capitalist economic order as the only properly, or 'fully developed', political state: witness Marx's pronouncement that 'when, in the course of development, class distinctions have disappeared, . . . the public power will lose its political character.'[53]

In Locke's theory the political right of the individual remains a conceptual hypothesis. However, the social contract is the point at which the symbolic giving up of the right to the 'political', representative, liberal government takes place, and a closer look at Locke's version of the social contract will give some broad, general indication of a conception of the political that is compatible with the retention of the 'natural' right of political judgement and action by citizens. A comparison with Rousseau's theory is also pertinent here.[54] Rousseau's conjectural history of the state of nature denounces the liberal social contract as a fraud through which individuals voluntarily enchain themselves. In *The Social Contract* he offers an alternative version of the social contract story in which citizens do not alienate their political right to representatives but retain it themselves within a participatory or 'radical' democracy.

Locke's two-stage social contract is often presented as involving, firstly, the formation of a society and, secondly, the formation of a political society. This interpretation rests on the mistaken view that Locke's state of nature is asocial. In the first stage of the contract a new political community is created out of the 'dispersed' political society of the state of nature; i.e. individuals give up their political right to the community. The question that has to be asked here is, what kind of 'giving up' is this? As Rousseau tells us, it is very different from that of the second stage of the contract where the political right is passed on to a few representatives. The new political community is composed of the contracting individuals (who else?) so that the 'giving up' is to themselves. They 'give up' their individual 'natural' political right to themselves in a different capacity, a collective capacity as citizens of the new political community.

> The act of association consists of a reciprocal commitment between society and the individual, so that each person, in making a contract, as it were, with himself, finds himself doubly committed, first as a member of the sovereign body in relation to individuals, and secondly, as a member of the state [political community] in relation to the sovereign.[55]

After the single-stage, participatory social contract, individuals 'regain' their political right every time that they act as citizens in their participatory democracy, i.e. act collectively together to decide on and implement the political good of their community. The 'natural' individual political right thus ceases to be a paradoxical fiction and a merely formal status, and gains actual expression. The political sphere within a participatory democracy ceases to be a reified abstraction standing, separately and autonomously, over and above and external to the rest of social life. Rather, it is brought into being whenever citizens gather together to make political decisions. Political life is thus rooted in, and forms an integral part of, social life as a whole. It is distinct from the private aspects of social life, where individuals act singularly, but it is no longer, as in liberal theory, dualistically counterposed against the private sphere of social life; instead it is dialectically interrelated with it.

The Lockeian, liberal-democratic response to this very brief sketch would be that there is no point in suggesting that it could form the beginnings of a basis to develop an alternative democratic conception of the political, because, empirically, its implications are nonsensical. Rousseau's claim that if there is to be a free, just and equal democratic political community, then there can be no second stage to the contract, no representatives in the liberal sense and, hence, no liberal-democratic state, is empirically absurd. However, the plausibility of this response is greatly enhanced by the 'spell' cast by the modern state. Opponents of radical democracy see the political community in terms of one unit only, in terms of the state. The alternatives then become either a – clearly absurd – assembly of millions, or a – clearly realistic – giving up of citizens' political right to a few representatives who assemble to make decisions, representatives who embody the political interest of the community.[56]

The development of an alternative conception of the political must thus be integrated with empirical arguments about the feasibility of moving beyond the liberal-democratic state to a political community composed of a multiplicity of participtory or self-managed units (perhaps to be called councils). In such a system, political authority 'moves neither from above nor below, but [is] horizontally directed so that the federated units mutually check and control their powers.'[57] But, it is likely to be demanded here, surely even a self-managing democracy could not escape from the second stage of the social contract; surely representatives would be necessary within the participatory units and thus the 'natural' political right cannot lose its paradoxical character?

This objection, too, gains much of its force because 'representative' has become so well identified with representation within the liberal-democratic state. Or, to put this another way, we have long since ceased to treat Rousseau's distinction between the 'sovereign' and the 'government' as worthy of serious consideration. For Rousseau the 'government', i.e. representatives who are agents or officers of the citizens (the 'sovereign') of a participatory unit, is 'an intermediary body established between the subjects [individuals] and the sovereign [citizens] for their mutual communication'.[58] These representatives are not the bearers of the alienated political right of the citizens, nor are they parties to the contract, i.e. there is no second stage. To move to the second stage would turn the contract into one 'which stipulates between the two parties the conditions under which the one undertakes to command and the other to obey. It will be admitted, I am sure, that this is a strange way of contracting'.[59] 'Representatives' compatible with a self-managing democracy and its appropriate conception of the political 'are not the people's masters'. When acting on behalf of the political community in specific spheres and for specific periods, 'they are only doing their duty as citizens, without having any sort of right to argue terms.' These representatives are strictly accountable for what they do. It is citizens collectively who alone retain the right to make political decisions and who, therefore, are not merely spectators of their representatives but the active creators and controllers of their own political life.[60]

If it is granted that the empirical feasibility of a self-managing democracy is, at the least, an open question, two further objections, relevant to themes of this chapter, will probably be advanced. The first is Wolin's objection that to 'deny the state', and to replace it with a decentralized federation of participatory councils, will further accentuate the tendency towards the 'chopping up of political man' that began with the sublimation of the political and the development of liberalism. This objection takes it for granted that liberal-democratic citizenship is something more than a fiction and that it does provide some meaningful, general and unifying point of reference for the individual. In fact the 'private citizen' of liberal democracy is encouraged to see her various roles and capacities as separate and fragmented, as embodying different and often competing 'interests'; housewife, mother, consumer, factory worker, secretary, motorist, friend, lover . . . how does 'private citizenship' bring them together? In contrast, an enlarged and actual citizenship in a multiplicity of participatory units could give concrete experience of the complex of interrelationships between different social spheres, roles and capacities.

The second objection is that by drawing many 'private' organizations and areas into political life, by treating, e.g., the enterprise as one of the self-managing units of a participatory democracy, the 'natural' rights or freedoms of the individual will be diminished, not enlarged. I do not want to rehearse here the arguments against the liberal view of freedom as purely negative freedom; rather I raise this point in order to distinguish my argument from the slogan I cited in my introductory remarks, 'the personal is the political'.

This is not to say that it is not an effective slogan – liberal democracies give short shrift to Locke's 'property in your own person' when women demand that it should apply also to their bodies – but to argue that it should not be seen as more than a slogan. As an alternative to the liberal-democratic conception of the political it merely mirrors its adversary; it tries to end the dualistic separation of private and political life by opposing to it the assimilation of the two spheres. The interrelationship of the personal and the political spheres can be recognized, as can the fact that any relationship can, in certain circumstances, have political effects, but this is not the same as arguing that the criteria and principles that should order our interactions and decision-making as citizens should be exactly the same as those that should underlay our relationships with friends and lovers. This is to try to transform the technocratic, procedural 'political method' of a 'a polity . . . systematically denuded of a set of public moral values'[61] by the claim that the morality of the personal is all that we need. A public or political morality, principles of political right on which members of a self-managing democracy can self-consciously draw to order their political practice, has also to be developed along with a participatory conception of the political. Moreover, 'the personal' is as much a part of liberal democracy as the fiction of citizenship and the reification of the political. The transformation of liberal democracy requires the transformation of *both* spheres of social life and an appreciation of their distinctiveness *within* their dialectical interrelationship.

Hannah Arendt has said of the self-managing councils that 'whether this system is a pure utopia. . . . I cannot say.'[62] So far, the councils have been defeated by the state and buried by its theorists and historians. Is a self-managing, participatory democracy indeed a utopia? Political theory alone cannot answer this question: but let Rousseau have the last word; we should never forget that 'the boundaries of the moral [social] realm are less narrow than we think; it is our own weaknesses, our vices and our prejudices that limit them.'[63]

NOTES

1 G. Sartori, *Democratic Theory* (Wayne State University Press, Detroit, 1962), pp. 362, 370.
2 B. Crick, *In Defence of Politics* (Penguin Books, Harmondsworth, Middlesex, 1964), revised ed., pp. 29, 145, 164. Without this institutional context it is difficult to know what to make of Crick's descriptions such as that on p. 161. Cf. B. M. Barry, *Sociologists, Economists and Democracy* (Macmillan, London, 1970) p. 59 (footnote), on 'the "pluralist" theory of constitutional government . . . sometimes called "liberal democracy". . . . Crick . . . confusingly calls the same phenomenon "politics".'
3 Crick *In Defence of Politics*, pp. 17, 24.
4 J. Plamenatz, *Man and Society* (Longmans, London, 1963), vol. I, p. 241.
5 K. Marx, 'On the Jewish Question', in *Writings of the Young Marx on Philosophy and Society*, ed. L. D. Easton and K. M. Guddat, (Anchor Books, New York, 1967), pp. 225–6 (italics in the original).
6 D. Easton, *The Political System*, 2nd ed. (Knopf, New York, 1971), p. 134.
7 R. A. Dahl, *Modern Political Analysis* (Prentice Hall, Englewood Cliffs, NJ. 1963), p. 6.
8 S. Wolin, *Politics and Vision: Continuity and Innovation in Western Political Thought* (Allen & Unwin, London, 1961), p. 290.

9 Ibid., p. 363.
10 Ibid., p. 305.
11 Ibid., p. 306.
12 Ibid., p. 368.
13 Ibid., pp. 430–2.
14 Ibid., p. 306.
15 Ibid., pp. 307–8.
16 Ibid., p. 306.
17 Ibid., p. 434.
18 Ibid., p. 294.
19 R.Ashcraft, 'Locke's State of Nature: Historical Fact or Moral Fiction?', *American Political Science Review*, 62(3) (1968), pp. 898–915.
20 Ibid., pp. 900–1.
21 Paragraph references in brackets in the text are to J. Locke, *Two Treatises of Government*, ed. P. Laslett, 2nd ed., (Cambridge University Press, Cambridge, 1967), II.
22 On the importance of the invention of money for Locke's argument see C. B. Macpherson, *The Political Theory of Possessive Individualism* (Oxford University Press, Oxford, 1962), pp. 203–11, 233–5.
23 Macpherson, *Possessive Individualism*, p. 242, reflects the argument that the 'pleasant' and 'unpleasant' picture of the state of nature correspond to the pre- and post-monetary stages on the grounds that both appear in the period immediately preceding civil society. But Locke's theory of resistance to arbitrary government demands that the bonds of trust and the mutual obligations between the members of society (the 'pleasant' or formal picture) never disappear; 'society' continues, despite the difficulties of the second stage of the state of nature or an arbitrary ruler in civil society.
24 For an excellent discussion of this aspect of Locke's theory see G. J. Schochet, 'The Family and the Origins of the State in Locke's Political Philosophy', in *John Locke: Problems and Perspectives* (Cambridge University Press, Cambridge, 1969). Schochet, p. 88, notes Locke's terminological confusion but he overlooks Locke's distinction between 'political' and 'government'.
25 Schochet, 'Origins of the State', p. 92.
26 J. Dunn, *The Political Thought of John Locke* (Cambridge University Press, Cambridge, 1969), p. 106.
27 It is not necessary to accept Macpherson's argument about differential rationality to agree that Locke does provide 'a positive moral basis for capitalist society' (p. 221). Whether he 'set out' to do so is another matter; see the arguments of Dunn, *The Political Thought of John Locke*, chaps 15–17, and, on Locke's attitude to the labourer, E. J. Hundert, 'The Making of *Homo Faber*: John Locke Between Ideology and History', *Journal of the History of Ideas*, 33 (1972), pp. 3–22.
28 On 'direct' political judgement see H. C. Mansfield Jr, 'Hobbes and

the Science of Indirect Government', *American Political Science Review*, 65 (1971), pp. 97–110.

29 See S. Lukes, *Individualism* (Blackwell, Oxford, 1973).

30 J. Locke, *A Letter on Toleration* (Oxford University Press, Oxford, 1968), ed. J. W. Gough, p. 89.

31 Wolin, *Politics and Vision*, p. 338. Religion played a larger role in Locke's theory than these remarks suggest; in this sense his theory is less modern than Hobbes's. See R. Ashcraft, 'Faith and Knowledge in Locke's Philosophy', in *John Locke: Problems and Perspectives*, ed. J. W. Yolton (Cambridge University Press, Cambridge, 1969).

32 See J. A. Schumpeter, *Capitalism, Socialism and Democracy* (Allen & Unwin, London, 1943), chap. 12, on the democratic 'political method'.

33 See the discussion in M. Walzer, *Obligations: Essays on Disobedience, War and Citizenship* (Simon & Schuster, New York, 1971), chap. 10. The phrase comes from Hobbes's *Leviathan*. ed. C. B. Macpherson (Penguin Books, Harmondsworth, Middlesex, 1968), chap. XXIX, p. 375.

34 See E. M. Wood, *Mind and Politics: An Approach to the Meaning of Liberal and Socialist Individualism* (University of California Press, Berkeley, 1972), p. 156.

35 One of Wolin's (p. 304), criticisms of liberalism is that government – or political decision making – has been subsumed 'under the principle of the division of labor'; i.e. it becomes another area of professional or technical expertise, not of principled deliberation. See also the arguments in J. Habermas, 'Technology and Science as "Ideology"', in *Towards a Rational Society* (Heinemann, London, 1971), although Habermas's argument that the legitimation or ideology has changed seems to me to overlook the extent to which liberal-democratic theory survives as a theory of the state and the political, and the extent to which the technocratic state was inherent in liberalism from its origins. Cf. A. Ryan's comment on James Mill's political theory, that politics is 'dispensible' if a more efficient means can be found, in 'Two Concepts of Politics and Democracy', in *Machiavelli and the Nature of Political Thought*, ed. M. Fleischer (Atheneum, New York, 1972), p. 110.

36 Cf. Wood, *Mind and Politics*, pp. 152–3.

37 In his early discussion of Hegel's political theory, Marx saw universal suffrage as the means through which the separation of civil society and the state would be transcended; K. Marx, *Critique of Hegel's 'Philosophy of Right'* (Cambridge University Press, Cambridge, 1970), ed. J. O'Malley, p. 121.

38 R. A. Dahl, *Who Governs?* (Yale University Press, New Haven, 1961), pp. 223–5.

39 Rousseau was well aware of this problem. In the first part of *The Discourse on Inequality*, he argues, especially against Hobbes, that non-social 'individuals' in the state of nature would be bereft of all

recognizably human qualities. Rousseau does not attempt to explain how such a situation is overcome and society 'instituted'; in the second part of *The Discourse*, he assumes the social nature of individuals and offers a conjectural history of the origins of government – which is a salutary contrast to that of Locke.

40 C. Pateman, 'Political Obligation and Conceptual Analysis', *Political Studies*, 21 (1973), pp. 199–218.

41 This has given rise to problems over the status of non-state 'primitive' societies: 'the recent discovery of the existence and importance of organised government in even the most "primitive" societies has not been without, once again, some considerable confusion between government in general and political systems in particular', Crick, *In Defence of Politics*, p. 180.

42 Wolin, *Politics and Vision*, p. 5.

43 Ibid., p. 417.

44 See the discussion in R. Miliband, *The State in Capitalist Society* (Weidenfeld & Nicholson, London, 1969).

45 H. Arendt, *The Human Condition* (Anchor Books, New York, 1959), p. 27.

46 Ibid., p. 55.

47 Ibid., p. 61.

48 See H. Arendt, *On Revolution* (Penguin Books, Harmondsworth, Middlesex, 1973), chap. 6; and 'Thoughts on Politics and Revolution' in *Crises of the Republic* (Penguin Books, Harmondsworth, Middlesex, 1973).

49 It is also for this reason that Arendt, in *On Revolution*, states that factory councils were misguided and a failure since councils must be 'political' bodies (although it is not clear that she maintains this position in 'Thoughts on Politics'; see pp. 189–90). I have excluded Arendt from my wider discussion, however, because her position is far more complex than that of Wolin, and, despite the insistence on the 'autonomy' of the political, she is sharply critical of liberalism and liberal democracy.

50 See the discussion of this problem in A. Wolfe, 'New Directions in the Marxist Theory of Politics', *Politics and Society*, 4(2) (1974), especially pp. 146–51; Wolfe helpfully compares Marx's analysis of the commodity with his comments on the liberal state.

51 G. Balandier, *Political Anthropology* (Penguin Books, Harmondsworth, Middlesex, 1972), p. 187.

52 See T. Skillen, 'The Statist Conception of Politics', *Radical Philosophy*, 2 (1972), pp. 2–6.

53 K. Marx and F. Engels, 'The Communist Manifesto', in *Selected Works*, vol. I (Lawrence & Wishart, London, 1968), p. 53.

54 See also Wood's discussion of Rousseau; *Mind and Politics*, p. 152 and pp. 162–73.

55 J. J. Rousseau, *The Social Contract*, tr. M. Cranston (Penguin Books, Harmondsworth, Middlesex, 1968), I. chap. 7, p. 62.

56 It is sometimes suggested that the liberal-democratic state could be turned into a participatory democracy through technology; by the installation of voting devices in every home so that instant referenda could be taken on all political issues (see, e.g. R. P. Wolff, *In Defense of Anarchism* (Harper & Row, New York, 1970), pp. 34–7; and P. Singer, *Democracy and Disobedience* (Oxford University Press, Oxford, 1973), pp. 106–7. This suggetion does not, however, overcome the problems of 'private citizenship'. A more logical conclusion of this argument is drawn by Asimov in his story 'Franchise' in *Earth is Room Enough* (Panther Books, London, 1960), where one 'representative' voter is chosen by computer and tied into electronic equipment to vote for all the rest. (I owe this reference to my colleague Dennis Altman.)

57 Arendt, 'Thoughts on Politics', p. 188.

58 Rousseau, *The Social Contract*, III, chap. 1, p. 102.

59 Ibid., chap. 16, p. 144.

60 Ibid., chap. 18, p. 146. Compare: 'The Commune was to be a working, not a parliamentary, body, executive and legislative at the same time . . . [All] public servants, . . . were to be elective, responsible and revocable, . . . universal suffrage was to serve the people, constituted in Communes, as individual suffrage serves any other employer in the search for the workmen and managers in his business.' K. Marx, 'The Civil War in France', *Selected Works*, pp. 291–2. Some further comments on liberal-democratic representation can be found in my 'A Contribution to the Political Theory of Organizational Democracy', *Administration and Society*, 7(1) (1975), especially pp. 15–18.

61 J. B. Elshtain, 'Moral Woman and Immoral Man: A Consideration of the Public-Private Split and its Political Ramification', *Politics and Society*, 4(4) (1974), p. 471. This excellent discussion also deals, from a different starting point, with some of the problems raised above.

62 Arendt, 'Thoughts on Politics', p. 189.

63 Rousseau, *The Social Contract*, III, chap. 12, p. 136.

6

Feminist Critiques of the Public/Private Dichotomy

The dichotomy between the private and the public is central to almost two centuries of feminist writing and political struggle; it is, ultimately, what the feminist movement is about. Although some feminists treat the dichotomy as a universal, trans-historical and trans-cultural feature of human existence, feminist criticism is primarily directed at the separation and opposition between the public and private spheres in liberal theory and practice.

The relationship between feminism and liberalism is extremely close but also exceedingly complex. The roots of both doctrines lie in the emergence of individualism as a general theory of social life; neither liberalism nor feminism is conceivable without some conception of individuals as free and equal beings, emancipated from the ascribed, hierarchical bonds of traditional society. But if liberalism and feminism share a common origin, their adherents have often been opposed over the past two hundred years. The direction and scope of feminist criticism of liberal conceptions of the public and the private have varied greatly in different phases of the feminist movement. An analysis of this criticism is made more complicated because liberalism is inherently ambiguous about the 'public' and the 'private', and feminists and liberals disagree about where and why the dividing line is to be drawn between the two spheres, or, according to certain contemporary feminist arguments, whether it should be drawn at all.

Feminism is often seen as nothing more than the completion of the liberal or bourgeois revolution, as an extension of liberal principles and rights to women as well as men. The demand for equal rights has, of course, always been an important part of feminism. However, the attempt to universalize liberalism has more far-reaching consequences than is often appreciated because, in the end, it inevitably challenges liberalism itself.[1] Liberal-feminism has radical implications, not least in challenging the separation and opposition between the private and public spheres that is fundamental to liberal theory and practice. The liberal contrast between private and public is more than a distinction between two kinds of social activities. The public sphere, and the principles that govern it, are seen as separate from, or independent of, the relationships in the private sphere. A familiar illustration of this claim is the long controversy between liberal and radical political scientists about participation, the radicals denying the liberal claim that the social inequalities of the private sphere are irrelevant to questions about the political equality, universal suffrage and associated civil liberties of the public realm.

Not all feminists, however, are liberals; 'feminism' goes far beyond liberal-feminism. Other feminists explicitly reject liberal conceptions of the private and public and see the social structure of liberalism as the political problem, not a starting point from which equal rights can be claimed. They have much in common with the radical and socialist critics of liberalism who rely on 'organic' theories (to use Benn and Gaus's terminology[2]) but they differ sharply in their analysis of the liberal state. In short, feminists, unlike other radicals, raise the generally neglected problem of the patriarchal character of liberalism.

Liberalism and Patriarchalism

Benn and Gaus's account of the liberal conception of the public and private illustrates very nicely some major problems in liberal theory. They accept that the private and the public are central categories of liberalism, but they do not explain why these two terms are crucial or why the private sphere is contrasted with and opposed to the 'public' rather than the 'political' realm. Similarly, they note that liberal arguments leave it unclear whether civil society is private or public but, although they state that in both of their liberal models the family is paradigmatically private, they fail to pursue the question why, in this case, liberals usually also see civil society as private. Benn and Gaus's account of liberalism also illustrates its abstract, ahistorical character and, in what is omitted and taken for granted, provides a good example of the theoretical discussions that feminists are now sharply criticizing. The account bears out Eisenstein's claim that 'the ideology of public and private life' invariably presents 'the division between public and private life, . . . as reflecting the development of the bourgeois liberal state, not the patriarchal ordering of the bourgeois state'.[3]

The term 'ideology' is appropriate here because the profound ambiguity of the liberal conception of the private and public obscures and mystifies the social reality it helps constitute. Feminists argue that liberalism is structured by patriarchal as well as class relations, and that the dichotomy between the private and the public obscures the subjection of women to men within an apparently universal, egalitarian and individualist order. Benn and Gaus's account assumes that the reality of our social life is more or less adequately captured in liberal conceptions. They do not recognize that 'liberalism' is patriarchal-liberalism and that the separation and opposition of the public and private spheres is an unequal opposition between women and men. They thus take the talk of 'individuals' in liberal theory at face value although, from the period when the social contract theorists attacked the patriarchalists, liberal theorists have excluded women from the scope of their apparently universal arguments.[4] One reason why the exclusion goes unnoticed is that the separation of the private and public is presented in liberal theory as if it applied to all individuals in the same way. It is often claimed – by anti-feminists today, but by feminists in the nineteenth century, most of whom accepted the doctrine of 'separate spheres' – that the two spheres are separate, but equally important and valuable. The way in which women and men are differentially located within private life and the public world is, as I shall indicate, a complex matter, but underlying a complicated reality is the belief that women's natures are such that they are properly subject to men and their proper place is in the private, domestic sphere. Men properly inhabit, and rule within, both spheres. The essential feminist argument is that the doctrine of 'separate but equal', and the ostensible individualism and egalitarianism of liberal theory, obscure the patriarchal reality of a social structure of inequality and the domination of women by men.

In theory, liberalism and patriarchalism stand irrevocably opposed to each other. Liberalism is an individualist, egalitarian, conventionalist doctrine; patriarchalism claims that hierarchical relations of subordination necessarily follow from the natural characteristics of men and women. In fact, the two doctrines were successfully reconciled through the answer given by the contract theorists in the seventeenth century to the subversive question of who counted as free and equal individuals. The conflict with the patriarchalists did not extend to women or conjugal relations; the latter were excluded from individualist arguments and the battle was fought out over the relation of adult sons to their fathers.

The theoretical basis for the liberal separation of the public and the private was provided in Locke's *Second Treatise*. He argued against Filmer that political power is conventional and can justifiably be exercised over free and equal adult individuals only with their consent.

Political power must not be confused with paternal power over children in the private, family sphere, which is a natural relationship that ends at the maturity, and hence freedom and equality, of (male) children. Commentators usually fail to notice that Locke's separation of the family and the political is also a sexual division. Although he argued that natural differences between men, such as age or talents, are irrelevant to their political equality, he agrees with Filmer's patriarchal claim that the natural differences between men and women entail the subjection of women to men or, more specifically, wives to husbands. Indeed, in Locke's statement at the beginning of the *Second Treatise* that he will show why political power is distinctive, he takes it for granted that the rule of husbands over wives is included in other (non-political) forms of power. He explicitly agrees with Filmer that a wife's subordination to her husband has a 'Foundation in Nature' and that the husband's will must prevail in the household as he is naturally 'the abler and the stronger'.[5] But a natural subordinate cannot at the same time be free and equal. Thus women (wives) are excluded from the status of 'individuals' and so from participating in the public world of equality, consent and convention.

It may appear that Locke's separation of paternal from political power can also be characterized as a separation of the private from the public. In one sense this is so; the public sphere can be seen as encompassing all social life apart from domestic life. Locke's theory also shows how the private and public spheres are grounded in opposing principles of association which are exemplified in the conflicting status of women and men; natural subordination stands opposed to free individualism. The family is based on natural ties of sentiment and blood and on the sexually ascribed status of wife and husband (mother and father). Participation in the public sphere is governed by universal, impersonal and conventional criteria of achievement, interests, rights, equality and property – liberal criteria, applicable only to men. An important consequence of this conception of private and public is that the public world, or civil society, is conceptualized and discussed in liberal theory (indeed, in almost all political theory) in abstraction from, or as separate from, the private domestic sphere.

It is important to emphasize at this point that the contemporary feminist critique of the public–private dichotomy is based on the same Lockean view of the two categories; domestic life is as paradigmatically private for feminists as it is in (this interpretation of) Locke's theory. However, feminists reject the claim that the separation of the private and the public follows inevitably from the natural characteristics of the sexes. They argue that a proper understanding of liberal social life is possible only when it is accepted that the two spheres, the domestic (private) and civil society (public), held to be separate and opposed, are inextricably interrelated; they are the two sides of the single coin of liberal-patriarchalism.

If, at one theoretical level, feminists and liberals are in conflict over a shared conception of the public and the private, at another level they are at odds about these very categories. There is another sense in which the private and public are far from synonymous with Locke's paternal and political power. Precisely because liberalism conceptualizes civil society in abstraction from ascriptive domestic life, the latter remains 'forgotten' in theoretical discussion. The separation between private and public is thus re-established as a division *within* civil society itself, within the world of men. The separation is then expressed in a number of different ways, not only private and public but also, for example, 'society' and 'state', or 'economy' and 'politics', or 'freedom' and 'coercion' or 'social' and 'political'.[6] Moreover, in *this* version of the separation of private and public, one category, the private, begins to wear the trousers (to adapt J. L. Austin's patriarchal metaphor for once in an appropriate context). The public or political aspect of civil society tends to get lost, as, for example, Wolin points out in *Politics and Vision*.[7]

The uncertain position of the public sphere develops for very good reason; the apparently universal criteria governing civil society are actually those associated with the liberal conception of the male individual, a conception which is presented as that of *the* individual. The individual is the owner of the property in his person, that is to say, he is seen in abstraction from his ascribed familial relations and those with his fellow men. He is a 'private' individual, but he needs a sphere in which he can exercise his rights and opportunities, pursue his (private) interests and protect and increase his property. If all men ('individuals') are so to act in an orderly fashion, then, as Locke is aware, a public 'umpire' (rather than a hidden – private? – hand), or a representative, liberal state, is required to make and enforce publicly known, equitable laws. Because individualism is, as Benn and Gaus remark, 'the dominant mode of liberal theory and discourse', it is not surprising either that the private and the public appear as the 'obvious' pair of liberal categories, or that the public gets stripped of its trousers and civil society is seen, above all else, as the sphere of private interest, private enterprise and private individuals.[8]

In the late twentieth century the relation between the capitalist economy and the state no longer looks like that between Locke's umpire and civil society and confusion abounds about the boundary between the private and public. But the confusion is unlikely to be remedied from within a theory which 'forgets' that it includes another boundary between private and public. One solution is to reinstate the political in public life. This is the response of Wolin or of Habermas in his rather opaque discussion of the 'principle' of the public sphere, where citizens can form reasoned political judgements.[9] Unlike these theorists, feminist critiques insist that an alternative to the liberal conception must also encompass the relationship between public and domestic life. The question that feminists raise is why the patriarchal character of the separation of a depoliticized public sphere from private life is so easily 'forgotten'; why is the separation of the two worlds located within civil society so that public life is implicitly conceptualized as the sphere of men?

The answer to this question can be found only by examining the history of the connection between the separation of production from the household and the emergence of the family as paradigmatically private. When Locke attacked (one aspect of) patriarchalism, husbands were heads of households but their wives played an active, independent part in numerous areas of production. As capitalism and its specific form of sexual as well as class division of labour developed, however, wives were pushed into a few, low-status areas of employment or kept out of economic life altogether, relegated to their 'natural', dependent, place in the private, familial sphere.[10] Today, despite a large measure of civil equality, it appears natural that wives are subordinate just because they are dependent on their husbands for subsistence, and it is taken for granted that liberal social life can be understood without reference to the sphere of subordination, natural relations and women. The old patriarchal argument from nature and women's nature was thus transformed as it was modernized and incorporated into liberal-capitalism. Theoretical and practical attention became fixed exclusively on the public area, on civil society – on 'the social' or on 'the economy' – and domestic life was assumed irrelevant to social and political theory or the concerns of men of affairs. The fact that patriarchalism is an essential, indeed constitutive, part of the theory and practice of liberalism remains obscured by the apparently impersonal, universal dichotomy between private and public within civil society itself.

The intimate relation between the private and the natural is obscured when, as in Benn and Gaus's account, the private and the public are discussed in abstraction from their historical development and also from other ways of expressing this fundamental structural separation within liberalism. I have already observed that, when the separation is located within civil society, the dichotomy between private and public is referred to in a variety of ways (and a full account of liberalism would have to explain these variations). Similarly, the feminist understanding of the private and the public, and the feminist critique of their separation and opposition, are sometimes presented in these terms, but the argument is also formulated using the categories of nature and culture, or personal and political, or morality and power, and, of course, women and men and female and male. In popular (and academic) consciousness the duality of female and male often serves to encapsulate or represent the series (or circle) of liberal separations and oppositions: female, or – nature, personal, emotional, love, private, intuition, morality, ascription, particular, subjection; male, or – culture, political, reason, justice, public, philosophy, power, achievement, universal, freedom. The most fundamental and general of these oppositions associates women with nature and men with culture, and several contemporary feminists have framed their critiques in these terms.

Nature and Culture

Patriarchalism rests on the appeal to nature and the claim that women's natural function of child-bearing prescribes their domestic and subordinate place in the order of things. J. S. Mill wrote in the nineteenth century that the depth of the feelings surrounding the appeal to nature was 'the most intense and most deeply-rooted of all those which gather round and protect old institutions and customs'.[11] In the 1980s, when women in the liberal democracies have won citizenship and a large measure of legal equality with men, the arguments of the organized anti-feminist movement illustrate that the appeal to nature has lost none of its resonance. From the seventeenth century a question has been persistently asked by a few female voices: 'If all men are born free, how is it that all women are born slaves?'[12] The usual answer, vigorously presented by Mary Wollstonecraft in the *Vindication of the Rights of Women* in 1792, and today by feminist critics of the sexism of children's books, schooling and the media, is that what are called women's natural characteristics are actually, in Wollstonecraft's phrase, 'artificial', a product of women's education or lack of it. However, even the most radical changes in educational practice will not affect women's natural, biological capacity to bear children. This difference between the sexes is independent of history and culture, and so it is perhaps not surprising that the natural difference, and the opposition between (women's) nature and (men's) culture, has been central to some well-known feminist attempts to explain the apparently universal subordination of women. Arguments focusing on nature/culture fall into two broad categories, the anthropological and the radical feminist.[13]

In one of the most influential anthropological discussions, Ortner argues that the only way to explain why the value universally assigned to women and their activities is lower than that assigned to men and their pursuits is that women are 'a symbol' of all 'that every culture defines as being of a lower order of existence than itself'.[14] That is, women and domestic life symbolize nature. Humankind attempts to transcend a merely natural existence so that nature is always seen as of a lower order than culture. Culture becomes identified as the creation and the world of men because women's biology and bodies place them closer to nature than men, and because their child-rearing and domestic tasks, dealing with unsocialized infants and with raw materials, bring them into closer contact with nature. Women and the domestic sphere thus appear inferior to the cultural sphere and male activities, and women are seen as necessarily subordinate to men.

It is unclear whether Ortner is arguing that women's domestic activities symbolize nature, are part of nature or, rather, place women in a mediating position between nature and culture. She argues that the opposition between women/nature and men/culture is itself a cultural construct and not given in nature; 'Woman is not "in reality" any closer to (or further from) nature than man – both have consciousness, both are mortal. But there are certainly reasons why she appears that way.'[15] However, Ortner fails to give sufficient weight to the fundamental fact that men and women are social and cultural beings, or to its corollary that 'nature' always has a social meaning, a meaning that, moreover, varies widely in different societies and in different historical periods. Even if women and their tasks have been universally devalued, it does not follow that we can understand this important fact of human existence by asking questions in universal terms and looking for general answers formulated in terms of universal dichotomies. The distinction between domestic, private women's life and the public world of men does not have the same meaning in pre-modern European society as in present liberal-capitalism, and to see both the latter and hunter-gatherer societies from the perspective of a general opposition between nature and culture, or public and private, can lead only to an emphasis on biology or 'nature'. Rosaldo recently criticized arguments about women's subordination that, like Ortner's, implicitly rest on the question, 'how did it begin?' She points out that to seek a universally applicable answer inevitably opposes 'woman' to 'man', and gives rise to a separation of domestic life from 'culture' or 'society' because of the 'presumably panhuman functions' thus attributed to women.[16]

The most thorough attempt to find a universal answer to the question of why it is that women are in subjection to men, and the most stark opposition between nature and culture, can be found in the writings of the radical feminists who argue that nature is the single cause of men's domination. The best-known version of this argument is Firestone's *The Dialectic of Sex*, which also provides an example of how one form of feminist argument, while attacking the liberal separation of private and public, remains within the abstractly individualist framework which helps constitute this division of social life. Firestone reduces the history of the relation between nature and culture or private and public to an opposition between female and male. She argues that the origin of the dualism lies in 'biology itself – procreation',[17] a natural or original inequality that is the basis of the oppression of women and the source of male power. Men, by confining women to reproduction (nature), have freed themselves 'for the business of the world'[18] and so have created and controlled culture. The proposed solution is to eliminate natural differences (inequalities) between the sexes by introducing artificial reproduction. 'Nature' and the private sphere of the family will then be abolished and individuals, of all ages, will interact as equals in an undifferentiated cultural (or public) order.

The popular success of *The Dialectic of Sex* owes more to the need for women to continue to fight for control of their bodies and reproductive capacity than to its philosophical argument. The key assumption of the book is that women necessarily suffer from 'a fundamentally oppressive biological condition'.[19] but biology, in itself, is neither oppressive nor liberating; biology, or nature, becomes either a source of subjection or free creativity for women only because it has meaning within specific social relationships. Firestone's argument reduces the social conceptions of 'women' and 'men' to the biological categories of 'female' and 'male', and thus denies any significance to the complex history of the relationship between men and women or between the private and public spheres. She relies on an abstract conception of a natural, biological female individual with a reproductive capacity which puts her at the mercy of a male individual, who is assumed to have a natural drive to subjugate her.[20] This contemporary version of a thorough Hobbesian reduction of individuals to their natural state leads to a theoretical dead-end, not perhaps a surprising conclusion to an argument that implicitly accepts the patriarchal claim that women's subordination is decreed by nature. The way forward will not be found in a universal dichotomy between nature and culture, or between female and male individuals. Rather, as Rosaldo argues, it is necessary to develop a feminist theoretical perspective that takes account of the social relationships between women and men in historically specific structures of domination and subordination; and, it might be added, within the context of specific interpretations of the 'public' and 'private'.

Morality and Power

The long struggle to enfranchise women is one of the most important theoretical and practical examples of feminist attacks on the dichotomy between the private and public. Suffragist arguments show how the attempt to universalize liberal principles leads to a challenge to liberalism itself, and this is particularly well, if implicitly, illustrated in the writing of J. S. Mill. Despite the enormous amount of attention given to voting over the past thirty years, remarkably little attention has been paid by either theoretical or empirical students of politics to the political meaning and consequences of manhood and womanhood suffrage. In recent feminist literature, however, two different views can be found about the implications of the enfranchisement of women for the separation between the public and the private. There is disagreement whether the suffrage movement served to reinforce the sexual separation in social life or whether, rather despite itself, it was one means of undermining it. In the mid-nineteenth century, when feminism emerged as an organized social and political movement, the argument from nature had been elaborated into the doctrine of separate spheres; men and women, it was claimed, each naturally had a separate but complementary and equally valuable social place. The most striking difference between the early feminists and suffragists and contemporary feminists is that almost everyone in the nineteenth century accepted the doctrine of separate spheres.

The early feminists bitterly opposed the grossly unequal position of women but the reforms they struggled to achieve, such as an end to the legal powers of husbands that made their wives into private property and civil non-persons, and the opportunity to obtain an education so that single women could support themselves, were usually seen as means to equality for women who would remain with their own private sphere. The implicit assumption was that the suffrage, too, meant different things to men and women. This comes out clearly in one of the most passionately sentimental, and anti-feminist, statements of the doctrine of separate spheres. In 'Of Queens' Gardens', Ruskin argues that

> The man's duty, as a member of the commonwealth, is to assist in the maintenance, in the advance, in the defence of the state. The woman's duty, as a member of the commonwealth, is to assist in the ordering, in the comforting, and in the beautiful adornment of the state.[21]

Citizenship for women could thus be seen as an elaboration of their private, domestic tasks and one of the suffragists' main arguments was that the vote was a necessary means to protect and strengthen women's special sphere (an argument that gained weight at the end of the century as legislatures increasingly interested themselves in social issues related to women's sphere). Moreover, both the most ardent anti-suffragists and vehement suffragists agreed that women were weaker, but more moral and virtuous, than men. The anti-suffragists argued that, therefore, enfranchisement would fatally weaken the state because women could not bear arms or use force; the suffragists countered by claiming that women's superior morality and rectitude would transform the state and usher in a reign of peace. All this has led Elshtain to argue that it was precisely because the suffragists accepted the assumptions of the doctrine of separate spheres that they 'failed, even on their own terms'. Far from raising a challenge to the separation of the public and private, they merely 'perpetuated the very mystifications and unexamined presumptions which served to rig the system against them'.[22]

Much of Elshtain's argument is conducted in terms of the duality of morality and power, one way of formulating the separation of private and public when this is located *within* civil society. Liberal theorists often contrast the political sphere (the state), the sphere of power, force and violence, with society (the private realm), the sphere of voluntarism, freedom and spontaneous regulation.[23] However, the argument about the implications of women's moral superiority, and Elshtain's use of the duality of morality and power, refer rather to the more fundamental separation of the private, domestic sphere from public life or civil society. The opposition between morality and power then counterposes physical force and aggression, the natural attributes of manliness, which are seen as exemplified in the military force of the state, against love and altruism, the natural attributes of womanhood, which are, paradigmatically, displayed in domestic life where the wife and mother stands as the guardian of morality.[24] Was the struggle for womanhood suffrage locked in the separation and dichotomies of patriarchal-liberalism, within the duality of morality and power (which, again, is one way of expressing the doctrine of separate spheres), to the extent suggested by Elshtain? To vote is, after all, a political act. Indeed, it has come to be seen as *the* political act of a liberal-democratic citizen, and citizenship is a status of formal civil or public equality.

A different assessment of the suffrage movement is presented in recent work by DuBois, who argues that the reason that both sides of the struggle for enfranchisement saw the vote as the key feminist demand was that the vote gave women 'a connection with the social order not based on the institution of the family and their subordination within it . . . As citizens and voters, women would participate directly in society as individuals, not indirectly through their subordinate position as wives and mothers.[25] DuBois emphasizes that the suffragists did not question women's 'peculiar suitability' for domestic life, but the demand for the vote constituted a denial that women were naturally fit *only* for private life. The demand for the suffrage thus reached to the heart of the mutual accommodation between patriarchalism and liberalism since to win the vote meant that, in one respect at least, women must be admitted as 'individuals'. This is why DuBois can argue that women's claim for a public, equal status with men, 'exposed and challenged the assumption of male authority over women'.[26] An important long-term consequence of women's enfranchisement, and the other reforms that have led to women's present position of (almost) formal political and legal equality with men, is that the contradiction between civil equality and social, especially familial, subjection, including the beliefs that help constitute it, is now starkly revealed. The liberal-patriarchal separation of the public and private spheres has become a political problem.

The dimensions of the problem are set out – very clearly, with the benefit of hindsight – in John Stuart Mill's feminist essay *The Subjection of Women* and his arguments for womanhood suffrage. Mill's essay shows that the assumption that an individual political status can be added to women's ascribed place in the private sphere and leave the latter intact, or even strengthened, is ultimately untenable. Or, to make this point another way, liberal principles cannot simply be universalized to extend to women in the public sphere without raising an acute problem about the patriarchal structure of private life. Mill shows theoretically, as the feminist movement has revealed in practice, that the spheres are integrally related and that women's full and equal membership in public life is impossible without changes in the domestic sphere.

In *The Subjection*, Mill argues that the relation between men and women, or more specifically between husbands and wives, forms an unjustified and unjustifiable exception to the liberal principles of individual freedom and equality, free choice, equality of opportunity and allocation of occupations by merit that (he believes) govern other social and political and institutions in nineteenth-century Britain. The social subordination of women is 'a single relic of an old world of thought and practice exploded in everything else'.[27] At the beginning of the essay Mill attacks the appeal to nature and argues that nothing can be known about the natural differences, if any, between women and men until evidence is available about their respective attributes within relationships and institutions where they interact as equals instead of as superiors and inferiors. Much of Mill's argument is directed against the legally sanctioned powers of husbands which placed them in the position of slave-masters over their wives. Legal reform should turn the family from a 'school of despotism' into a 'school of sympathy in equality' and a 'real school of the virtues of freedom'.[28] However, as recent feminist critics have pointed out, in the end he falls back on the same argument from nature that he criticizes. Although Mill argues that in the prevailing circumstances of women's upbringing, lack of education and occupational opportunities, and legal and social pressures, they do not have a free choice whether or not to marry, he also assumes that, even after social reform, most women will still choose marital dependence. He states that it will generally be understood that when a woman marries she has chosen her 'career', just like a man entering a profession: 'she makes choice of the management of a household, and the bringing up of a family, as the first call upon her exertions . . . She renounces [all occupations] not consistent with the requirements of this.'[29] The question why, if marriage is a 'career', liberal arguments about (public) equality of opportunity have any relevance to women, is thus neatly begged.

Mill introduced the first measure for womanhood suffrage into the House of Commons in 1867. He advocated votes for women for the same two reasons that he supported manhood suffrage; because it was necessary for self-protection or the protection of interests and because political participation would enlarge the capacities of women. However, it is not usually appreciated that Mill's acceptance of a sexually ascribed division of labour, or the separation of domestic from public life, cuts the ground from under his argument for enfranchisement. The obvious difficulty for his argument is that women as wives will be largely confined to the small circle of the family so they will find it hard to use their votes to protect their interests. Women will not be able to learn what their interests are without experience outside domestic life. This point is even more crucial for Mill's argument about individual development and education through political participation. Mill, in what Benn and Gaus call his 'representative liberal text', refers to the development of a 'public spirit' by citizens.[30] In *The Subjection* he writes of the elevation of the individual 'as a moral, spiritual and social being' that occurs under 'the ennobling influence' of free government.[31] This is a large claim to make for the periodic casting of a ballot and Mill did not think that such consequences would arise from the suffrage alone. He writes that 'citizenship', and here I take him to be referring to universal suffrage, 'fills only a small place in modern life, and does not come near the daily habits or inmost sentiments'.[32] He goes on to argue that the (reformed) family is the real school of freedom. However, this is no more plausible than the claim about liberal-democratic voting. A despotic, patriarchal family is no school for democratic citizenship; but neither can the egalitarian family, on its own, substitute for participation in a wide variety of social institutions (especially the workplace) that Mill, in his other social and political writings, argues is the necessary education for citizenship. How can wives who have 'chosen' private life develop a public spirit? Women will thus exemplify the selfish, private beings, lacking a sense of justice, who result, according to Mill, when individuals have no experience of public life.

Mill's ultimate failure to question the 'natural' sexual division of labour undermines his argument for an equal public status for women. His argument in *The Subjection* rests on an extension of political principles to the domestic sphere – which immediately brings the separation of the private and public, and the opposition between the principles of association in the two spheres, into question. He would not have remained Benn and Gaus's 'exemplary' liberal theorist if he had not, at least in part, upheld the patriarchal-liberal ideology of the separation between public and private. On the other hand, by throwing doubt on the original Lockean separation of paternal and political power, and by arguing that the same political principles apply to the structure of family life as to political life, Mill also raises a large question about the status of the family. The language of 'slaves', 'masters', 'equality', 'freedom' and 'justice' implies that the family is a conventional, not a natural, association. Mill would not want to draw the conclusion that the family is political, but many contemporary feminists have done so. The most popular slogan of today's feminist movement is 'the personal is the political', which not only explicitly rejects the liberal separation of the private and public, but also implies that no distinction can or should be drawn between the two spheres

'The Personal is the Political'

The slogan 'the personal is the political' provides a useful point from which to comment on some of the ambiguities of the public and private in liberal-patriarchalism and also, in the light of some of its more literal feminist interpretations, to comment further on an alternative feminist conception of the political. Its major impact has been to unmask the ideological character of liberal claims about the private and public. 'The personal is the political' has drawn women's attention to the way in which we are encouraged to see social life in personal terms, as a matter of individual ability or luck in finding a decent man to marry or an appropriate place to live. Feminists have emphasized how personal circumstances are structured by public factors, by laws about rape and abortion, by the status of 'wife', by policies on child-care and the allocation of welfare benefits and the sexual division of labour in the home and workplace. 'Personal' problems can thus be solved only through political means and political action.

The popularity of the slogan and its strength for feminists arises from the complexity of women's position in contemporary liberal-patriarchal societies. The private or personal and the public or political are held to be separate from and irrelevant to each other; women's everyday experience confirms this separation yet, simultaneously, it denies it and affirms the integral connection between the two spheres. The separation of the private and public is both part of our actual lives and an ideological mystification of liberal-patriarchal reality.

The separation of the private domestic life of women from the public world of men has been constitutive of patriarchal-liberalism from its origins and, since the mid-nineteenth century, the economically dependent wife has been presented as the ideal for all respectable classes of society. The identification of women and the domestic sphere is now also being reinforced by the revival of anti-feminist organizations and the 'scientific' reformulation of the argument from nature by the sociobiologists.[33] Women have never been completely excluded, of course, from public life; but the way in which women are included is grounded, as firmly as their position in the domestic sphere, in patriarchal beliefs and practices. For example, even many anti-suffragists were willing for women to be educated, so that they could be good mothers, and for them to engage in local politics and philanthropy because these activities could be seen, as voting could not, as a direct extension of their domestic tasks. Today, women still have, at best, merely token representation in authoritative public bodies; public life, while not entirely empty of women, is still the world of men and dominated by them.

Again, large numbers of working-class wives have always had to enter the public world of paid employment to ensure the survival of their families, and one of the most striking features of post-war capitalism has been the employment of a steadily increasing number of married women. However, their presence serves to highlight the patriarchal continuity that exists between the sexual division of labour in the family and the sexual division of labour in the workplace. Feminist research has shown how women workers are concentrated into a few occupational areas ('women's work') in low-paid, low-status and non-supervisory jobs.[34] Feminists have also drawn attention to the fact that discussions of worklife, whether by *laissez-faire* liberals or Marxists, always assume that it is possible to understand economic activity in abstraction from domestic life. It is 'forgotten' that the worker, invariably taken to be a man, can appear ready for work and concentrate on his work free from the everyday demands of providing food, washing and cleaning, and care of children, only because these tasks are performed unpaid by his wife. And if she is also a paid worker she works a further shift at these 'natural' activities. A complete analysis and explanation of the structure and operation of capitalism will be forthcoming only when the figure of the worker is accompanied by that of the housewife.

Feminists conclude that the 'separate' liberal worlds of private and public life are actually interrelated, connected by a patriarchal structure. This conclusion again highlights the problem of the status of the 'natural' sphere of the family, which is presupposed by, yet seen as separate from and irrelevant to, the conventional relations of civil society. The sphere of domestic life is at the heart of civil society rather than apart or separate from it. A widespread conviction that this is so is revealed by contemporary concern about the crisis, the decline, the distintegration of the nuclear family that is seen as the bulwark of civilized moral life. That the family is a major 'social problem' is significant, for the 'social' is a category that belongs in civil society, not outside it, or, more accurately, it is one of the two sides into which civil society can be divided; the social (private) and the political (public). Donzelot has recently explored how the emergence of the social is also the emergence of 'social work' and a wide variety of ways of (politically) 'policing' the family, giving mothers a social status and controlling children.[35] Feminists, too, have been investigating how personal and family life is politically regulated, an investigation which denies the conventional liberal claim that the writ of the state runs out at the gate to the family home. They have shown how the family is a major concern of the state and how, through legislation concerning marriage and sexuality and the policies of the welfare state, the subordinate status of women is presupposed by and maintained by the power of the state.[36]

These feminist critiques of the dichotomy between private and public stress that the categories refer to two interrelated dimensions of the structure of liberal-patriarchalism; they do not necessarily suggest that no distinction can or should be drawn between the personal and political aspects of social life. The slogan 'the personal is the political' can, however, be taken literally. For example, Millett, in *Sexual Politics*, implicitly rejects Locke's distinction between paternal and political power. In political science the political is frequently defined in terms of power, but political scientists invariably fail to take their definition to its logical conclusion. Millett agrees with the definition but, in contrast, argues that all power is political so that, because men exercise power over women in a multitude of ways in personal life, it makes sense to talk of 'sexual politics' and 'sexual dominion . . . provides [the] most fundamental concept of power'.[37] The personal becomes the political. This approach illuminates many unpalatable aspects of sexual and domestic life, in particular its violence, that too frequently remain hidden, but it does not greatly advance the critique of patriarchal-liberalism. As the radical feminist attempts to eliminate nature, as one side of the dichotomy, so Millett seeks to eliminate power, thus echoing the suffragist vision of a moral transformation of politics. But this does nothing to question the liberal association (or identification) of the political with power, or to question the association of women with the 'moral' side of the duality.

Other feminists have also rejected the identification of the political with power. Sometimes, by standing liberal-patriarchalism on its head, it is merely claimed that, properly understood, political life is thus intrinsically feminine.[38] More fruitfully, the feminist rejection of 'masculine' power also rests on an alternative conception of the political. It is argued that the political is the 'area of shared values and citizenship',[39] or that it 'includes shared values and civic concerns in which power is only one aspect.'[40] These conceptions remain undeveloped in feminist writings, but they are closely related to the arguments of the critics of liberalism who deplore the depoliticization of civil society or liberalism's loss of a distinctive sense of the political. For instance, Habermas argues for public, shared communication so that substantive political problems can be rationally evaluated, and Wolin states that the 'public' and the 'common' are 'synonyms for what is political', so that 'one of the essential qualities of what is political . . . is its relationship to what is "public".'[41] These critics and some feminists agree that what is not personal is public – and that what is public is political. The implication is that there is no division within civil society, which is the realm of the public, collective, common political life of the community. The argument is usually developed, however, without any consideration of how this conception of the public-political sphere is related to domestic life, or any indication that such a problem arises. The feminists have posed, but have not yet answered, this fundamental question. What can be said is that although the personal is not the political, the two spheres are interrelated, necessary dimensions of a future, democratic feminist social order.

Conditions for a Feminist Alternative to Liberal-Patriarchalism

Feminist critiques of the liberal-patriarchal opposition of private and public raise fundamental theoretical questions, as well as the complex practical problems of creating a radical social transformation. But one objection to feminist arguments denies that our project is even sensible. Wolff has recently claimed, from a position sympathetic to feminism, that overcoming the separation of the two spheres presents an inherently insoluble problem. To 'struggle against the split' is pointless; the best that can be achieved is *ad hoc* adjustments to the existing order. The separation of public and private derives from two 'equally plausible and total incompatible conceptions of human nature'. One is that of 'man [sic] as essentially rational, atemporal, ahistorical', and the second is of 'man as essentially time bound, historically, culturally and biologically conditioned'.[42] To argue that everyone should be treated in the public world as if the facts of sex, class, colour, age and religion do not count, is to insist that we should deny the most basic human facts about ourselves and thus accentuate the inhumanity and alienation of the present. But Wolff's two conceptions are not of a single 'human' nature, and they are far from equally plausible; they represent the liberal-patriarchal view of the true natures of (private) women and (public) men. Human beings *are* time bound, biological and culturally specific creatures. Only from a liberal individualist perspective (one failing to see itself as a patriarchalist perspective) that abstracts the male individual from the sphere where his wife remains in natural subjection, then generalizes this abstraction as public man, can such an opposition of 'human' nature, of women and men, private and public, appear philosophically or sociologically plausible.

Feminists are trying to develop a theory of a social practice that, for the first time in the Western world, would be a truly general theory – including women and men equally – grounded in the interrelationship of the individual to collective life, or personal to political life, instead of their separation and opposition. At the immediately practical level, this demand is expressed in what is perhaps the most clear conclusion of feminist critiques; that if women are to participate fully, as equals, in social life, men have to share equally in child-rearing and other domestic tasks. While women are identified with this 'private' work, their public status is always undermined. This conclusion does not, as is often alleged, deny the natural biological fact that women, not men, *bear* children; it does deny the patriarchal assertion that this natural fact entails that only women can *rear* children. Equal parenting and equal participation in other activities of domestic life presuppose some radical changes in the public sphere, in the organization of production, in what we mean by 'work' and in the practice of citizenship. The feminist critique of the sexual division of labour in the workplace and in political organizations of all ideological persuasions, and its rejection of the liberal-patriarchal conception of the political, extends and deepens the challenge to liberal-capitalism posed by the participatory democratic and Marxist criticism of the past two decades, but also goes well beyond it.

The temptation, as Wolff's argument shows, is to suppose that if women are to take their place as public 'individuals', then the conflict is about the universalization of liberalism. But that is to ignore the feminist achievement in bringing to light the patriarchal character of liberalism and the ambiguities and contradictions of its conception of the private and public. A full analysis of the various expressions of the dichotomy between the private and the public has yet to be provided, together with a deeper exploration than is possible in this chapter of the implications of the double separation of domestic life from civil society and the separation of the private from public within civil society itself. Feminist critiques imply a dialectical perspective upon social life as an alternative to the dichotomies and oppositions of patriarchal-liberalism. It is tempting, as shown by feminists themselves, either to replace opposition by negation (to deny that nature has any place in a feminist order) or to assume that the alternative to opposition is harmony and identification (the personal is the political; the family is political). The assumptions of patriarchal-liberalism allow only these two alternatives, but feminist critiques assume that there is a third.

Feminism looks toward a differentiated social order within which the various dimensions are distinct but not separate or opposed, and which rests on a social conception of individuality, which includes both women and men as biologically differentiated but not unequal creatures. Nevertheless, women and men, and the private and the public, are not necessarily in harmony. Given the social implications of women's reproductive capacities,[43] it is surely utopian to suppose that tension between the personal and the political, between love and justice, between individuality and communality will disappear with patriarchal-liberalism.

The range of philosophical and political problems that are encompassed, implicitly or explicitly, in feminist critiques indicates that a fully developed feminist alternative to patriarchal-liberalism would provide its first truly 'total critique'.[44] Three great male critics of abstractly individualist liberalism already claim to have offered such a critique, but their claim must be rejected. Rousseau, Hegel and Marx each argued that they had left behind the abstractions and dichotomies of liberalism and retained individuality within community. Rousseau and Hegel explicitly excluded women from this endeavour, confining these politically dangerous beings to the obscurity of the natural world of the family; Marx also failed to free himself and his philosophy from patriarchal assumptions. The feminist total critique of the liberal opposition of private and public still awaits its philosopher.

NOTES

1 The subversive character of liberal-feminism has recently been uncovered by Z. Eisenstein, *The Radical Future of Liberal Feminism* (Longman, New York, 1981).
2 S. Benn and G. Gaus (eds), *Public and Private in Social Life* (Croom Helm, London and New York, 1983), chap. 2.
3 Eisenstein, *The Radical Future*, p. 223.
4 J. S. Mill is an exception to this generalization, but Benn and Gaus do not mention *The Subjection of Women*. It might be objected that B. Bosanquet, for example, refers in *The Philosophical Theory of the State* (Ch. X, 6), to 'the two persons who are [the] head' of the family. However, Bosanquet is discussing Hegel, and he shows no understanding that Hegel's philosophy rests on the explicit, and philosophically justified, exclusion of women from headship of a family or from participating in civil society or the state. Bosanquet's reference to 'two

persons' thus requires a major critique of Hegel, not mere exposition. Liberal arguments cannot be universalized by a token reference to 'women and men' instead of 'men'. On Hegel see P. Mills, 'Hegel and "The Woman Question": Recognition and Intersubjectivity', in *The Sexism of Social and Political Theory*, ed. L. Clark and L. Lange (University of Toronto Press, Toronto, 1979). (I am grateful to Jerry Gaus for drawing my attention to Bosanquet's remarks.)

5 J. Locke, *Two Treatises of Government*, ed. P. Laslett, 2nd ed. (Cambridge University Press, Cambridge, 1967), I, §47; II §82. The conflict between the social contract theorists and the patriarchalists is more fully discussed in T. Brennan and C. Pateman, ' "Mere Auxiliaries to the Commonwealth": Women and the Origins of Liberalism', *Political Studies*, 27 (1979), pp. 183–200.

6 Rawls's two principles of justice provide an example of this division. He states that the principles 'presuppose that the social structure can be divided into two more or less distinct parts'. He does not call these private and public, but the 'equal liberties of citizenship' are usually called 'political' liberties and the 'social and economic inequalities' of the second part are usually seen as part of the 'private' sphere. In Rawls's final formulation it is clear that the principles refer to civil society and that the family is outside their scope. Part (b) of the second principle, equality of opportunity, cannot apply to the family, and part (a), the difference principle, may not apply. A clever son, say, may be sent to university at the expense of other family members. (I owe this last point to my student, Deborah Kearns.) John Rawls, *A Theory of Justice* (Harvard University Press, Cambridge, MA, 1971), pp. 61, 302.

7 S. Wolin, *Politics and Vision* (Allen & Unwin, London, 1961).

8 It is also the sphere of privacy. J. Reiman, 'Privacy, Intimacy, and Personhood', *Philosophy and Public Affairs*, 6 (1976), p. 39, links 'owning' one's body to the idea of a 'self' and argues this is why privacy is needed. My comments in the text do not explain why liberal theorists typically write of the private and the public rather than the political. An explanation could only be found in a full examination of liberal ambiguities about the public and the political, which takes us far from the purpose of this chapter, although the problem arises again below in the context of the feminist slogan 'the personal is the political'.

9 J. Habermas, 'The Public Sphere', *New German Critique*, 6(3) (1974), pp. 49–55. However, Habermas, like other writers, ignores the fact that women are conventionally held to be deficient in reason and therefore unfit to participate in a public body.

10 In the present context these remarks must be very condensed. For amplification see Brennan and Pateman, ' "Mere Auxiliaries to the Commonwealth" ', in R. Hamilton *The Liberation of Women: A Study of Patriarchy and Capitalism*, (Allen & Unwin, London, 1978); H. Hartmann, 'Capitalism, Patriarchy and Job Segregation by Sex',

Signs, 1(3), pt 2 (Supp. Spring 1976) pp. 137–70; A. Oakley, *Housewife* (Allen Lane, London, 1974), chap. 2, 3.

11 J. S. Mill, 'The Subjection of Women' in *Essays on Sex Equality*, ed. A. Rossi, (University of Chicago Press, Chicago, IL, 1970), pp. 125–242, at p. 126.

12 M. Astell, 'Reflections on Marriage' (published 1706), cited in L. Stone, *The Family, Sex and Marriage in England: 1500–1800* (Weidenfeld & Nicholson, London, 1977), p. 240.

13 'Radical feminists' is the term used to distinguish the feminists who argue that the male–female opposition is the cause of women's oppression from 'liberal feminists' and 'socialist feminists'.

14 S. B. Ortner, 'Is Female to Male as Nature is to Culture?', in *Women, Culture and Society*, ed. M. Z. Rosaldo and L. Lamphere (Stanford University Press, Stanford, 1974), p. 72. Ortner says nothing about the writers over the past two centuries who have glorified nature and seen culture as the cause of vice and inequality. However, the meaning of 'nature' in these arguments is extremely complex and the relationship of women to nature is far from clear. Rousseau, for instance, segregates women and men even in domestic life because women's natures are seen as a threat to civil life (culture). For some comments on this question, see chap. 1.

15 Ortner, 'Is Female to Male as Nature is to Culture?', p. 87.

16 M. Z. Rosaldo, 'The Use and Abuse of Anthropology: Reflections on Feminism, and Cross-Cultural Understanding', *Signs*, 5(3) (1980), p. 409. Compare D. Haraway, 'Animal Sociology and a Natural Economy of the Body Politic, Part I: A Political Physiology of Dominance', *Signs*, 4(1) (1978), esp. pp. 24–5.

17 S. Firestone, *The Dialectic of Sex* (W. Morrow, New York, 1970), p. 8.

18 Ibid., p. 232. She also fails to distinguish 'culture' as art, technology, etc. from 'culture' as the general form of life of humankind.

19 Ibid., p. 255.

20 I owe the last point to J. B. Elshtain, 'Liberal Heresies: Existentialism and Repressive Feminism', in *Liberalism and the Modern Polity*, ed M. McGrath (Marcel Dekker, New York, 1978), p. 53.

21 J. Ruskin, 'Of Queens' Gardens', in *Free and Ennobled*, ed. C. Bauer and I. Pitt (Pergamon Press, Oxford, 1979), p. 17.

22 J. B. Elshtain, 'Moral Woman and Immoral Man: A Consideration of the Public-Private Split and its Political Ramifications', *Politics and Society*, 4 (1974), pp. 453–61.

23 A recent argument that relies on this contrast is J. Steinberg, *Locke, Rousseau and the Idea of Consent* (Greenwood Press, Westport, CT, 1978), esp. chaps. 5–7. Emphasis on consent gives an appearance of morality to the private sphere, which is far less evident when, as is usually the case, self-interest is seen as the governing principle of (private) civil society. If the division within civil society is seen as freedom (as self-interest) opposing power, the location of morality

within domestic life is more pointed but poses a serious problem of order for liberal public or civil society.

24 An acute problem about 'nature' and women's 'nature' now emerges because women are seen both as natural guardians of morality and as naturally politically subversive: see chap. 1.

25 E. DuBois, 'The Radicalism of the Woman Suffrage Movement', *Feminist Studies*, 3 (1/2) (1975), pp. 64, 66.

26 E. DuBois, *Feminism and Suffrage* (Cornell University Press, Ithaca, NY, 1978), p. 46.

27 Mill, *The Subjection*, p. 146.

28 Ibid., pp. 174–5.

29 Ibid., p. 179.

30 See Benn and Gaus, *Public and Private*, chap. 2, referring to Mill's *Considerations on Representative Government*.

31 Mill, *The Subjection*, p. 237.

32 Ibid., p. 174.

33 On sociobiology see, e.g., E. O. Wilson, *Sociobiology: The New Synthesis* (Harvard University Press, Cambridge, MA, 1975), and S. Goldberg, *The Inevitability of Patriarchy*, 2nd ed. (W. Morrow, New York, 1974). For a critique, see, e.g., P. Green, *The Pursuit of Inequality* (Martin Robertson, Oxford, 1981), chap. 5.

34 See, e.g., for Australia, K. Hargreaves, *Women at Work* (Penguin Books, Harmondsworth, Middlesex, 1982); for England, J. West (ed.), *Women, Work and the Labour Market* (Routledge & Kegan Paul, London, 1982); for America, Eisenstein, *The Radical Future of Liberal Feminism*, chap. 9.

35 J. Donzelot, *The Policing of Families* (Pantheon Books, New York, 1979). 'The most surprising thing is the status "the social" has won in our heads, as something we take for granted' (p. xxvi).

36 On marriage see, e.g., D. L. Barker, 'The Regulation of Marriage: Repressive Benevolence' in *Power and the State*, ed. G. Littlejohn et al. (Croom Helm, London, 1978); on rape see chap. 4, and A. G. Johnson, 'On the Prevalence of Rape in the United States', *Signs*, 6(1) (1980), pp. 136–46; on the welfare state see, e.g., E. Wilson, *Women and the Welfare State* (Tavistock, London, 1977).

37 K. Millett, *Sexual Politics* (Hart-Davis, London, 1971), pp. 25, 26.

38 N. McWilliams, 'Contemporry Feminism, Consciousness Raising and Changing Views of the Political' in *Women in Politics*, ed. J. Jaquette (Wiley, New York, 1974), p. 161.

39 Ibid.

40 L. B. Iglitzin, 'The Making of the Apolitical Woman: Femininity and Sex-Stereotyping in Girls' in Jaquette, *Women in Politics*, p. 34.

41 J. Habermas, 'The Public Sphere', and Wolin, *Politics and Vision*, pp. 9, 2.

42 R. P. Wolff, 'There's Nobody Here but Us Persons' in *Women and Philosophy*, ed. C. Gould and M. Wartofsky (Putnams, New York,

1976), pp. 137, 142–3. Wolff also objects to the feminist struggle against the separation of private and public because it builds normative assumptions about human nature into the advocacy of new forms of social institutions – an oddly misplaced objection in the light of the assumption about women's and men's nature embodied in patriarchal-liberalism.

43 See R. P. Petchesky, 'Reproductive Freedom: Beyond "A Woman's Right to Choose",' *Signs*, 5(4) (1980), pp. 661–85.

44 I have taken the phrase from R. M. Unger, *Knowledge and Politics* (Free Press, New York, 1975). Unger's claim to have provided a total critique of liberalism must also be rejected. He fails to see that the antinomies of theory and fact, reason and desire, and rules and values are, at the same time, expressions of the patriarchal antinomy between man and woman. He states (p. 59) that 'the political form of the opposition of formal reason to arbitrary desire is the contrast between public and private existence' – but it is also the opposition between the 'nature' of men and women.

7

The Civic Culture: A Philosophic Critique

Empirical democratic theory no longer constitutes the orthodoxy for writers on democracy that was the case when *The Civil Culture*[1] was written, but its basic assumptions are still widely accepted. *The Civic Culture* provides one of the best single 'case studies' from which to build a general critique of the post-war school of empirical theory through an understanding of the way in which these assumptions shaped conclusions about democratic theory and practice. There are, of course, many specific differences between individual theorists in the school, but these are overshadowed by a common theoretical perspective within which empirical findings are analysed. Studies of empirical theory are also characterized, as in *The Civic Culture*, by the inclusion of a concluding chapter in which the significance of data on individual political attitudes and activities for 'normative' democratic theory is addressed. The final chapter of *The Civic Culture* reflects the widespread confidence of the late 1950s and early 1960s in the Anglo-American political system, and is typical in its celebration of the role of political apathy and disinterest. Unlike some other examples of the genre, however, *The Civic Culture* contains evidence about the socialization process through which individual attitudes are developed. This evidence is crucial to a critique of empirical theory and to the development of a democratic theory that can move decisively beyond its theoretical inadequacy and political complacency.

Empirical democratic theory has been much criticized, but the critics and the empirical theorists have often tended to talk past each other on some fundamental issues. The critics wish to defend a tradition of 'normative' democratic theory that is rejected as old-fashioned and, more importantly, unscientific, by the empirical theorists. The critics have tended to be timid in the face of the claims of 'science' and 'objectivity' –

even though it has been remarked how rarely this scientific approach has produced critical conclusions[2] – and so have tended to neglect the task of tackling the empirical theorists on their own ground. The central claim that must be challenged is that, in the light of the data revealed by empirical investigations, it is indeed unrealistic to cling to traditional conceptions of democratic theory and the democratic citizen. Ironically, as *The Civic Culture* reveals, the interpretation of empirical data is one of the major weaknesses of empirical democratic theory. It is also a weakness that cannot be remedied without abandoning some basic assumptions of the theory. Despite the claims of empirical theorists, they have not produced a convincing account of the relationship between the pattern of attitudes and activity revealed in their findings and the political structure of the liberal democracies.

Empirical theorists have shown little curiosity about their own theoretical antecedents. Both sides of the controversy about democratic theory have been hampered by the widely accepted belief that there is a classical theory of democracy to be accepted, rejected, or, at the very least, drastically modified.[3] It is not difficult to see that the so-called classical theory can refer to either of two very different traditions of argument about the nature and place of popular participation in political life. The first is the classical liberal theory of constitutional, representative government, to which the empirical theory of democracy, following J. A. Schumpeter's conception of the democratic political method,[4] is direct heir. The second is the neglected classical theory of participatory democracy to be found, for example, in the writings of John Stuart Mill and, pre-eminently, Jean-Jacques Rousseau. Because these two traditions have not been distinguished, the empirical theorists have shown little awareness that their arguments are a contemporary reworking of the liberal classical theory, which explains why their arguments received such an enthusiastic reception. It was not so much a new theory[5] as a mid-twentieth-century version of the liberal theory that developed as, and continues to be, the political theory of the Anglo-American system. Another consequence of the myth of one classical theory is that democratic theory has become identified with liberal theory, and the existing liberal-democratic system – that is, liberal representative government plus universal suffrage – has become identified with democracy. *The Civic Culture* illustrates this confusion of two different political traditions. It is therefore not surprising that its critics have so often accused the allegedly scientific empirical theory of being essentially ideological and celebrating the status quo. It is true that in the preface Almond and Verba state that 'our conclusions ought not to lead the reader to complacency about democracy in . . . Britain and the United States,' yet their historical viewpoint, their interpretation of their findings and the concluding chapter of the study all invite the very complacency that they warn against.

One of the virtues of Almond and Verba's sociological approach is that,[6] in principle, they treat liberal democracy as a system and aim to elucidate the relationship between the civic culture and the political structure. They are not successful in this aim, however, because their theoretical perspective runs counter to any such endeavour. Liberal theory, on the one hand, focuses on the 'institutional arrangements' stressed by Schumpeter, and treats the political culture as a given. The social inequalities of the political culture of the liberal democracies are treated as separate from, and irrelevant to, the formal equality of citizenship. On the other hand, because liberal theory is also essentially individualist, when, as in *The Civic Culture*, attention is directed to political culture, this is treated as a matter of individual attributes and attitudes that can be correlated with levels of political participation in abstraction from the political structure or institutional arrangements. The implicit adherence of empirical theorists of democracy to an individualist, liberal theory means that they are unable to recognize and discuss as *problems* some of the fundamental questions raised by their empirical findings.

The most important illustration of this failure is the persistent neglect of the significance of the relationship between class, or SES (socio-economic status), sex and 'participatory' political orientations and political activity, which is one of the best attested findings in political science and confirmed by the evidence in *The Civic Culture*. Almond and Verba do not ask why such a relationship exists, or what relevance it might have for their characterization of the civic culture as 'democratic'. Their findings are treated as one aspect of political reality that must be accepted, and, although the correlation between class and civic orientations is reported, it is presented only as a matter of individual attitudes and attributes that happen to be patterned in a specific manner. Yet the most striking finding in *The Civic Culture* is that civic culture is systematically divided along lines of class and sex. The relationship between such a culture and the formal equality institutionalized in the political structure is never confronted or seen as a problem. Or, to make this point in another way, the historical development of the civic culture is presented as if it were in fact as liberal ideology tells us that it is, the development of a system in which the political method works to the advantage of, and protects the interests of, all citizens. But *empirical* theorists should at least be able to ask whether the finding that SES is so closely related to civic orientations and participation casts doubt on that particular view of history.

One reason why empirical theorists' interpretation of their own evidence tends to go unchallenged is that the classical democratic theory, which suggests an alternative interpretation, is so neglected. Classical participatory democratic theory is grounded in an appreciation of the mutual interrelationship between political culture and political structure[7] and, because it embodies the traditional and normative view that a democracy is a system in which all citizens participate, it explicitly raises the character of the civic culture as a problem. As I shall show in this chapter, however, a critical examination of the argument of *The Civic Culture* also reveals that the problem exists. The first sections of my discussion look at the historial perspective and conception of 'political culture' in *The Civic Culture*. I then turn to the central problem of the evidence on political competence, its relation to SES and the rationality of political inactivity, and the three dimensions of political culture. Finally, the question of the democratization of the civic culture and the concept of civic participation are considered.

In the argument that follows I shall concentrate on the evidence in *The Civic Culture* about Britain and the United States of America because the authors take these countries as their model for, and see them as the main carriers of, the civic culture, and they see Britain as fundamentally important for its historical development.[8]

The Historical Perspective

One of the most striking features of the book is that although the civic culture is described from the opening sentence of chapter 1 as 'the political culture of democracy', the meaning of democracy itself is never discussed. One reason for this omission, and for the way in which the civic culture is presented as a *problem*, is the historical perspective within which the civic culture is discussed. This historical perspective is not an unfamiliar one to readers of post-war democratic theory; it emphasizes the collapse of constitutional regimes between the wars and the threats to democratic stability posed by the development of totalitarian systems. Almond and Verba also stress the gradual development of the civic culture over a long period of time in Great Britain out of 'a series of encounters between modernization and traditionalism' (p. 7). The traditional political orientations of citizens were fused with modern participatory orientations to form the nice balance of the civic culture, although the authors do not make clear when it was that the civic culture could unequivocally be said to have emerged. The problem about the civic culture, as posed by Almond and Verba, does not concern Britain and America, where the civic culture already exists, and where it is taken for granted that the political culture is 'democratic'. Rather, the problem is that of the maintenance and strengthening of the civic culture in countries such as Italy, Germany and Mexico (examined in *The Civic Culture*), where its existence is precarious, and also its future development in countries of the third world, where it does not yet exist.

There are two important consequences of this historical perspective for the arguments of *The Civic Culture*. First, by taking the findings from Great Britain and the United States on individual civic attitudes and social relationships as unproblematic, Almond and Verba are inhibited from asking questions about the implications of their data for the liberal-democratic system and possible developments within it. The 'participation explosion' (p. 4) of the latter half of the twentieth century is relevant to the developing countries, not to Britain or the United States. Second, this particular perspective tells us very little about the historical background of the civic culture. Except for some extremely general remarks about the gradual emergence of the civic culture in Great Britain, there is little to be learned about its development or that of the idea of a 'civic culture'. The discussion is abstract and ahistorical because of the lack of a perspective placing the present conception of the civic culture in the context of the development of both Western, liberal-capitalist society and the political theory of that society, namely, liberal theory.[9] Despite the resemblances between Almond and Verba's concern with the worldwide diffusion of the civic culture and the nineteenth-century British concern with the export of British political institutions, there is no appreciation in *The Civic Culture* of the historical continuity in the conception of the role of the citizen in liberal theory from the time of Hobbes and Locke, through nineteenth-century liberal theory, to empirical democratic theory of the second half of the twentieth century.

The main thrust of liberal theory has always been to give a well-defined but minimal role to the citizen. The focus has been on the role of representative government, or what Almond and Verba call, more broadly, the political elites. It also has to be kept in mind that liberal political theory developed as the theory of, indeed as part of, Western capitalist society. In Schumpeter's words: 'democracy in the sense of our theory of competitive leadership presided over the process of political and institutional change by which the bourgeoisie reshaped, and from its own point of view rationalized, the social and political structure that preceded its ascendency.'[10] As liberal theory developed, the political role allotted to the citizen was extended from the complete non-participation of Hobbes's theory to the participation consequent upon the emergence of competitive elections and universal suffrage.[11] Yet there has been no substantial change in the basic structure of the theory, or in the conception of the citizen, within which this extension of participation has been encompassed. By the nineteenth century James Mill was calling a more popularly elected representative government 'the grand discovery of modern times'.[12] The argument became firmly established that regular competitive elections, or the sanction of loss of office, would ensure that representatives protected and furthered the interests of all citizens. Liberal theory became liberal democratic when it was recognized that the whole adult community must therefore exercise the sanction, and universal suffrage was admitted. The idea of popular control of political representatives is absolutely central to any theory of democracy (see p. 476), but it must be emphasized that popular participation was added to liberal theory primarily as a way of placing a limitation on political representatives, not as something essential and valuable in its own right. Political participation is still seen as a necessary protective device, a cost that must be paid at least occasionally by some citizens, but ideally as seldom as possible; it is not an integral part of the individual citizen's life.

This brief sketch does, I hope, establish the historical antecedents of the arguments of *The Civic Culture*. Like most other post-war writers, Almond and Verba see 'democracy' in liberal terms as the 'political method' whereby 'individuals acquire the power to decide by means of a competitive struggle for the people's vote'.[13] Periodic electoral participation is crucial in ensuring that political elites actually are responsive to citizens; interelectoral pressure-group activity and other actions aimed at influencing governments are a supplement to this. The participatory democratic tradition argues that citizens should not merely vote for representatives but take part in actual political decision-making. One would expect that revisions of democratic theory that deny the importance of an active role for citizens and stress the contribution of political apathy to the stability of the system would be concerned to take issue with participatory theory. However, the myth that there is only one classical theory of democracy has had the curious result that often, as in *The Civic Culture*, what is really being revised – if anything at all – is liberal-democratic theory itself.

Almond and Verba's version of the classical myth is couched in terms of what they call the 'rationality-activist' model of the pattern of political attitudes and political activity that would exist according to 'the norms of democratic ideology' (p. 473). The only specific source they give for this model is an American civics textbook (presumably written for school-children), but the important point is that, as described, the rationality-activist view is in no way incompatible with liberal-democratic theory. The citizen has to be 'involved and active in politics, informed about politics, and influential' (p. 474), but this is involvement and activity *within* the existing liberal-democratic system of competitive elections. Strangely enough, Almond and Verba remark that a democratic political system is one where 'the ordinary citizen participates in political decisions' (p. 178), and they talk of the citizen who is able to participate in non-governmental areas of social life expecting to 'participate in political decisions as well' (p. 328). Not surprisingly, they give no indication of how such participation by the civic citizen of liberal democracies takes place, except in terms of the election of decision-makers and attempts to influence (not participate in) their decisions. Earlier liberal writers were never very explicit about the standards of political activity and interest to which citizens should, ideally, conform, but it is clear that those standards were concerned with electoral participation. When Almond and Verba and other writers have looked at the results of empirical investigations into citizens' political orientations, they have argued that these show that the 'rationality-activist' version of democratic ideology must have set standards that were 'unreasonably high' (p. 475). Democratic theory, that is, *liberal-democratic theory*, should therefore be rewritten. Only minimal levels of activity and interest, and largely apolitical attitudes, are required from most citizens; anything more would threaten the smooth working of the political system.

Thus in *The Civic Culture* we find an account of the proper role of the democratic citizen that is concerned with the way in which the citizen's activity and participatory orientations are 'balanced' or 'managed' by subject and parochial orientations, so that citizens display the inactivity and deference that enables political elites to govern unhindered. Although the precise content of the balance is not specified,[14] Almond and Verba actually refer to the adherence by citizens to a belief in active citizenship and a belief that elites can be influenced by citizens as a 'myth' (pp. 183, 481). They add that if the myth is to be effective 'it cannot be pure myth. It must be an idealization of real behavioral patterns.' (p. 485) But it is indeed a myth of participation that empirical democratic theory requires – not citizens' beliefs and actions that are reasonably held and grounded in the facts of political life. The civic culture of the 'potentially active citizen' (p. 481) must never become more than an unrealized potentiality. Provided enough citizens vote to keep the electoral machinery in operation and political elites alternating in office, the myth, it is claimed, is enough to ensure that elites act as they should in the interests of all the citizenry: 'they act responsively not because citizens are actively making demands, but in order to keep them from becoming active.' (p. 487).

The place of the civic citizen of the second half of the twentieth century remains, as it has always done in liberal theory, primarily the private sphere of life. Ordinary citizens, unlike political elites, enter political life only on special occasions, such as elections, or when their interests seem unusually and vitally threatened. The separation of the political sphere and popular political participation from other spheres of social life is a central structural feature of liberal theory and it works to obscure the mutual interaction of political culture and political structure on which *The Civic Culture* focuses. The contemporary version of the liberal conception of the citizen is nicely and revealingly stated by Dahl:

> Among his [sic] resources for influencing officials, *homo civicus* discovers the ballot. . . . in fact he may doubt its value and rarely if ever employ it, . . . Or he may see the ballot as a useful device for influencing politicians. . . . But the chances are very great that political activity will always seem rather remote from the main focus of his life. . . . as a strategy to achieve his gratifications indirectly, political action will seem considerably less efficient than working at his job, . . . planning a vacation, moving to another neighborhood or city, . . . *Homo civicus* is not, by nature, a political animal.[15]

But this description of *Homo civicus* merely serves to raise the question ignored by the authors of *The Civic Culture*: what exactly is *democratic* about the civic culture? This is a question to which I shall return.

The Conception of 'Political Culture'

Almond and Verba's conception of 'political culture' is an essentially Parsonsian one.[16] In general, they argue, 'political culture' refers to individuals' 'attitudes toward the political system and its various parts, and attitudes toward the role of the self in the system' (p. 13). It is concerned with *'psychological orientation toward social objects . . . the political system as internalized in the cognitions, feelings, and evaluations'* of citizens. The political culture is the pattern formed by the social distribution of these attitudes (p. 14). This suggests that the 'civic culture' is a description of orientations as they presently exist, and this is also suggested by the overall argument of the study. But what exactly is the status of the 'civic culture'? Is it a description? Or is it an abstract model of orientations that we should expect to find in the political culture of a democracy? The latter interpretation is suggested by the argument that certain countries can be more civic than others. As I shall indicate, one of the problems with *The Civic Culture* is that it hovers uneasily between these two possibilities.

Almond and Verba derive the threefold classification of the dimensions of 'orientations' or 'internalized aspects' of political culture from Parsons and Shils: cognitive orientations refer to 'knowledge of and belief about the political system'; affective orientations to 'feelings about the political system'; evaluational orientations to judgements and opinions that involve a 'combination of value standards . . . with information and feelings' (p. 15). If all three dimensions of political culture are kept in mind, some consideration of the mutual, dialectical interaction of political culture and political structure cannot be avoided. The cognitive dimension, for example, refers to individuals' knowledge and beliefs about the political structure; that is, it contains a built-in reference to the impact of structure on culture. However, as will become clear when Almond and Verba's discussion of citizen competence is considered, they concentrate on psychological or affective orientations.

I argued above that it is the diffusion of the civic culture that is seen as a problem in *The Civic Culture*. It might appear, however, that there is a problem for the United States and Britain after all because, Almond and Verba claim, their investigation is directed toward the question of whether there is 'a democratic political culture – a pattern of political attitudes that fosters democratic stability, that in some way "fits" the democratic political system.' (p. 473) One of the most significant aspects of the problem of political stability is the 'relationship between political culture and political structure', and an 'assumption of congruence' between the two should be avoided (p. 34). This is a very odd position for the authors of *The Civic Culture* to adopt. As Almond and Verba imply in their discussion of the gradual development of the civic culture, the political culture and political structure of the liberal democracies have developed together. Moreover, they take the United States and Great Britain as their model of 'stable' democracies, and it is hard to see how this stability could have been maintained if political structure and political culture did not 'fit' each other; it is the lack of such nice congruence that poses problems for stability in, say, Italy or Mexico. Almond and Verba seem to see neither how circular their arguments are nor that the problem of fit is hardly a problem at all.

Nor is it at all clear how the typology of political cultures, the parochial, subject and participant, and the 'mixed' civic culture, presented in chapter 1, are derived. The authors state that 'rather than inferring the properties of democratic culture from political institutions or social conditions, we have attempted to specify its content by examining attitudes in a number of operating democratic systems.' (p. 12) Yet their presentation of the civic culture is as much a logical inference from a conception of democracy as it is a result of empirical investigation. Indeed, it could scarely be otherwise, since liberal-democratic theory is the theory of the political system of the civic culture; it developed along with that system. It would be strange if a stable system did not exhibit a congruence between its political culture and political structure *and* a congruence between the actual pattern of citizens' political attitudes and those that the theory of the system tells us should exist. Thus the conception of a civic political culture appears to be a model that is derived from a specific conception of democracy – a model that would be confirmed in an empirical investigation of a system that is *ex-hypothesis* stable and democratic. Moreover, unless a specific conception of democracy is *already* at hand, how are we, or Almond and Verba, to know that the civic culture is not simply a participatory culture, but a participatory political culture '*plus something else*' (p. 31)? In the absence of such a model, puzzlement arises and the notion of a civic culture appears arbitrary; 'I am not even sure why we should regard the [civic] values as "appropriate" or "congruent" for such systems, other than because we have discovered them there.'[17] That the civic culture is a mixed culture is both an assumption or a premise which structures the argument of *The Civic Culture* as a whole and a conclusion. The empirical evidence presented in the body of the study confirms the assumptions about the civic culture with which the book begins – and these assumptions are then presented later, in chapter 15, as conclusions about the proper role of the citizen in a democracy.

In their opening discussion, Almond and Verba state that the conception of political culture provides 'the connecting link between micro- and macropolitics' (p. 33), between individual political attitudes and the operation of the political structure. This seems to me to be a mistaken view of political culture. If, as Almond and Verba intend, one is going to investigate the interaction between culture and structure, it is difficult to see how political culture itself can provide a link when it is one side of the process to be investigated. Something else is needed to provide the link between political culture and structure, and to provide a basis for an explanation of their interaction. It is the notion of political socialization that serves as a 'connecting link' between the micro and macro levels. I do not find Almond and Verba's discussion of political culture as a 'link' easy to follow, but it seems to assume what they are trying to avoid, namely, the assumption of congruence between political culture and structure. The authors state that they have 'defined the political culture as the particular incidence of patterns of political orientation in the population of a political system'. (p. 33) It is possible to establish 'what propensities for political behavior exist in the political system as a whole, and in its various parts, among special orientation groups (i.e., subcultures), or at key points of initiative or decision in the political structure (i.e., role cultures). . . . we can [locate] . . . attitudinal and behavioral propensities in the political structure of the system.' (p. 33)

If political culture itself is to provide a link with political structure, it would seem that it must in some sense be both separate from and congruent with, or even identical to, political structure. The latter is the Parsonsian approach: Parsons has said that a 'fundamental' proposition about 'action systems' is that 'their structure as treated within the frame of reference of action *consists* in institutionalized patterns of normative culture.'[18] As I have already noted, Almond and Verba's use of 'orientations' follows Parsons's essentially psychological conception (in fact, if not in principle). Orientations (culture) are internalized and hence become institutionalized – or part of structure. Thus no question of lack of congruence arises. Nor does political socialization need to be seen as a link beween culture and political structure, because no link is really needed. Or political culture, rather oddly, can serve as such.

On this account political socialization appears as a neutral mechanism underlying the existing social distribution of orientations. There is no problem about the social pattern of political culture or the content of political orientations. The pattern remains only to be described and the notion of political socialization makes this possible. Two problems arise at this point: the civic culture as a model is required if the democratic culture is to be described. How else do we know what to look for? Second, the assumption has to be made that it is, in principle, open for any individual to be socialized into specific orientations. If there is no congruence between culture and structure, the actual pattern of political culture is a contingent matter. As I shall indicate in the next section of this chapter, however, the evidence of *The Civic Culture* is that the distribution of individual political orientations is related to SES; it is not random. Therefore, the pattern of the civic culture does actually pose a problem. Why should such a relationship with class exist? But the approach of *The Civic Culture* requires that the civic pattern can only be described and accepted – not explained. No problem will be recognized, or an opening for an explanation emerge, all the time that political socialization is treated as a neutral notion to be applied externally by the political scientist or theorist, rather than as the link between political culture and structure. From the system perspective of *The Civic Culture*, political socialization should be seen as a major mechanism in the maintenance of the 'stable' distribution of the civic culture, which is so important for the smooth operation of the liberal-democratic political method.

The Politically Competent Citizen

A democratic political culture, *The Civic Culture* states, 'should consist of a set of beliefs, attitudes, norms, perceptions, and the like, that support participation'. (p. 178) I now want to review briefly some of the data of the study concerning the extent to which citizens feel that they ought to participate and feel themselves competent to do so. Almond and Verba argue that 'belief in one's competence is a key political attitude', that the 'self-confident citizen appears to be the democratic citizen' (p. 257) and that beliefs about political competence have significant consequences for the operation of the political system. To the extent to which citizens feel politically competent they believe they can exert influence over political representatives, that is, 'the degree to which governmental officials act to benefit [a] group or individual because the officials believe that they will risk some deprivation . . . if they do not so act.' (p. 180)

One important finding is that citizens who feel subjectively competent are more likely than those lacking in a sense of competence to be politically active and actually to try to influence political elites (see table 3, p. 188). It is found that individuals' level of education and their occupational status and sex make a difference to how subjectively competent they feel (see figure 1, p. 206; figure 3, p. 210; table 7, p. 212). At the local political level, the feelings of competence of similar educational groups in the different countries 'resemble one another at least as much as, and perhaps more than, do different educational groups within the same nation.' (p. 208) Almond and Verba comment on the general relationship between feelings of political competence and higher levels of education and occupational status that 'whether or not one believes himself [sic] capable of influencing a local or national regulation depends a lot on who he is within his own country.' (pp. 212–13)

When respondents were divided according to their scores on a scale measuring feelings of subjective competence, it was found that those who scored highest were the most likely to be 'committed to democratic values'. They were, for instance, more likely to believe that ordinary citizens should play an active role in the community than those with lower-scores. But even among the highest-scoring respondents, the level of education made a difference; in the United States, for example, 53 per cent of those scoring high on the subjective competence scale with only primary education thought that citizens ought to be active, compared with 67 per cent of high scorers who had a secondary, or above, level of education (see table 7, p. 256). A similar pattern emerged among respondents questioned about whether or not they thought 'elections were necessary'; those most likely to agree were those highest in subjective competence and with higher levels of education (see table 6, p. 254). Such citizens, in both the United States and Great Britain, were also the most likely to report a 'feeling of satisfaction' when they voted (see table 3, p. 243).

The Civic Culture also tells us something about the socialization process that tends to produce persons with feelings of subjective political competence. The essential question is 'whether there is a close relationship between the roles that a person plays in non-political situations and his role in politics.' (p. 327) Almond and Verba look at socialization within the authority structures of non-governmental institutions and organizations and its relationship to feelings of political competence. Their argument is that participation inside non-governmental authority structures can be seen as training for participation in politics and as developing politically relevant skills. Individuals can be expected to 'generalize' from experiences outside political life to politics; if they have participated within non-political authority structures they will expect to do so in the political sphere also (pp. 327–8).

The authority structures with which Almond and Verba are concerned are those of the family, the school and the workplace. Many studies of political socialization have concentrated on childhood socialization. It seems more plausible, however, to argue, with Almond and Verba, that, whatever the significance of the earliest years in the general formation of individual personality, later periods are of more importance for political life when, for example, the individual absorbs a multitude of informal exposures to politically relevant material. The young (and the mature) adult's experience and observation of political life itself or, to put it another way, the impact of the operation of the political structure on the individual's attitudes, is also very important. Authority structures especially relevant for political socialization in the later years are those that are 'closer in time and in kind to the political system' (p. 325). Socialization within authority structures 'remote' from that of the political system may provide an 'inadequate training for the performance of civic activites' (p. 328). Almond and Verba are not, however, concerned with the extent to which, say, the authority structure of the workplace is *in fact* analogous to that of the political sphere, even though they do state that they are interested in how far a democratic political system depends on 'democratic substructures in the society' (p. 363). As with political competence, what they are investigating is how far individuals believe or feel that they were or are able to participate within non-political authority structures, and how far this belief is 'transferred' or 'generalized' to the political sphere itself.

In the United States and Great Britain (as in the other three countries investigated), persons who score highest on the subjective competence scale are most likely to remember participating in the family or at school. For example, in Great Britain 70 per cent of family participants scored high on the subjective competence scale, whereas only 51 per cent of family non-participants did so (see table 18, p. 348; table 20, p. 354). This relationship does not hold, however, for those with education at the secondary level or above. In the case of both family participation and informal school participation, it is less educated respondents who 'generalize' from these areas to political participation. Almond and Verba comment that persons with lower educational attainment are also less likely to have learned participatory skills, or the 'norm that one ought to participate', and are less likely to interact with others in contexts where political competence is expected of them. For these individuals the family and the school are important areas of socialization because there are no other areas, such as higher education, that can 'substitute' (pp. 349, 355).

In the workplace, the relationship between participation and the sense of subjective competence is found at all educational levels (p. 365), and the relationship is stronger than with the earlier forms of participation (pp. 371–2). The authors state that the structure of authority in the workplace is 'probably the most significant – and salient – structure of that kind with which the average man finds himself in daily contact.' (p. 363) Respondents who report that they are consulted about job decisions and feel free to protest about decisions in their workplace are likely to feel highly politically competent. But the kind of job that the individual does makes a difference; in the United States, of workers who report that they are consulted, 70 per cent of those in unskilled jobs score high on the political competence scale, whereas 82 per cent of those in white collar jobs do so (see table 24, p. 364). The importance of the relationship between workplace participation and the sense of subjective political competence becomes clearer when the data on the cumulative effect of participation are taken into account. Those respondents whose remembered participation in family or school is now reinforced by participation in the workplace are more likely to feel highly competent than those now in a non-participatory workplace (see tables 26, 27, p. 367).

It was, however, also found that workplace participation, unlike higher education, could not substitute for participation within the family or school. Where individuals could participate at their place of work, earlier participation still made a difference in levels of competence; on the other hand, for individuals with higher education, participation in the family and at school was largely irrelevant for feelings of political competence. Workplace participation is related to political competence through the 'generalization' process, and differs from higher education – which, *The Civic Culture* suggests, is a complex process, involving such things as the learning of politically relevant skills, the 'inculcation of participatory norms', and the placing of individuals in contexts where participation is expected. Higher education, Almond and Verba argue, is a 'many-sided experience' which can 'increase an individual's potentiality to participate' (pp. 370–1).

Another area of adult political socialization is voluntary associations – 'small political systems' (p. 313) – which are also of great importance as mediators between the individual and political elites. Those with higher education in America and Britain, as in the other three countries, are most likely to be organizational members (see table 4, p. 304), and membership of voluntary organizations is associated with a high score on the political competence scale. Members who belong to organizations that they regard as political are more likely to be high scorers, and so are persons in such organizations with education of at least secondary level (see table 6, p. 308). Almond and Verba also investigated differences between active and passive organizational members, for, as they note, some large organizations may appear very remote to their members, and passive members may receive little or no training in participation. It is the most active members who are likely to be highly subjectively competent (and again there is a relationship with levels of education), and membership of more than one organization has a cumulative effect on political competence (see table 12, p. 317; table 14, p. 321). These data lead the authors to comment that 'pluralism, even if not explicitly political pluralism, may indeed be one of the most important foundations of political democracy.' (p. 322)

The Civic Culture and SES

There are two major and related failings in Almond and Verba's discussion of political competence and its significance for democracy. First, no explanation is offered for the striking relationship that emerges between SES and feelings of political competence. The concluding commentary of *The Civic Culture* is conducted as if the nice balance of the civic culture rested on a randon distribution of the appropriate orientations among all citizens. Thus the social pattern of the civic culture is regarded as unproblematic. Second, the question of how this pattern interacts with the political structure is never answered. The aim of *The Civic Culture* is to investigate this relationship in a more exact and systematic fashion than earlier discussions of 'national character', and Almond and Verba state that much of the existing literature 'fails to make the connection between the psychological tendencies of individuals and groups, and political structure and process' (p. 33). But, because *The Civic Culture* remains within the liberal theoretical framework, it shares in this failing; in the final chapter the pattern of the civic culture is counterposed against, not related to, the operation of the political structure of liberal democracy.

Almond and Verba regret the fact that *The Civic Culture* contains no index of the SES of respondents' parents, but, they continue, it can be assumed that the individual's level of education is related to the SES of parents (p. 334) – and, it might be added, to the individual's own future status. As illustrated above, *The Civic Culture* reveals a consistent relationship between levels of political competence and levels of education and, where this is considered, occupational status. This relationship might have been expected. Almond and Verba tend not to relate their findings to other studies (except in a general sense for the purpose of casting doubt on the 'rationality-activist' model of the citizen) but the connection between SES, or class, and political participation was well established before the publication of *The Civic Culture*.[19] Moreover, ordinary observation of political life in the liberal democracies would suggest such a relationship. Almond and Verba, as noted, remark that whether citizens feel competent depends on 'who they are', and they also refer, for example, to 'the sharp differences in political attitudes that one observes among respondents from various social backgrounds.' (p. 337) They even go so far as to state that 'the educated classes possess the keys to political participation and involvement' and that citizens of low educational attainment 'tend to constitute subject and parochial subcultures' (pp. 381, 386), but their discussion of the findings ignores the significance of this. In the aggregation of data, and in the conclusions of *The Civic Culture*, it is assumed that all citizens can be treated equally as 'carriers' of the civic political culture.

Throughout *The Civic Culture* it is also assumed that there are no problems in talking about *the* political culture or *the* civic culture of Britain and the United States. The implication is not only that there is a model of the civic culture at hand, but also that the model is relevant across the whole community. Yet the finding that the orientations of the civic culture are distributed according to SES suggests that, if there are not two political cultures, then the civic culture is, at the least, a systematically *divided* political culture. This is not only a matter of 'subcultures', or random groupings sharing the attributes of the civic culture to a different extent, but a broad social differentiation of upper and lower SES groups or classes. The nice balance of the civic culture, set out in the final chapter of the book is, in fact, a balance based on the virtual absence of working-class citizens from political life. The balance rests on the division between the civic orientations of predominantly upper SES citizens (and it should not be forgotten that political elites tend also to be drawn from this same background) and the less civic political culture of the bulk of the citizenry.

That the orientations of the civic culture are found mostly among individuals from higher SES backgrounds, and that it is also these individuals who are likely to belong to voluntary associations and to be politically active, is not a finding that *empirical* theorists of democracy can take for granted. Such findings suggest that political apathy is not, as one writer dismissively claimed, 'nobody's fault'[20] – so that no question of an explanation arises – but that it is a socially structured and maintained phenomenon; what might be called a non-participation syndrome exists.[21] It is precisely this syndrome that needs to be explained; why lower SES – and female sex – lack of civic orientations and political inactivity tend to be associated.

The findings of *The Civic Culture* suggest that an explanation, and hence an account of the 'stability' of the division of the civic culture, should be looked for within the socialization process inside the authority structures of everyday life. This explanation depends on the notion of political socialization as the link between political culture and political structure, and as an integral part of their mutual interaction.

Citizens from lower SES backgrounds are unlikely to participate in family and school (although within this group the relationship between participation and political competence holds) and, most importantly of all, in view of the closeness of the authority structure of the workplace to political life, they tend to go into the unskilled, blue-collar and routinized white-collar jobs where participation is least likely to occur. Thus, at all stages in the socialization process, their lack of a sense of competence receives further reinforcement. Nor are these lower SES citizens likely to go on to receive higher education, which 'substitutes' for participation in family and school. The very nature of the workplace participation with which Almond and Verba are concerned (and I shall comment further on this) makes it a very weak competitor with the many-sided advantages that higher education brings – not the least of which is that higher education also leads to occupations where workplace participation can be expected. The cumulative effect of the political socialization process for most lower SES citizens is that it 'fits' them for their place, a not very 'civic' place, in the liberal-democratic political culture. It allows them to occupy the politically inactive side of the balance of the civic culture.

The difference between SES groups is not the only systematic division of the civic culture to emerge from the data of *The Civic Culture*. The balance of the civic culture is also based on sex. The civic culture is a male culture. The findings show that women (in all countries) generally rank lower than men on all the indices of political attitudes and activity associated with the civic culture (pp. 388–97). Why is there such a division between the sexes? This can, in part, be explained by the differing socialization of men and women.[22] In both Britain and America, women are less likely than men to participate in the family and at school, are less likely to go on to higher education and, when they enter the paid labour force, are much less likely to have higher-status jobs and experience of work-place participation. Thus women, too, will tend to be on the inactive side of the civic balance. Nevertheless, Almond and Verba state that in the United States and Britain 'politically competent, aware, and active women seem to be an essential component of the civic culture.' (p. 399) Once again, they are switching to the civic culture as a model; compared with women in the three other countries investigated, women in the United States and Britain appear as more active, or civic. Yet, as a description of the Anglo-American political culture, the civic culture remains sexually divided, and it is this fact that poses a problem – even though *some* active women might be needed, just as *some* active men are required if there is to be a balanced culture.

Earlier, I criticized Almond and Verba for circular arguments but, in one sense, their argument is not circular enough. Nowhere in *The Civic Culture* is there an explanation of the circle of the non-participation syndrome, or the relationship among low SES, female sex, lack of civic orientations and low levels of political participation. The implicit assumption is that the correlation is a contingent matter. Nor is the relationship between the social inequalities underlying the pattern of the civic culture and the formal political equality of liberal democracy confronted; it remains a fortunate coincidence, and Britain and America are happy countries, because the democratic civic culture and democratic political institutions are found together.

In view of the fact that the civic culture is a political culture divided on the basis of SES and sex, the question that I posed earlier must be asked again: what is democratic about the civic culture? The answer can only be very little at all, except that it encompasses universal suffrage. The civic culture is a democratic culture that reverses the central focus of democracy since its origins in ancient times, although it retains the traditional assumption that democracy can exclude half of humankind. 'Democracy' refers to a political system based on an active and central role by the people, the *demos*, in political life and political decision-making. The civic culture rests not on the participation of the people, but on their non-participation. Its political focus is on the role of the upper SES (male) citizens, as participants and decision-makers. The balance of the civic culture is one that allows these elites 'to get on with governing' in the absence of a politically active people. The responsiveness of elites, necesssary in a democracy, is ensured, it is claimed, because there is a *potential* for activity by citizens, not because they are or need to be active.

Almond and Verba are able to characterize the civic culture as 'democratic' because they are implicitly falling back on the identification of liberal and democratic theory, and the model of the civic culture that this identification supplies. Moreover, liberal theory, from Locke's government of property-holders, through James Mill's references to the wise and virtuous middle classes, to the 'civic' citizens of the present study, has always argued that it is middle- and upper-class males who are best 'fitted' for political participation and decision-making. *The Civic*

Culture, and other empirical theories of democracy, may parade this argument in a scientific costume, but what they are doing is offering us a more sophisticated but very familiar answer to the problem of how liberalism can accommodate universal suffrage, without disturbing social inequalities or the predominant political role of the (male) middle class. The approach of *The Civic Culture* obscures the need to ask important questions concerning not just the stable maintenance of the balance of the civic culture, but whether the implicit liberal model of the civic culture is the only feasible model of civic political life, and the possibility of democratic development of the civic culture.

I shall turn to the latter questions later. To prepare the way it is necessary, first, to say something more about political socialization and the interpretation of the findings of *The Civic Culture*. So far I have followed Almond and Verba's discussion and have looked in only one direction, from culture to political structure, and have emphasized the affective dimension of the civic culture, the subjective feeling of political competence. As their own introductory discussion of political culture argues, however, there is more than one dimension involved, and furthermore, if the relationship of political culture and political structure is our concern, then some attention must be paid to the impact of structure on culture.

The Dimensions of Political Culture and the Generalization Argument

There are many passing references in *The Civic Culture* to the impact of political structure, but, as with the relationship between SES and civic orientations, its significance for the civic culture is not pursued. Nor are two dimensions of the three-fold classification of the political culture, the evaluative and the cognitive, given more than passing attention.

Almond and Verba state that they do not wish to deny 'the importance of the political system itself as a source of individuals' attitudes toward that system' (p. 368), but the source is never given due weight. In Britain and America individuals who score high on the political competence scale are most likely to express 'a general attachment to the political system' (p. 251; also table 5). They also are likely to 'believe that a democratic participatory system is the proper system to have.' (pp. 254–5; also tables 6 and 7) The differences in extent of 'normative allegiance' to their political systems among political competents in the five countries, as Almond and Verba point out, reflect the history of each country. Nevertheless, the authors fail to take into account the evaluative dimension of political culture, and the learning of political norms during political socialization, in their discussion. I have argued that the civic culture as a model is implicitly derived from liberal theory, but citizens of the Anglo-American liberal democracies have their own, albeit often not well-formulated, models of the proper role of the citizen; they learn about liberal theory, the theory of their own political system, during the socialization process. The abstract nature of much of Almond and Verba's discussion of the civic culture is related to their neglect of the role of liberal theory or ideology in the stability of the interaction of political culture and structure. It is not only academics who identify democracy with liberal democracy. Almond and Verba's presentation of a divided civic culture as one democratic culture gains plausibility because the division is encompassed within a general acceptance of the existing system as 'democracy'.[23]

Once the evaluative dimension of political culture in Britain and America is considered, the relationship between the sense of political competence and the political structure becomes more complex than is suggested in Almond and Verba's analysis. The question that needs to be asked is whether or not the replies to questions designed to measure feelings of competence might also be reflecting an acceptance of the 'norms of democratic ideology', or the evaluative dimension of political culture. Respondents might be replying on the basis of what they have learned of liberal theory during the political socialization process, what they have learned about how the political system ought to work, and what they are held to be able to do if faced, for example, with the prospect of an unjust law.[24] Feelings of competence are likely to develop in a complicated fashion, to be closely linked both to the citizen's understanding of the liberal-democratic theory of his or her political role, and to the citizen's own experience of, and observation of, the working of the political system.

The possibility that the evaluative dimension is relevant to replies to questions aiming to elicit information about feelings of competence illuminates certain features of the findings of *The Civic Culture*. Respondents were asked what they thought they could do if their national legislature or local government was considering a law they regarded as harmful or unjust, and whether, if they attempted to change it, they thought they would succeed or not. The fairly high proportion of citizens who see themselves as politically competent might appear to reflect, as Almond and Verba remark, 'a somewhat unrealistic belief in their opportunities to participate' (p. 182). If, however, a sense of competence is not the only thing that is being tapped, the proportion is less remarkable. Furthermore, Almond and Verba themselves are not entirely unambiguous in their view of political competence. They make the significant statement that someone who has participated in non-governmental areas of social life is more likely '*to accept the belief* that he is a competent citizen.' (p. 369, italics added) It is not that such participants' beliefs that they are politically competent are reasonably held on the basis of their experience of and assessment of the political system. Instead, they are likely to accept the ideological assumption that citizens are able to influence political elites. And that is a rather different matter. It is, though, quite in keeping with Almond and Verba's view of the belief in citizens' political influence as a myth which 'whether true or not, . . . is believed' (p. 487)

The third, cognitive, dimension of political culture is important for Almond and Verba's argument that political competence is rooted in a process of 'generalization' by individuals from their experiences of participation or non-participation in family, school and workplace. This implies that individuals arrive at their political beliefs in disregard of the political system. Their beliefs are based purely on their non-political experiences. This argument, even given the doubts about the rationality of ordinary citizens that have so exercised political scientists and political sociologists, is rather difficult to swallow. There is no doubt that such experiences are important in developing the individual's general self-confidence and abilities for effective action in social life, but this is not to accept the argument that the feeling of political competence is based on no more than 'projections of . . . underlying disposition toward all authority'.[25] One obvious additional factor is that individuals may believe what they are taught about the liberal-democratic political system; another is that they may autonomously come to an assessment of the political system as more or less responsive to any attempt by them to participate and to exercise influence on elites.

Almond and Verba do touch upon the latter factor (e.g. see discussion on p. 368) but they do not consider the relationship of this cognitive dimension of political culture to their generalization argument. One interesting question about the civic culture is why the large gap exists between the proportion of respondents who feel politically competent and the proportion who have actually tried to influence political elites. In the United States 67 per cent of citizens feel politically competent, and in Great Britan, 57 per cent; but only 33 per cent and 18 per cent, respectively, have actually tried to influence their local elites (see tables 2, 3, pp. 186, 188). Almond and Verba's interpretation of, and explanation for, this gap is that it is a necessary ingredient in the 'balance' of the civic culture to 'allow governmental elites to act' (p. 481). Individuals believe in the myth of citizen influence, or in the 'values associated with a democratic system' (p. 257). It is argued, as noted earlier, that belief in this myth is sufficient to ensure popular control of political elites. In other words, the underlying assumption of Almond and Verba's argument is that the system actually works as liberal theory tells us that it should, and that citizens believe this to be the case.

This is why Almond and Verba can suggest that it is rational for many of those who feel competent to act not to do so. There is no need for them to act on the basis of the generalization that they make from experiences in non-political areas of social life. To expect to find anything but a large divergence between political competence and political activity is to set our standards of citizenship 'unreasonably high'. Almond and Verba argue that 'standards' and 'theories of politics' should be 'drawn from the realities of political life' (p. 475). This implies that 'the realities' are there, self-evidently, to be drawn upon. But before anything conclusive can be said about standards, a convincing interpretation and characterization of reality itself is required, in particular the reality of the close relationship between competence and SES.

Almond and Verba argue that widespread failure to act politically is connected with the costs involved, which usually means that 'it may just not be worth it' to participate (p. 476). Citizens have many important non-political interests and, given the time and effort required to engage in the complex business of political activity, it is irrational for citizens to pay the cost of doing so (p. 475) – especially when the myth of competence works for them. It is true that individuals always have to make a choice about which activities they are to undertake, but it really is remarkable that 'reality' happens to be such that 'rationality' works so neatly in a class-based (and sex-based) fashion. It is not a random cross-section of citizens who find it 'rational' not to pay the 'costs' of participation, but lower SES citizens. The problem of the 'disappearing' competents is much more complicated than Almond and Verba lead us to believe. The balance of the civic culture is between the rationality of the working-class (and female) tendency not to be politically active, and the male and middle-class rational participation. For the latter, political activity may be regarded as a benefit, not a cost. A. O. Hirschman, for example, cites the case of stockholders who prefer to use their stock to try to influence corporations, rather than 'exiting' from them.[26] Stockholders, like other recent activists on public goods issues, tend to be drawn from middle-class backgrounds, and thus fit neatly into the balance of the civic culture and divided rationality about political activity.

Why should there be such a division among citizens? The socialization process examined in the last section has thrown some light on to this. The cognitive dimension of political culture suggests another explanation: there may be a differential evaluation of the political system by members of different SES groups. Hence it would be rational for them to act differently. Indeed, replies of respondents from different SES backgrounds to questions designed to measure feelings of political competence and other orientations suggest that this differential evaluation exists. The replies of working-class citizens indicate scepticism that the system actually operates as it is held to.[27] Thus a straightforward explanation of political inactivity is available – providing that the correlation between SES and participation is not forgotten. Working-class citizens believe that participation 'may just not be worth it', and moreover, their withdrawal from political life is legitimized by the liberal conception of the 'naturally' inactive citizen.

Almond and Verba's argument completely neglects the association between class and participation and implies that social status is irrelevant to which side of the balance a citizen occupies, or to the citizen's view of the rationality of action or inaction. That class-based differences in evaluation of the political system are rational has now received confirmation from *Participation in America*, a large-scale empirical study which shares an author, Sidney Verba, with *The Civic Culture*. The study finds that the responsiveness of political elites, or 'concurrence', goes disproportionately to the most politically active citizens, to the upper SES groups. The general conclusion of the study is that *'participation helps those who are already better off.'*[28] The position of those who are already socially advantaged is maintained and reinforced through political participation, and the empirical data recorded in *The Civic Culture* reflect this basic fact. It is no surprise that feelings of political competence, political activity and allegiance to the liberal-democratic system and to 'democratic norms' are closely correlated with high SES; middle-class citizens have good reason to be full members of the civic culture. The real surprise is that empirical theorists of democracy have exhibited so little curiosity about the social character of the balance of the liberal-democratic political culture. Neglect of the evaluative and cognitive dimensions of political culture has led to a simplified view of the individual's orientations, especially those of working-class citizens and women. Although upper SES citizens (especially males) can appear as unambiguously civic citizens, the orientations of other citizens are a contradictory mixture, reflecting both a 'rational' evaluation of the operation of the political system and the worth of participation, and an acceptance of the 'values associated with a democratic system'. In Britain and the United States 'the uneducated tend to share with the educated a common affective and normative allegiance to the political system' (p. 387), but this is encompassed within a common identification of democracy with the existing system. Citizens from all classes learn something of liberal ideology, and the argument of *The Civic Culture* gives us no help in disentangling the various dimensions of citizens' responses which apparently measure their feelings of competence.

It took nine years from the publication of *The Civic Culture* for a major investigation to appear that was specifically focused on the relationship of social inequality to liberal democracy. Empirical democratic theorists have failed to ask the questions, not difficult or obscure questions, that empirical findings have demanded, and still demand. It is now no longer so easy to ignore the significance of the well-documented connection between SES and political participation, nor is it so easy to ignore the question of the distribution of the 'responsiveness' of elites. It was not that inequality, poverty and discrimination did not exist at the end of the 1950s – writers of that period could have paused and wondered how the political system actually looked to ordinary citizens, what political participation actually meant to them (a few of them did so) – but inequalities were not then forced to the attention of academic writers as they have been since the dramatic events of the mid-1960s. A few riots, lootings, sit-ins and protests even from *women* concentrate the mind wonderfully. But what is still not clear is whether they sufficiently concentrate the minds of empirical theorists looking at political culture or at aspects of social inequality through the spectacles provided by liberal theory.[29]

Despite the aim of the study, liberal democracy is not treated in *The Civic Culture* as a complex system. Social inequality, or the civic culture, is not systematically related to the operation of the political structure and the maintenance of a stable system. Rather, the myth of citizenship is both presented as a myth and taken as an accurate characterization of liberal democracy, so that the evidence revealing the socially divided nature of the civic culture can be glossed over. Empirical democratic theory, and the argument of *The Civic Culture*, thus mystifies and obscures, rather than clarifies, the significance of its own data, and fails to explain why there is a fit between the balance of the civic culture and the political structure of liberal democracy.

The Democratic Development of the Civic Culture

Almond and Verba see the further development of the civic culture primarily as a matter of its diffusion to countries outside the liberal democracies. But there is also an important question to be asked about its future development in Britain and the United States; namely, whether the civic culture can be shared by the whole of the citizenry, or whether a culture divided by SES and sex is the best approximation to a democratic culture that can be achieved. The crucial problem then arises of how a democratization of the civic culture might be achieved.

In their discussion of 'the future of the civic culture', Almond and

Verba emphasize education as a possible substitute in the new nations for the long development of the civic culture in the liberal democracies. The importance of education, especially higher education, and its relationship to feelings of political competence have already been indicated. Schooling in the liberal democracies, however, does not do a great deal to cut across the class and sex divisions of the civic culture; in fact, it is now one of the major channels for its reinforcement. Although development of the schooling systems of the new nations may provide a short cut toward a liberal civic culture, in the developed world schooling, in its present form, is unlikely to provide an avenue for the *democratic* development of the civic culture.

Almond and Verba argue that, in the new nations, formal education might be supplemented by developing 'other channels of political socialization' (p. 502). No more than minor adjustments are required to the civic culture in Britain or the United States; the former could absorb an increase in the participatory orientations, and the latter an increase in the deferential orientations. The crucial point about this suggestion, however, is that it is presented as an adjustment within the orientations of single individuals. Indeed, the final chapter of *The Civic Culture* refers almost exclusively to the 'mixture' of orientations of *each individual*, rather than to the social pattern of the 'balance' of the civic culture.[30] However, the mixture of orientations is *not* randomly distributed across all individuals; middle-class males are likely to be 'participant' citizens, whereas 'parochial' and 'subject' orientations tend to be characteristic of working-class females. The individualist theoretical perspective of *The Civic Culture* persistently obscures the class division of the civic culture. Yet it is the social (class and sex) balance or mixture of the culture that is basic to its stable fit into the political structure – as the empirical data presented by Almond and Verba clearly reveal. The authors, however, ignore their own findings and, when they briefly turn from the balance of orientations within individuals, their only comment about the social pattern of the civic culture is that 'some individuals believe they are competent and some do not; some individuals are active and some are not.' (p. 485) Hidden behind that 'some' are the systematic social divisions of the civic culture.

The argument of *The Civic Culture* cannot encompass democratic development of the political culture of America and Britain. If participant orientations were to be spread across the whole population, the balance of the civic culture would disappear; it '*depends upon the inconsistencies between political norms and perceptions, . . . and political behavior.*' (p. 482) But, as I have shown, the middle class tend not to be, and have no reason to be, 'inconsistent' in their political lives. They feel competent and allegiant, and are likely to be politically active. It is working-class citizens who are most likely to show a discrepancy between their orientations and their behaviour. To change the relevant balance across class and sex, to democratize the civic culture, would therefore require some radical changes in the institutional structure of liberal democracy; the divided culture and the structure have developed together as a complex 'democratic' system, with its appropriate 'channels of socialization'. A democratization of the civic culture, a change in the balance, therefore implies a democratization of the authority structures of liberal democracy.

The empirical findings presented in *The Civic Culture* lead to this conclusion. High levels of the feeling of competence are associated with participation in everyday life, but at present low SES citizens and women are unlikely to have opportunities to participate, especially in the workplace. If, as Almond and Verba argue, pluralism is an important foundation of liberal democracy, *democratic pluralism*, or the democratization of everyday life, is equally imporant for the development of a democratic political culture, and as a basis for participatory democracy.

There is now a considerable body of additional evidence to support the evidence of *The Civic Culture* on the importance of the authority structure of the workplace for more general political attitudes, and the impact of participation within organizations and associations of various kinds on feelings of competence.[31] It is particularly noteworthy that Almond and Verba's workplace 'participation' took place within the existing non-democratic authority structure of capitalist enterprises (although they imply that the workplace can be regarded as a 'democratic substructure'). Their respondents were asked whether or not they were 'consulted' about decisions concerning their jobs, and whether or not they felt free to protest about such decisions. This is a very weak and minimal sense of participation, at best amounting to no more than pseudo-participation.[32] Almond and Verba, however, are not alone in finding that even pseudoparticipation does have wide-ranging psychological consequences for those involved.[33] For this reason participatory techniques have been used for group therapy purposes, and 'participative' management is now well established as an advanced capitalist management technique, a technique that does not require any changes in the overall authority structure of the enterprise. Nevertheless, the relationship between the weakest forms of participation and levels of the sense of political competence shows that the democratization of the workplace is a necessary basis for the diffusion of participatory political orientations throughout the population. It would also provide a training ground, in a familiar context, for participation in democratic political life.

A feeling of political competence is not, however, sufficient for active citizenship. As I have already argued, participation must also be worthwhile, and this raises some complex and important questions about the implications of workplace democracy. Empirical theorists of democracy have recently begun to turn their attention to participation in the workplace, but their discussions illustrate why many radicals are suspicious of, or opposed to, schemes to increase participation. Many recent discussions suggest that workplace participation may merely extend the divided civic culture or consolidate social inequality over a wider area, rather than changing the balance and extending democracy. Robert Dahl, for example, now argues that industrial democracy can form part of polyarchy, or liberal democracy. In *After the Revolution?* he presents workplace democracy as 'one solution too obvious to be ignored' to the problems generated by the 'corporate leviathans' and the 'appropriation of public authority by private rulers'.[34] Dahl also argues that if individuals found that participation 'contributed to their own sense of competence and helped them to control an important part of their daily lives, then lassitude and indifference toward participation might change into interest and concern.' He is pessimistic about the extent to which interest would develop, however, and suggests that it is most likely that 'technicians and lower executives' rather than blue-collar workers would participate.[35]

The evidence about participation in the workplace, including evidence from Yugoslavia, supports Dahl's pessimism. The social pattern of participation resembles that in wider political life, with higher-status, better-educated and skilled males most likely to be active. Before the conclusion is accepted that, after all, lower SES individuals and women are 'naturally' apolitical creatures, and the divided civic culture is the best approximation to 'democracy' that can be achieved, some further questions must be considered.

Dahl is not concerned with the development of a democratic political culture, but with the power of 'private rulers'. This is a fundamental problem, but it is not self-evident that the problem discussed in this chapter is solved if private capitalist rulers are replaced by an elected central managing board, or a workers' council. Of course, this would be a very real change in the capitalist organization of production (especially given the extensive interrelationship between the corporate leviathans and the liberal-democratic state apparatus). Nevertheless, to elect a government in each enterprise is to introduce liberal democracy into a new context: and it is precisely the fact that *liberal* democracy and the divided civic culture fit each other that gives rise to the problem of *democracy*. There is no good reason to suppose that the introduction of an elected council in the enterprise will of itself have very different consequences from liberal elected representative government in the state; it will tend to provide another avenue through which the already socially advantaged may participate.

Investigations of the Yugoslav system of workers' self-management tend to bear this out. Sidney Verba (with Goldie Shabad) has recently investigated participation in workers' councils in Yugoslavia and has found that a close relationship beween SES and participation exists: 'the better-educated and more affluent citizen is more likely to become a member of a workers' council', although more skilled blue-collar workers participate in workers' councils than in other forms of political activity. Verba and Shabad direct attention to two factors that underlie the evidence that 'participation in workers' councils, of the . . . kinds of activity [investigated], is the one most biased in favor of the "haves" in Yugoslav society.'[36] First, only workers in the socialist sector are eligible to participate in workers' councils, and they tend to come from higher SES backgrounds; second, the League of Communists is a less important channel for participation in workers' councils than in other areas. (Although league membership, too, is biased in favour of upper SES individuals, it is generally 'both a necessary and sufficient condition of regular political activity in Yugoslavia'.[37]) Verba and Shabad also argue that participation in workers' councils is seen as a technocratic activity, based on skills and expertise, rather than as a matter of political commitment. This raises wider questions about the reasons for the similarity of the pattern of participation in the civic cultures of Britain and America and in Yugoslavia's self-management system.

The analysis of *The Civic Culture* fails to look beyond the aggregation of individual characteristics; similarly, Verba and Shabad's discussion of Yugoslavia does not relate the association between SES and participation to the wider social structure. In one vital area the liberal democracies and Yugoslavia are alike. Both liberal-capitalism and Yugoslav self-management since the economic reforms of 1965, are based on the market, which suggests that the relationship between Yugoslav political culture and political structure will, in some crucial respects, resemble that of the civic culture and its political structure. Indeed, in another investigation of Yugoslav political life, it is commented that the Yugoslavs 'have instituted equality to the extent that citizens enjoy the same formal political rights, and liberty to the degree that people are free to be economically unequal. This compromise between liberty and equality is called liberalism.'[38] To the extent that the Yugoslav system is a variant of liberalism, or a system of formal political equality within substantive social inequality, it raises exactly the same problem of the development of democratic participation as the civic culture does.

Yugoslav workers' self-management involves more than the election of a central workers' council; each enterprise is decentralized into work units with their own councils. Significantly enough, the evidence indicates that despite the correlation between SES and participation in workers' councils, many ordinary workers do wish for more participation within their own work units.[39] The general conclusion that can be drawn from the empirical data is that if the civic culture is to be democratized, some very radical changes are required that go far beyond the multiplication of miniature liberal democracies. A vote for a central managing body in the enterprise will have little relevance for many workers if all else remains the same. The daily organization of work itself is especially important, as Braverman has shown;[40] if the sexual and other divisions on which the capitalist organization of production is built are not challenged, the balance of orientations is unlikely to be greatly disturbed.

The development of a democratic political culture demands, in short, a radical restructuring of all aspects of the organizations and associations of everyday life to provide opportunities for worthwhile participation for all citizens. If such a restructuring is to be achieved, it also requires that we begin to look at political life, and the concepts that help constitute it, from a democratic rather than a liberal perspective. I have emphasized how the identification of democracy with liberal representative government prevents the recognition of key problems of democratic theory as problems. Another illustration of this is the problem of the status of participation in the workplace. Dahl remarks that it 'is an absurdity' to see economic enterprises as 'private'.[41] Yet to see them as part of the political sphere – as the notion of 'democratization' itself suggests – is to step outside the liberal theoretical framework within which empirical theorists are working.[42] Liberal theory draws a sharp separation between the political and other areas of social life, especially the economic (a separation that is breached once participation in the workplace is surveyed along with conventional forms of political activity). The argument that the foundations of a democratic political culture lie in the democratization of everyday life is also an argument that the political needs to be reconceptualized.

If participation in the workplace is seen as a technocratic activity, or a matter for experts, rather than as part of the *political* life of citizens, then the apparent 'naturalness' and unproblematic character of a socially divided civic culture will be reinforced. Zukin argues that the increasing shift of power in Yugoslavia toward a technocratic elite is one reason for the withdrawl of lower SES citizens from political activity; they are 'refusing to be manipulated'.[43] Or, like citizens from similar backgrounds in the civic culture, they do not regard it as 'rational', or worthwhile, to participate in an activity for which they lack expertise. Nor is it only participation in Yugoslav workers' councils that is seen as technocratic or a matter for experts; in the liberal democracies elections are held to 'place experts in office for a fixed term, subject to the right of the citizen to protest if he dislikes what they do and to replace them at the next election.'[44] The liberal conception of political life, as Wolin has emphasized, is that government is part of the social division of labour.[45] As in other areas, it is 'economical' to have experts in the procedure or technique of managing the liberal political method elected to office – although it is far from clear in what this expertise consists.

This conception of representation and political elites underlies Almond and Verba's ideological arguments about the 'myth' of citizens' political influence and political apathy in *The Civic Culture*. It is rational not to participate, and so save the costs of activity, because experts will look after political life for you, with the myth ensuring their responsiveness. I have already shown how this claim ignores the fact that the division of political labour, like the division of labour in general, is grounded in sex and class, but it should also be stressed that the liberal conception of political elites as experts obscures another basic problem. From a liberal perspective it is finding well-qualified experts and ensuring their efficiency through the electoral sanction that is the problem; the fact of expertise itself is seen as 'politically neutral'.[46] But a *democratic* theorist, perhaps especially an empirical democratic theorist, cannot regard political expertise as unproblematic. The ancient and radical idea was that in a democracy *all citizens* were experts about their own political life, no matter what their special knowledge and skills in other areas. This idea has now been cast aside. 'Democracy' is now held to be a system where citizens alienate their right to decide about their own political lives to non-political experts (usually, today, lawyers and other professionally qualified men). It is hardly surprising that, in view of this conception of the political and citizenship, working-class individuals and women feel it is not worthwhile to be active; their skills and knowledge are not seen as politically relevant, either in the politics of the state or in the workplace.

Changes in the liberal-democratic political structure and changes in political consciousness and political concepts are integrally related to each other. No headway will be made in developing *democratic* theory and practice until it is recognized that liberal theory is part of the problem. An understanding of the relationship between the capitalist economy, or Yugoslav self-management, and their respective political structures will not be obtained merely by adding bits and pieces of 'participation' to liberal theory, or investigating the correlates of individual participation. The participatory classical theorists offer insights for an alternative approach, and present alternative conceptions of 'representation', 'government' and the structure of a 'political' community. Empirical theorists argue as if only one technocratic conception of political life exists in democratic theory. But Rousseau offers us a systematic critique of this liberal conception, and presents an alternative democratic theory in which citizens retain political authority in their own hands; they act as their own government. Elected representatives are not precluded, but although they may act on behalf of citizens, representatives do not decide for them.[47] They are not experts to whom citizens alienate their political authority: 'the holders of the executive power are not the people's masters but its officers.'[48]

The conventional argument against taking participatory theory seriously is that it is empirically unrealistic; that, for example, it is to 'talk as if people are willing to participate in decisions without any regard for the costs of time: . . . The cost is, plainly, that the time might be used in doing something else – often, in fact, something a great deal more interesting and important than going to a meeting.'[49] The reference to 'going to a meeting' indicates a failure of imagination. There are other ways to participate if political activity begins to become part of everyday life, not something extra to it. The objections that appeal to the empirical facts and the realities and treat participatory democracy as inherently impossible ignore the basic problem about that reality: why it is that the costs appear to weigh so much more heavily on women and the working class. This is not to deny that people can usually engage in only one thing at a time, but to insist that the divided civic culture is *not* a 'natural fact' about our social world, and that there *are* good reasons to look beyond liberal theory and practice. In the abstract it is very difficult to say anything definite about participation within an alternative socio-political context, but it is only if, in a participatory system, a certain proportion of (randomly distributed) citizens choose not to participate that theorists would be justified in writing of the 'naturally' apolitical individual.

Civic Participation

The word *civic* appears in the title of the book, yet readers are not told why this particular description of the pattern of political orientations in Britain and America was chosen. Nor does *The Civic Culture* explain why 'civic' participation takes a particular form. I shall consider the latter question first.

The 'consolidation' of the civic culture, Almond and Verba argue, meant that the 'working classes could enter into politics and, in a process of trial and error, find the language in which to couch their demands and the means to make them effective.' (p. 8) Certainly, the welfare state has brought a great improvement to the lives of working-class people, although in the recession of the late 1970s this improvement does not appear so far-reaching as it did a decade or more earlier. But the 'language' that the working class has 'found' is the language of liberal, representative politics and its competing interest groups, with all this implies for ideas about democracy and the form of political theory from which individuals make sense of the world. It is a language that maintains that the working class has the means to achieve its demands in a system in which 'participation helps those who are already better off.' In other words, it is assumed in *The Civic Culture* that the liberal-democratic political method provides a successful mechanism within which interests are protected and the demands of ordinary citizens are met. Civic participation is therefore participation associated with the electoral system. There is no room for, or need to ask, substantive political questions about the form that civic or democratic participation might take.

The Civic Culture and other empirical democratic theory of its period gave no hint that a 'participation explosion' was imminent with the civic culture itself. Nor have empirical investigators paid attention to 'protests and demonstrations'. W. R. Schonfeld has pointed out that there has been an 'extremely curious' lack of criticism of this omission,[50] a lack that reflects the widespread acceptance by other theorists of the perspective upon participation provided by empirical theory, a perspective that contains no means of assessing 'unorthodox' political activity that goes outside conventional electoral and interelectoral activity. The political method of liberal democracy is unrelated to specific political criteria or specific principles of political morality or right; that is precisely why Schumpeter's conception of democracy has proved so congenial to value-free and scientific empirical theory. This means that theorists are caught in a perpetual present, where established forms of electoral participation can be described and called 'democratic', but nothing substantive can be said about other activities, or about possible future developments of democratic political action.

Although unorthodox activities take widely differing forms, they are either ignored or dismissed as 'undemocratic',[51] or, as in the case of civil (civic?) disobedience – typically engaged in by middle-class 'civic' citizens – so defined as to be robbed of all political impact. As Barry has caustically commented of one such account, it reduces political action to the level of the threat of the little girl in the English children's stories: 'If you don't do it I'll scream and scream until I make myself sick.'[52] If a democratic theory and practice is to be developed as an alternative to existing liberal democracy, it is necessary that political theorists turn their attention to the formulation of criteria that will enable us to distinguish *democratic* forms from the variety of activities that extend over urban guerrillas, factory occupations, squatting, civil disobedience, the setting up of self-help organizations, electoral participation and acts of individual witness. As part of this task it is also necessary to consider what counts as political activity. In *The Civic Culture*, participation in the workplace is treated as a non-political arena to develop orientations and skills necessary in political life; but, as argued above, the extension of democratic participation to wider areas of social life should be seen as political participation and as integral to active citizenship.

In using the word *civic* to describe electoral participation, Almond and Verba presumably wish to draw upon its association with valuable and valued political ideals. The culture (and the structure that it fits) is one in which all citizens are able freely to act politically and attain their goals in a peaceful and mutually responsible fashion. The characterization of the liberal-democratic system as 'civic' or 'democratic' appropriates these ideals to liberalism, but again, there is no reason why this identification should so easily be accepted. I take it that the civic culture can be seen as standing in the tradition of civic humanism, which J. G. A. Pocock presents as a tradition in which 'the development of the individual towards self-fulfillment is possible only when the individual acts as a citizen, that is as a conscious and autonomous participant in an autonomous decision-taking political community.'[53] This account of civic political life is more appropriate to a participatory democratic system than the socially divided civic culture, notwithstanding that critics of the school of theorizing to which *The Civic Culture* belongs are often accused of throwing away the valuable liberal 'civic' heritage.

This accusation misunderstands both the arguments of the critics and the historical tradition to which they belong (a tradition which exists alongside liberal theory and emerged as part of the same socio-economic developments). The misunderstanding is exacerbated because the 'realistic' alternatives in political life are often presented, as in the opening of *The Civic Culture*, as two only: either existing liberal democracy or totalitarianism. In addition, criticism of social inequality and its integral connection with the liberal-democratic political method is frequently misrepresented as an attack on civil liberty and all liberal values. Critics of empirical theory are not rejecting the entire history and culture of liberalism, but building from it. Their fundamental argument is that liberal theory has held out a promise to *all* citizens that has not been, and cannot be, fulfilled. If the promise is to be realized, democratization of the civic culture, development beyond liberal democracy is necessary, Parekh has stated this position nicely:

> Liberalism . . . is only one of many possible ways of defining liberal values, and it is possible to hold liberal values – that is, to be a liberal with a small 'l' – and yet to interpret and justify them differently from the way Liberalism does. . . . Indeed, it is perfectly intelligible for a person not to be a Liberal precisely because he is a liberal; that is to say, it is precisely because he believes that the modern Liberal society cannot safeguard the traditional liberal values which he cherishes that he might want to overthrow it.[54]

If liberal values are to be interpreted and justified differently, a theoretical alternative to conventional empirical theory must be developed. This does not imply the neglect of empirical research, but rather that it should throw light on to basic problems of political participation and democracy. At present, empirical theory all too often obscures or denies the existence of problems, and presents evidence of socially structured inequalities as 'natural facts' about the world that constitute insurmountable barriers to increased participation by the presently inactive. If empirical research is to help rather than hinder our understanding of the civic culture, it must be interpreted in a new framework; the individualist basis of liberal theory must be left behind. The aggregation of individual correlates of political activity will not illuminate the relationship between political structure because the basic *problem*, the fact that the structure is grounded in class and sex divisions, never appears as such. Rather, systematically structured inequalities appear as individual psychological and personal attributes that happen to be distributed in a particular way.

During the 1970s a welcome change occurred in political theory; important political problems (both 'traditional' and new) are being discussed, and the comforting arguments of earlier years are being more widely questioned. Yet although 'theoretical self-consciousness'[55] is more widespread, a great deal remains to be done to produce a worthwhile empirical democratic theory. Once that is achieved we shall really have a theory that enables us to understand our own social and political world, and that can 'help us decide what to do [politically] and how to go about doing it.'[56] Until then, we shall still lack a 'democratic' theory that is the theory of civic participatory practice of the people and for the people.

NOTES

1 G. A. Almond and S. Verba, *The Civic Culture: Political Attitudes and Democracy in Five Nations* (Princeton University Press, Princeton, NJ, 1963); references in parentheses in the text are to this book.
2 On writers who want to be both 'value-neutral' and 'impeccable champions of conventional pluralist democracy', see C. Bay, 'Politics and Pseudopolitics', in *Apolitical Politics*, ed. C. A. McCoy and J. Playford (T. Y. Crowell, New York, 1967), p. 19.
3 This is discussed in my *Participation and Democratic Theory* (Cambridge University Press, Cambridge, 1970), esp. pp. 16–21.
4 J. A. Schumpeter, *Capitalism, Socialism and Democracy* (Allen & Unwin, London, 1943), chap. 22.
5 This was the label given to empirical theory in one of the best-known critiques: G. Duncan and S. Lukes, 'The New Democracy', *Political Studies*, 11 (1963), pp. 156–77. It is also known as the 'elitist theory', the 'contemporary theory', 'polyarchy', etc.

6 The description is that of B. M. Barry, *Sociologists, Economists and Democracy* (Collier-Macmillan, London, 1970).

7 For a discussion of some examples of this theory, see Carole Pateman, *Participation*, chap. 2.

8 I do not specifically consider Almond and Verba's notion of 'stability'. It seems, as Barry notes (*Sociologists*, p. 86), to mean no more than 'the infrequency of unconstitutional changes of regime'.

9 See B. Jessop, *Traditionalism, Conservatism and British Political Culture* (Allen & Unwin, London, 1974), p. 255.

10 Schumpeter, *Capitalism*, p. 297.

11 And even this was not seen as essential in Schumpeter's account; see Schumpeter, *Capitalism*, pp. 244–5.

12 J. Mill, *An Essay on Government* (Cambridge University Press, Cambridge, 1937), p. 34.

13 Schumpeter, *Capitalism*, p. 269.

14 For this criticism, see Barry, *Sociologists*, pp. 49–50; Jessop, *Traditionalism*, pp. 53–5; and the comments of D. Kavanagh, *Political Culture* (Macmillan & Co., London, 1972), p. 65.

15 R. A. Dahl, *Who Governs? Democracy and Power in an American City* (Yale University Press, New Haven, CT, 1961), pp. 224–5.

16 The concept of 'political culture' is also discussed in Carole Pateman, 'Political Culture, Political Structure and Political Change', *British Journal of Political Science*, 1 (1973), pp. 291–305.

17 Kavanagh, *Political Culture*, p. 66.

18 T. Parsons et al., *Theories of Society* (The Free Press, New York, 1961), p. 36 (Parsons's italics).

19 For references to earlier investigations, see L. W. Milbrath, *Political Participation: How and Why Do People Get Involved in Politics?* (Rand McNally, Chicago, IL, 1965), pp. 113–14, 116.

20 G. Sartori, *Democratic Theory* (Wayne State University Press, Detroit, MI, 1962), p. 88.

21 This concept is developed in chap 5 of my unpublished doctoral thesis 'Participation and Recent Theories of Democracy', Oxford University, 1971.

22 Almond and Verba also argue that cultural norms about 'the traditional female status' are getting weaker in all countries (pp. 399–400). Such optimism has hardly been borne out. Moreover, Almond and Verba do not mention the discrimination that exists against women in political (and social and economic) life. The socialization explanation is certainly not the whole story. The other sources cited by Almond and Verba on women's political attitudes and activity should be treated with extreme caution. Political scientists, especially in the period of *The Civic Culture*, have either usually ignored women or merely repeated myths and stereotypes; see M. Goot and E. Reid, *Women and Voting Studies: Mindless Matrons or Sexist Scientism?* Sage Contemporary Political Sociology Series, vol. 1 (Sage Publications, Beverly Hills, CA, 1975); S. C. Bourque and

  J. Grossholtz, 'Politics an Unnatural Practice: Political Science Looks at Female Participation', *Politics and Society*, Winter 1974, pp. 225–66.

23 For an investigation and interpretation of the British political culture in similar terms, using the conceptions of 'hegemony' and 'dominant' and 'peripheral' value systems, see Jessop, *Traditionalism*.

24 This also raises a whole range of complex questions about the interpretation of replies to surveys like that of *The Civic Culture*, and the relationship of respondents to interviewers, which cannot be dealt with in the scope of this chapter. For a very different approach to the problem of citizens' lack of feelings of competence, and their evaluation of the political structure, see R. Sennett and J. Cobb, *The Hidden Injuries of Class* (Alfred A. Knopf, New York, 1972).

25 Barry, *Sociologists*, pp. 93–4.

26 A. O. Hirschman, ' "Exit, Voice and Loyalty": Further Reflections and a Survey of Recent Contributions', *Social Science Information*, 13 (1974), pp. 7–26. (I am grateful to Gabriel Almond for bringing this to my attention.) The rational withdrawal of low SES citizens into political inactivity can be seen as an exit from the political system. M. Walzer, *Obligations: Essays on Disobedience, War and Citizenship* (Simon & Schuster, New York, 1971), p. 266, calls attention to the inactive citizen who is involved 'in a kind of boycott of the political system'.

27 See Pateman, 'Political Culture', pp. 299–310); also, the evidence presented by M. Mann, 'The Social Cohesion of Liberal Democracy', *American Sociological Review*, 35 (1970), pp. 423–37.

28 S. Verba and N. H. Nie, *Participation in America: Political Democracy and Social Equality* (Harper & Row, New York, 1972), p. 338 (italics added).

29 The conclusions and arguments of *Participation in America* suggest not: I have discussed this study in a review essay, 'To Them That Hath, Shall Be Given', in *Politics*, 9(2) (1974), pp. 139–45.

30 Almond and Verba also argue that the 'balance' is between 'apparent contradictions' (p. 476). But these so-called contradictions would exist in any democratic system; there is always a need, for example, for citizens both to participate in decision making and to obey decisions. Nor is there any reason to suppose that social trust (pp. 284–8) would be lacking if inequality decreased and the benefits of participation were more equitably distributed.

31 A review of some of this evidence can be found in Pateman, *Participation*. See also P. Blumberg, *Industrial Democracy: The Sociology of Participation* (Constable, London, 1968); M. L. Kohn and C. Schooler, 'Class Occupation and Orientation', *American Sociological Review*, 34 (1969), pp. 659-78; L. Lipsitz, 'Work Life and Political Attitudes', *American Political Science Review*, 58 (1964), pp. 951–62.

32 On 'pseudoparticipation', see Pateman, *Participation*.

33 Blumberg, *Industrial Democracy* (esp. chap. 5), reviews much of the evidence. It is significant that pre-war experiments that were extremely influential for 'democratic management' were conducted by Lewin with young (male) children.
34 R. A. Dahl, *After the Revolution? Authority in a Good Society* (Yale University Press, New Haven, CT, 1970), pp. 115, 134.
35 Ibid., p. 136. There is now a large literature on industrial democracy to supplement the evidence in my *Participation*. See for example, G. D. Garson, *On Democratic Administration and Socialist Self-Management*, Sage Professional Papers in Administrative and Policy Studies, vol. 2 (Sage Publications, Beverly Hills, CA, 1974); the volumes of *Participation and Self-Management* (1972–3), Institute for Social Research, Zagreb, Yugoslavia; G. Hunnius, G. D. Garson, J. Case (eds), *Workers' Control* (Random House Vintage Books, New York, 1973); J. Vanek (ed) *Self-Management* (Penguin Books, Harmondsworth, Middlesex, 1975); M. Poole, *Workers' Participation in Industry*, rev. ed. (Routledge & Kegan Paul, London, 1978).
36 S. Verba and G. Shabad, 'Workers' Councils and Political Stratification: The Yugoslav Experience', *American Political Science Review*, 72(1) (1978), p. 85. See also S. Verba and G. Shabad, 'Workers' Councils and Political Participation', paper presented to the Annual Meeting of the American Political Science Association, 1975.
37 Verba and Shabad, 'Workers' Council and Political Stratification', p. 87.
38 S. Zukin, *Beyond Marx and Tito: Theory and Practice in Yugoslav Socialism* (Cambridge University Press, Cambridge, 1975), p. 250.
39 Ibid., pp. 189–90.
40 H. Braverman, *Labor and Monopoly Capitalism: The Degradation of Work in the Twentieth Century* (Monthly Review Press, New York, 1974).
41 Dahl, *After the Revolution?*, p. 120.
42 Many writers on industrial democracy insist that it cannot be the same as (political) democracy; for example, E. Rhenman, *Industrial Democracy and Industrial Management* (Tavistock, London, 1968), p. 42.
43 Zukin, *Beyond Marx and Tito*, p. 190; see also p. 178.
44 Dahl, *After the Revolution?*, p. 38.
45 S. Wolin, *Politics and Vision* (Allen & Unwin, London, 1961), p. 304.
46 Dahl, *After the Revolution?* p. 34.
47 For further comments on 'representation', see Carole Pateman, 'A Contribution to the Political Theory of Organizational Democracy', *Administration and Society* 7 (1975), pp. 15–18. Aspects of Rousseau's critique of liberal theory are discussed in Pateman, *The Problem of Political Obligation* (Polity Press, Cambridge, 1985; University of California Press, Berkely, CA, 1985), chap. 7.
48 J.-J. Rousseau, *The Social Contract*, tr. M. Cranston (Penguin Books, Harmondsworth, Middlesex, 1968), p. 146.

49 Dahl, *After the Revolution?*, p. 44.

50 W. R. Schonfeld, 'The Meaning of Democratic Participation', *World Politics*, 28 (1975), pp. 134–58.

51 The civic culture is called a 'culture of moderation' (p. 500), but the narrow view of 'democratic' activities, and the inability to discuss the relationship between class and sex and these activities as a problem, hardly encourages a moderate response.

52 B. M. Barry, *The Liberal Theory of Justice: A Critical Examination of the Principal Doctrines of 'A Theory of Justice' by John Rawls* (Oxford University Press, Oxford, 1973), p. 153.

53 J. G. A. Pocock, 'Civic Humanism and Its Role in Anglo-American Thought', in *Politics, Language and Time* (Methuen, London, 1972), p. 85. Pocock places Rousseau in this tradition, and argues (p. 103) that civic humanism 'provided the point of departure for the concept of alienation' – not a concept usually associated with liberal theory.

54 B. Parekh, 'Liberalism and Morality', in *The Morality of Politics*, ed. B. Parekh and R. N. Berki, (Allen & Unwin, London, 1972), p. 83. See also S. Lukes, *Individualism* (Blackwell, Oxford, 1973), part 3.

55 W. E. Connolly, 'Theoretical Self-Conciousness', *Polity*, 6 (1973), pp. 5–35.

56 J. Plamenatz, 'The Use of Political Theory', in *Political Philosophy* ed. A. Quinton, (Oxford University Press, London, 1967), p. 29.

8

The Patriarchal Welfare State

According to Raymond Williams's *Keywords*, 'the Welfare State, in distinction from the Warfare State, was first named in 1939.'[1] The welfare state was set apart from the fascist warfare state, defeated in the Second World War, and so the welfare state was identified with democracy at the christening. In the 1980s most Western welfare states are also warfare states, but this is not ordinarily seen as compromising their democratic character. Rather, the extent of democracy is usually taken to hinge on the *class* structure. Welfare provides a social wage for the working class, and the positive, social democratic view is that the welfare state gives social meaning and equal worth to the formal juridical and political rights of all citizens. A less positive view of the welfare state is that it provides governments with new means of exercising power over and controlling working-class citizens. But proponents of both views usually fail to acknowledge the sexually divided way in which the welfare state has been constructed. Nor do most democratic theorists recognize the *patriarchal* structure of the welfare state; the very different way that women and men have been incorporated as citizens is rarely seen to be of significance for democracy.[2] Even the fact that the earliest developments of the welfare state took place when women were still denied, or had only just won, citizenship in the national state is usually overlooked.[3]

I do not want to dispute the crucial importance of class in understanding the welfare state and democracy. To write about the welfare state is, in large part, to write about the working class. However, my discussion treats class in a manner unfamiliar to most democratic theorists, who usually assume that the welfare state, democracy and class can be discussed theoretically without any attention to the character of the relation between the sexes. I shall suggest some reasons why and how the patriarchal structure of the welfare state has been repressed from theoretical consciousness. I shall also consider the connection between employment and citizenship in the patriarchal welfare state, the manner in which 'women' have been opposed to the 'worker' and the 'citizen', and a central paradox surrounding women, welfare and citizenship. By 'the welfare state' here, I refer to the states of Britain (from which I shall draw a number of my empirical and historical examples), Australia and the United States. In the more developed welfare states of Scandinavia, women have moved nearer to, but have not yet achieved, full citizenship.[4]

For the past century, many welfare policies have been concerned with what are now called 'women's issues'. Moreover, much of the controversy about the welfare state has revolved and continues to revolve around the question of the respective social places and tasks of women and men, the structure of marriage and the power relationship between husband and wife. So it is not surprising that the Reagan administration's attack on the welfare state was seen as prompted by a desire to shore up the patriarchal structure of the state; the Reagan budgets, 'in essence, . . . try to restabilize patriarchy . . . as much as they try to fight inflation and stabilize capitalism.'[5] The difficulties of understanding the welfare state and citizenship today without taking the position of women into account are not hard to illustrate, because contemporary feminists have produced a large body of evidence and argument that reveals the importance of women in the welfare state and the importance of the welfare state for women.

Women are now the majority of recipients of many welfare benefits. In 1980 in the United States, for example, 64.8 per cent of the recipients of Medicare were women, while 70 per cent of housing subsidies went to women, either living alone or heading households;[6] and by 1979, 80 per cent of the families receiving Aid to Families with Dependent Children (AFDC) were headed by women (the number of such families having grown fourfold between 1961 and 1979).[7] A major reason why women are so prominent as welfare recipients is that women are more likely than men to be poor (a fact that has come to be known as 'the feminization of poverty'). In the United States, between 1969 and 1979, there was a decline in the proportion of families headed by men that fell below the official poverty line while the proportion headed by women grew rapidly.[8] By 1982 about one-fifth of families with minor children were headed by women, but they constituted 53 per cent of all poor families,[9] and female heads were over three times as likely as male heads to have incomes below the poverty line.[10] By 1980 two out of every three adults whose incomes were below the poverty line were women. The National Advisory Council on Economic Opportunity reported in 1980 that, if these trends continued, the entire population of the poor in the United

States would be composed of women and children by the year 2000.[11] In Australia women are also likely to be poor. A survey for the Commission of Inquiry into Poverty in 1973 found that, of the groups with 'disabilities', fatherless families were poorest; 30 per cent of such families were below the poverty line, and another 20 per cent only marginally above it.[12] Nor had the situation improved by 1978–9: 41 per cent of women who were single parents were then below the poverty line.[13]

The welfare state is now a major source of employment for women. For instance, in Britain the National Health Service is the biggest single employer of women in the country; about three-quarters of NHS employees, and 90 per cent of NHS nurses, are women.[14] In 1981 there were more than five million jobs in the public health, education and welfare sector in Britain (an increase of two million from 1961) and three-fifths of these jobs were held by women.[15] In the United States in 1980 women occupied 70 per cent of the jobs at all levels of government concerned with social services, which was a quarter of all female employment and about half of all professional jobs occupied by women. Employment is provided largely at state and local levels in the United States. The federal government subsidizes the warfare state where there are few jobs for women; only 0.5 per cent of the female work force is employed on military contracts. One estimate is that, for each billion dollar increase in the military budget, 9,500 jobs are lost to women in social welfare or the private sector.[16]

Women are also involved in the welfare state in less obvious ways. Negotiations (and confrontations) with welfare state officials on a day-to-day basis are usually conducted by women; and it is mothers, not fathers, who typically pay the rent, deal with social workers, take children to welfare clinics and so forth. Women are also frequently in the forefront of political campaigns and actions to improve welfare services or the treatment of welfare claimants. The services and benefits provided by the welfare state are far from comprehensive and, in the absence of public provision, much of the work involved, for example, in caring for the aged in all three countries is undertaken by women in their homes (something to which I shall return).

Finally, to put the previous points into perspective, there is one area of the welfare state from which women have been largely excluded. The legislation, policy-making and higher-level administration of the welfare state have been and remain predominantly in men's hands. Some progress has been made; in Australia the Office of the Status of Women within the (Commonwealth) Department of Prime Minister and Cabinet monitors cabinet submissions, and the Women's Budget Program requires all departments to make a detailed assessment of the impact of their policies on women.

Hegel's Two Dilemmas

To gain some insight into why the welfare state can still be discussed without taking account of these factors, it is useful to begin by looking at Donald Moon's account[17] of the welfare state as a response to 'Hegel's dilemma'. Hegel was the first political theorist to set out the moral dilemma that arises when citizenship is undermined by the operation of the capitalist market. The market leaves some citizens bereft of the resources for social participation and so, as Moon states, as 'undeserved exiles from society'. Citizens thrown into poverty lack both the means for self-respect and the means to be recognized by fellow citizens as of equal worth to themselves, a recognition basic to democracy. Poverty-stricken individuals are not and – unless the outcome of participation in the market is offset in some way, cannot be – full citizens. The moral basis of the welfare state lies in the provision of resources for what T. H. Marshall called the 'social rights' of democratic citizenship. For Moon, then, Hegel's dilemma is concerned with the manner in which the participation of some individuals as workers in the capitalist economy (or, in Hegel's terminology, in the sphere of civil society) can make a mockery of their formal status as equal citizens. In contemporary terms, it is a problem of class or, more exactly, now that mass unemployment could well be a permanent feature of capitalist economies, a problem of an underclass of unemployed social exiles. There is no doubt that this is an important problem, but Moon's reading of Hegel focuses on only *part* of the dilemma with which Hegel was faced.

In addition to the category of citizens who become social exiles through the accident that they can find no one to buy their labour-power at a living wage, Hegel also had to deal with a category of beings who are exiles because they are *incapable* of being incorporated into civil society and citizenship. According to Hegel – and to almost all the modern theorists who are admitted to the 'tradition of Western political philosophy' – women naturally lack the attributes and capacities of the 'individuals' who can enter civil society, sell their labour-power and become citizens.[18] Women, Hegel held, are natural social exiles. Hegel therefore had to find an answer to *two* dilemmas, and his theory gives a moral basis to both class division and sexual division. The welfare state could not provide a solution to the problem of women. Hegel's response was simultaneously to reaffirm the necessity of women's exile and to incorporate them into the state. Women are not incorporated as citizens like men, but as members of the family, a sphere separate from (or in social exile from) civil society and the state. The family is essential to civil society and the state, but it is constituted on a different basis from the rest of conventional social life, having its own ascriptive principles of association.

Women have now won the formal status of citizens, and their contemporary social position may seem a long way removed from that prescribed by Hegel. But Hegel's theory is still very relevant to the problem of patriarchy and the welfare state, although most contemporary political theorists usually look only at the relation between civil society and the state, or the intervention that the public power (state) may make in the private sphere (economy or class system). This view of 'public' and 'private' assumes that two of Hegel's categories (civil society and state) can be understood in the absence of the third (family). Yet Hegel's theory presupposes that family/civil society/state are comprehensible only in *relation* to each other – and then civil society and the state become 'public' in contrast to the 'private' family.

Hegel's social order contains a double separation of the private and public: the *class* division between civil society and the state (between economic man and citizen, between private enterprise and the public power); and the *patriarchal* separation between the private family and the public world of civil society/state. Moreover, the public character of the sphere of civil society/ state is constructed and gains its meaning through what it excludes – the private association of the family. The patriarchal division between public and private *is also a sexual division*. Women, naturally lacking the capacities for public participation, remain within an association constituted by love, ties of blood, natural subjection and particularity, and in which they are governed by men. The public world of universal citizenship is an association of free and equal individuals, a sphere of property, rights and contract – and of men, who interact as formally equal citizens.

The widely held belief that the basic structure of our society rests on the separation of the private, familial sphere from the public world of the state and its policies is both true and false. It is true that the private sphere has been seen as women's proper place. Women have never in reality been completely excluded from the public world, but the policies of the welfare state have helped ensure that women's day-to-day experience confirms the separation of private and public existence. The belief is false in that, since the early twentieth century, welfare policies have reached across from public to private and helped uphold a patriarchal structure of familial life. Moreover, the two spheres are linked because men have always had a legitimate place in both. Men have been seen both as heads of families – and as husbands and fathers they have had socially and legally sanctioned power over their wives and children – and as participants in public life. Indeed, the 'natural' masculine capacities that enable them, but not their wives, to be heads of families are the same capacities that enable them, but not their wives, to take their place in civil life.

Moon's interpretation of Hegel illustrates the continuing strength of Hegel's patriarchal construction of citizenship, which is assumed to be universal or democratic citizenship. The exiles from society who need the welfare state to give moral worth to their citizenship are male workers. Hegel showed deep insight here. Paid employment has become the key to citizenship, and the recognition of an individual as a citizen of equal worth to other citizens is lacking when a worker is unemployed. The history of the welfare state and citizenship (and the manner in which they have been theorized) is bound up with the history of the development of 'employment societies'.[19] In the early part of the nineteenth century, most workers were still not fully incorporated into the labour market; they typically worked at a variety of occupations, worked on a seasonal basis, gained part of their subsistence outside the capitalist market and enjoyed 'Saint Monday'. By the 1880s full employment had become an ideal, unemployment a major social issue, and loud demands were heard for state-supported social reform (and arguments were made against state action to promote welfare).[20] But who was included under the banner of 'full employment'? What was the status of those 'natural' social exiles seen as properly having no part in the employment society? Despite many changes in the social standing of women, we are not so far as we might like to think from Hegel's statement that the husband, as head, 'has the prerogative to go out and work for [the family's] living, to attend to its needs, and to control and administer its capital.'[21]

The political significance of the sexual division of labour is ignored by most democratic theorists. They treat the public world of paid employment and citizenship as if it can be divorced from its connection with the private sphere, and so the masculine character of the public sphere has been repressed. For example, T. H. Marshall first presented his influential account of citizenship in 1949, at the height of the optimism in Britain about the contribution of the new welfare state policies to social change – but also at the time (as I shall show) when women were being confirmed as lesser citizens in the welfare state. Marshall states that 'citizenship is a status bestowed on those who are full members of a community',[22] and most contemporary academic discussions of citizenship do not question this statement. But, as shown graphically and brutally by the history of blacks in the United States, this is not the case. The formal status of citizen can be bestowed on, or won by, a category of people who are still denied full social membership.

Marshall noted that the Factory Acts in the nineteenth century 'protected' women workers, and he attributes the protection to their lack of citizenship. But he does not consider 'protection' – the polite way to refer to subordination – of women in the private sphere or ask how it is related to the sexual division of labour in the capitalist economy and citizenship. Nor does the 'in some important respects peculiar' civil status of married women in the nineteenth century inhibit his confidence in maintaining, despite the limited franchise, 'that in the nineteenth century citizenship in the form of civil rights was universal', and that, in economic life, 'the basic civil right is the right to work'. Marshall sees the aim of the 'social rights' of the welfare state as 'class-abatement': this is 'no longer merely an attempt to abate the obvious nuisance of destitution in the lowest ranks of society. . . . It is no longer content to raise the floor-level in the basement of the social edifice, . . . it has begun to remodel the whole building.'[23] But the question that has to be asked is, are women in the building or in a separate annex?

Citizenship and Employment

Theoretically and historically, the central criterion for citizenship has been 'independence', and the elements encompassed under the heading of independence have been based on masculine attributes and abilities. Men, but not women, have been seen as possessing the capacities required of 'individuals', 'workers' and 'citizens'. As a corollary, the meaning of 'dependence' is associated with all that is womanly – and women's citizenship in the welfare state is full of paradoxes and contradicions. To use Marshall's metaphor, women are identified as trespassers into the public edifice of civil society and the state. Three elements of 'independence' are particularly important for present purposes, all related to the masculine capacity for self-protection: the capacity to bear arms, the capacity to own property and the capacity for self-government.

First, women are held to lack the capacity for self-protection; they have been 'unilaterally disarmed'.[24] The protection of women is undertaken by men, but physical safety is a fundamental aspect of women's welfare that has been sadly neglected in the welfare state. From the nineteenth century, feminists (including J. S. Mill) have drawn attention to the impunity with which husbands could use physical force against their wives,[25] but women/wives still find it hard to obtain proper social and legal protection against violence from their male 'protectors'. Defence of the state (or the ability to protect your protection, as Hobbes put it), the ultimate test of citizenship, is also a masculine prerogative. The anti-suffragists in both America and Britain made a great deal of the alleged inability and unwillingness of women to use armed force, and the issue of women and combat duties in the military forces of the warfare state was also prominent in the recent campaign against the Equal Rights Amendment in the United States. Although women are now admitted into the armed force and so into training useful for later civilian employment, they are prohibited from combat duties in Britain, Australia and the United States. Moreover, past exclusion of women from the warfare state has meant that welfare provision for veterans has also benefited men. In Australia and the United States, because of their special 'contribution' as citizens, veterans have had their own, separately administered welfare state, which has ranged from preference in university education (the GI bills in the United States) to their own medical benefits and hospital services, and (in Australia) preferential employment in the public service.

In the 'democratic' welfare state, however, employment rather than military service is the key to citizenship. The masculine 'protective' capacity now enters into citizenship primarily through the second and third dimensions of independence. Men, but not women, have also been seen as property-owners. Only some men own material property, but as 'individuals', all men own (and can protect) the property they possess in their persons. Their status as 'workers' depends on their capacity to contract out the property they own in their labour-power. Women are still not fully recognized socially as such property-owners. To be sure, our position has improved dramatically from the mid-nineteenth century when women as wives had a very 'peculiar' position as the legal property of their husbands, and feminists compared wives to slaves. But today, a wife's person is still the property of her husband in one vital respect. Despite recent legal reform, in Britain and in some of the states of the United States and Australia, rape is still deemed legally impossible within marriage, and thus a wife's consent has no meaning. Yet women are now formally citizens in states held to be based on the necessary consent of self-governing individuals.[26] The profound contradiction about women's consent is rarely if ever noticed and so is not seen as related to a sexually divided citizenship or as detracting from the claim of the welfare state to be democratic.

The third dimension of 'independence' is self-government. Men have been constituted as the beings who can govern (or protect) themselves, and if a man can govern himself, then he also has the requisite capacity to govern others. Only a few men govern others in public life – but all men govern in private as husbands and heads of households. As the governor of a family, a man is also a 'breadwinner'. He has the capacity to sell his labour-power as a worker, or to buy labour-power with his capital, and provide for his wife and family. His wife is thus 'protected'. The category of 'breadwinner' presupposes that wives are constituted as economic dependents or 'housewives', which places them in a subordinate position.

The dichotomy breadwinner/housewife, and the masculine meaning of independence, were established in Britain by the middle of the last century; in the earlier period of capitalist development, women (and children) were wage-labourers. A 'worker' became a man who has an economically dependent wife to take care of his daily needs and look after his home and children. Moreover, 'class', too, is constructed as a patriarchal category. 'The working class' is the class of working *men*, who are also full citizens in the welfare state.

This observation brings me back to Marshall's statement about the universal, civil right to 'work', that is, to paid employment. The democratic implications of the right to work cannot be understood without attention to the connections between the public world of 'work' and citizenship and the private world of conjugal relations. What it means to be a 'worker' depends in part on men's status and power as husbands, and on their standing as citizens in the welfare state. The construction of the male worker as 'breadwinner' and his wife as his 'dependent' was expressed officially in the Census classifications in Britain and Australia. In the British Census of 1851, women engaged in unpaid domestic work were 'placed . . . in one of the productive classes along with paid work of a similar kind.'[27] This classification changed after 1871, and by 1911 unpaid housewives had been completely removed from the economically active population. In Australia an initial conflict over the categories of classification was resolved in 1890 when the scheme devised in New South Wales was adopted. The Australians divided up the population more decisively than the British, and the 1891 Census was based on the two categories of 'breadwinner' and 'dependent'. Unless explicitly stated otherwise, women's occupation was classified as domestic, and domestic workers were put in the dependent category.

The position of men as breadwinner-workers has been built into the welfare state. The sexual divisions in the welfare state have received much less attention than the persistence of the old dichotomy between the deserving and undeserving poor, which predates the welfare state. This is particularly clear in the United States, where a sharp separation is maintained between 'social security', or welfare-state policies directed at 'deserving workers who have paid for them through "contributions" over their working lifetimes', and 'welfare' – seen as public 'handouts' to 'barely deserving poor people'.[28] Although 'welfare' does not have this stark meaning in Britain or Australia, where the welfare state encompasses much more than most Americans seem able to envisage, the old distinction between the deserving and undeserving poor is still alive and kicking, illustrated by the popular bogey-figures of the 'scrounger' (Britain) and the 'dole-bludger' (Australia). However, although the dichotomy of deserving/undeserving poor overlaps with the divisions between husband/wife and worker/housewife to some extent, it also obscures the patriarchal structure of the welfare state.

Feminist analyses have shown how many welfare provisions have been established within a two-tier system. First, there are the benefits available to individuals as 'public' persons by virtue of their participation, and accidents of fortune, in the capitalist market. Benefits in this tier of the system are usually claimed by men. Second, benefits are available to the 'dependents' of individuals in the first category, or to 'private' persons, usually women. In the United States, for example, men are the majority of 'deserving' workers who receive benefits through the insurance system to which they have 'contributed' out of their earnings. On the other hand, the majority of claimants in means-tested programmes are women – women who are usually making their claims as wives or mothers. This is clearly the case with AFDC, where women are aided because they are mothers supporting children on their own, but the same is also true in other programmes: '46 per cent of the women receiving Social Security benefits make their claims as wives.' In contrast: 'men, even poor men, rarely make claims for benefits solely as husbands or fathers.'[29] In Australia the division is perhaps even more sharply defined. In 1980–1, in the primary tier of the system, in which benefits are employment-related and claimed by those who are expected to be economically independent but are not earning an income because of unemployment or illness, women formed only 31.3 per cent of claimants. In contrast, in the 'dependents group', 73.3 per cent of claimants were women, who were eligible for benefits because 'they are dependent on a man who could not support them, . . . [or] should have had a man support them if he had not died, divorced or deserted them.'[30]

Such evidence of lack of 'protection' raises an important question about *women's* standard of living in the welfare state. As dependents, married women should derive their subsistence from their husbands, so that wives are placed in the position of all dependent people before the establishment of the welfare state; they are reliant on the benevolence of another for their livelihood. The assumption is generally made that all husbands are benevolent. Wives are assumed to share equally in the standard of living of their husbands. The distribution of income *within* households has not usually been a subject of interest to economists, political theorists or protagonists in arguments about class and the welfare state – even though William Thompson drew attention to its importance as long ago as 1825[31] – but past and present evidence indicates that the belief that all husbands are benevolent is mistaken.[32] Nevertheless, women are likely to be better off married than if their marriage fails. One reason why women figure so prominently among the poor is that after divorce, as recent evidence from the United States reveals, a woman's standard of living can fall by nearly 75 per cent, whereas a man's can rise by nearly half.[33]

The conventional understanding of the 'wage' also suggests that there is no need to investigate women's standard of living independently from men's. The concept of the wage has expressed and encapsulated the patriarchal separation and integration of the public world of employment and the private sphere of conjugal relations. In arguments about the welfare state and the social wage, the wage is usually treated as a return for the sale of *individuals'* labour-power. However, once the opposition breadwinner/housewife was consolidated, a 'wage' had to provide subsistence for several people. The struggle between capital and labour and the controversy about the welfare state have been about the *family wage*. A 'living wage' has been defined as what is required for a worker as breadwinner to support a wife and family, rather than what is needed to support himself; the wage is not what is sufficient to reproduce the worker's own labour power, but what is sufficient, in combination with the unpaid work of the housewife, to reproduce the labour-power of the present and future labour force.

The designer of the Australian Census classification system, T. A. Coghlan, discussed women's employment in his *Report* on the 1891 Census, and he argued that married women in the paid labour market depressed men's wages and thus lowered the general standard of living.[34] His line of argument about women's employment has been used by the trade union movement for the past century in support of bargaining to secure a family wage. In 1909 motions were put to the conferences of the Labour Party and Trades Union Congress in Britain to ban the employment of wives altogether, and as recently as 1982 a defence of the family wage was published arguing that it strengthens unions in wage negotiation.[35] In 1907 the family wage was enshrined in law in Australia in the famous Harvester judgement in the Commonwealth Arbitration Court. Justice Higgins ruled in favour of a legally guaranteed minimum wage – and laid down that a living wage should be sufficient to keep an unskilled worker, his (dependent) wife and three children in reasonable comfort.

Of course, a great deal has changed since 1907. Structural changes in capitalism have made it possible for large numbers of married women to enter paid employment, and equal-pay legislation in the 1970s, which in principle recognizes the wage as payment to an individual, may make it seem that the family wage has had its day. And it was always a myth for many, perhaps most, working-class families.[36] Despite the strength of the social ideal of the dependent wife, many working-class wives have always been engaged in paid work out of necessity. The family could not survive on the husband's wage, and the wife had to earn money, too, whether as a wage-worker, or at home doing outwork, or taking in laundry or lodgers or participating in other ways in the 'informal' economy. In 1976 in Britain the wages and salaries of 'heads of household' (not all of whom are men) formed only 51 per cent of household income.[37] The decline of manufacturing and the expansion of the service sector of capitalist economies since the Second World War have created jobs seen as 'suitable' for women. Between 1970 and 1980 in the United States over thirteen million women entered the paid labour force.[38] In Britain, if present trends in male and female employment continue, women employees will outnumber men in less than ten years.[39] Nevertheless, even these dramatic shifts have not been sufficient to make women full members of the employment society. The civil right to 'work' is still only half-heartedly acknowledged for women. Women in the workplace are still perceived primarily as wives and mothers, not workers.[40] The view is also widespread that women's wages are a 'supplement' to those of the breadwinner. Women, it is held, do not need wages in the same way that men do – so they may legitimately be paid less than men.

When the Commonwealth Arbitration Court legislated for the family wage, 45 per cent of the male work force in Australia were single.[41] Yet in 1912 (in a case involving fruit pickers) Justice Higgins ruled that a job normally done by women could be paid at less than a man's rate because women were not responsible for dependents. On the contrary, while many men received a family wage and had no families, and breadwinners were given the power to determine whether their dependents should share in their standard of living, many women were struggling to provide for dependents on a 'dependent's' wage. Eleanor Rathbone estimated that before and just after the Great War in Britain a third of women in paid employment were wholly or partially responsible for supporting dependents.[42] About the same proportion of women breadwinners was found in a survey of Victorian manufacturing industries in Australia in 1928.[43] Nevertheless, the classification of women as men's dependents was the basis for a living wage for women, granted in New South Wales in 1918; lower wages for women were enshrined in law and (until a national minimum wage for both sexes was granted in 1974) were set at 50–54 per cent of the male rate. Again in Britain, in the late 1960s and 1970s, the National Board for Prices and Incomes investigated low pay and argued that, as part-time workers, women did not depend on their own wage to support themselves.[44] In the United States, as recently as 1985, it was stated that 'women have generally been paid less [than men] because they would work for lower wages, since they had no urgent need for more money. Either they were married, or single and living at home, or doubling up with friends.'[45]

Women are prominent as welfare claimants because, today, it is usually women who are poor – and perhaps the major reason why women are poor is that it is very hard for most women to find a job that will pay a living wage. Equal-pay legislation cannot overcome the barrier of a sexually segregated occupational structure. Capitalist economies are patriarchal, divided into men's and women's occupations; the sexes do not usually work together, nor are they paid at the same rates for similar work. For example, in the United States, 80 per cent of women's jobs are located in only 20 of the 420 occupations listed by the Department of Labor.[46] More than half of employed women work in occupations that are 75 per cent female, and over 20 per cent work in occupations that are 95 per cent female.[47] In Australia in 1986, 59.5 per cent of women employees worked in the occupational categories 'clerical, sales and services'. In only 69 out of 267 occupational categories did the proportion of women reach a third or more.[48] The segregation is very stable; in Britain, for example, 84 per cent of women worked in occupations dominated by women in 1971, the same percentage as in 1951, and in 1901 the figure was 88 per cent.[49]

The economy is also vertically segregated. Most women's jobs are unskilled[50] and of low status; even in the professions women are clustered at the lower end of the occupational hierarchy. The British National Health Service provides a useful illustration. About one-third of employees are at the lowest level as ancillary workers, of whom around three-quarters are women. Their work is sex-segregated, so that the women workers perform catering and domestic tasks. As I noted previously, 90 per cent of NHS nurses are female but about one-quarter of senior nursing posts are held by men. At the prestigious levels, only about 10 per cent of consultants are female and they are segregated into certain specialities, notably those relating to children (in 1977, 32.7 per cent women).[51]

Many women also work part-time, either because of the requirements of their other (unpaid) work, or because they cannot find a full-time job. In Australia in 1986, 57.4 per cent of all part-time employees were married women.[52] In Britain two out of every five women in the work force are employed for thirty hours or less. However, the hourly rate for full-time women workers was only 75.1 per cent of men's in 1982 (and it is men who are likely to work overtime).[53] In 1980 women comprised 64 per cent of the employees in the six lowest paid occupations.[54] During the 1970s women's earnings edged slightly upward compared with men's in most countries, but not in the United States. In 1984 the median of women's earnings as full-time workers over a full year was $14,479, while men earned $23,218.[55] The growth in the service sector in the United States has largely been growth in part-time work; in 1980 almost a quarter of all jobs in the private sector were part-time. Almost all the new jobs appearing between 1970 and 1980 were in areas that paid less than average wages; in 1980 '51 per cent [of women] held jobs paying less than 66 per cent of a craft worker's wages'.[56]

Women's Work and Welfare

Although so many women, including married women, are now in paid employment, women's standing as 'workers' is still of precarious legitimacy. So, therefore, is their standing as democratic citizens. If an individual can gain recognition from other citizens as an equally worthy citizen only through participation in the capitalist market, if self-respect and respect as a citizen are 'achieved' in the public world of the employment society, then women still lack the means to be recognized as worthy citizens. Nor have the policies of the welfare state provided women with many of the resources to gain respect as citizens. Marshall's social rights of citizenship in the welfare state could be extended to men without difficulty. As participants in the market, men could be seen as making a public contribution, and were in a position to be levied by the state to make a contribution more directly, that *entitled* them to the benefits of the welfare state. But how could women, dependents of men, whose legitimate 'work' is held to be located in the private sphere, be citizens of the welfare state? What could, or did, women contribute? The paradoxical answer is that women contributed – welfare.

The development of the welfare state has presupposed that certain aspects of welfare could and should continue to be provided by women (wives) in the home, and not primarily through public provision. The 'work' of a housewife can include the care of an invalid husband and elderly, perhaps infirm, relatives. Welfare-state policies have ensured in various ways that wives/women provide welfare services gratis, disguised as part of their responsibility for the private sphere. A good deal has been written about the fiscal crisis of the welfare state, but it would have been more acute if certain areas of welfare had not been seen as a private, women's matter. It is not surprising that the attack on public spending in the welfare state by the Thatcher and Reagan governments goes hand-in-hand with praise for loving care within families, that is, with an attempt to obtain ever more unpaid welfare from (house)wives. The Invalid Care Allowance in Britain has been a particularly blatant example of the way in which the welfare state ensures that wives provide private welfare. The allowance was introduced in 1975 – when the Sex Discrimination Act was also passed – and it was paid to men or to single women who relinquished paid employment to look after a sick, disabled or elderly person (not necessarily a relative). Married women (or those cohabiting) were ineligible for the allowance.

The evidence indicates that it is likely to be married women who provide such care. In 1976 in Britain it was estimated that two million women were caring for adult relatives, and one survey in the north of England found that there were more people caring for adult relatives than mothers looking after children under 16.[57] A corollary of the assumption that women, but not men, care for others is that women must also care for themselves. Investigations show that women living by themselves in Britain have to be more infirm than men to obtain the services of home helps, and a study of an old people's home found that frail, elderly women admitted with their husbands faced hostility from the staff because they had failed in their job.[58] Again, women's citizenship is full of contradictions and paradoxes. Women must provide welfare, and care for themselves, and so must be assumed to have the capacities necessary for these tasks. Yet the development of the welfare state has also presupposed that women necessarily are in need of protection by and are dependent on men.

The welfare state has reinforced women's identity as men's dependents both directly and indirectly, and so confirmed rather than ameliorated our social exile. For example, in Britain and Australia the cohabitation rule explicitly expresses the presumption that women necessarily must be economically dependent on men if they live with them as sexual partners. If cohabitation is ruled to take place, the woman loses her entitlement to welfare benefits. The consequence of the cohabitation rule is not only sexually divided control of citizens, but an exacerbation of the poverty and other problems that the welfare state is designed to alleviate. In Britain today

> when a man lives in, a woman's independence – her own name on the weekly giro [welfare cheque] is automatically surrendered. The men become the claimants and the women their dependents. They lose control over both the revenue and the expenditure, often with catastrophic results: rent not paid, fuel bills missed, arrears mounting.[59]

It is important to ask what counts as part of the welfare state. In Australia and Britain the taxation system and transfer payments together form a tax-transfer system in the welfare state. In Australia a tax rebate is available for a dependent spouse (usually, of course, a wife), and in Britain the taxation system has always treated a wife's income as her husband's for taxation purposes. It is only relatively recently that it ceased to be the husband's prerogative to correspond with the Inland Revenue about his wife's earnings, or that he ceased to receive rebates due on her tax payments. Married men can still claim a tax allowance, based on the assumption that they support a dependent wife. Women's dependence is also enforced through the extremely limited public provision of child-care facilities in Australia, Britain and the United States, which creates a severe obstacle to women's full participation in the employment society. In all three countries, unlike Scandinavia, child-care outside the home is a very controversial issue.

Welfare-state legislation has also been framed on the assumption that women make their 'contribution' by providing private welfare, and, from the beginning, women were denied full citizenship in the welfare state. In America 'originally the purpose of ADC (now AFDC) was to keep mothers out of the paid labor force. . . . In contrast, the Social Security retirement program was consciously structured to respond to the needs of white male workers.'[60] In Britain the first national insurance, or contributory, scheme was set up in 1911, and one of its chief architects wrote later that women should have been completely excluded because 'they want insurance for others, not themselves'. Two years before the scheme was introduced, William Beveridge, the father of the contemporary British welfare state, stated in a book on unemployment that the 'ideal [social] unit is the household of man, wife and children maintained by the earnings of the first alone. . . . Reasonable security of employment for the breadwinner is the basis of all private duties and all sound social action.'[61] Nor had Beveridge changed his mind on this matter by the Second World War; his report, *Social Insurance and Allied Services*, appeared in 1942 and laid a major part of the foundation for the great reforms of the 1940s. In a passage now (in)famous among feminists, Beveridge wrote that 'the great majority of married women must be regarded as occupied on work which is vital though unpaid, without which their husbands could not do their paid work and without which the nation could not continue.'[62] In the National Insurance Act of 1946 wives were separated from their husbands for insurance purposes. (The significance of this procedure, along with Beveridge's statement, clearly was lost on T. H. Marshall when he was writing his essay on citizenship and the welfare state.) Under the act, married women paid lesser contributions for reduced benefits, but they could also opt out of the scheme, and so from sickness, unemployment and maternity benefits, and they also lost entitlement to an old-age pension in their own right, being eligible only as their husband's dependent. By the time the legislation was amended in 1975, about three-quarters of married women workers had opted out.[63]

A different standard for men and women has also been applied in the operation of the insurance scheme. In 1911 some married women were insured in their own right. The scheme provided benefits in case of 'incapacity to work', but, given that wives had already been identified as 'incapacitated' for the 'work' in question, for paid employment, problems over the criteria for entitlement to sickness benefits were almost inevitable. In 1913 an inquiry was held to discover why married women were claiming benefits at a much greater rate than expected. One obvious reason was that the health of many working-class women was extremely poor. The extent of their ill health was revealed in 1915 when letters written by working women in 1913–14 to the Women's Cooperative Guild were published.[64] The national insurance scheme meant that for the first time women could afford to take time off work when ill – but from which 'work'? Could they take time off from housework? What were the implications for the embryonic welfare state if they ceased to provide free welfare? From 1913 a dual standard of eligibility for benefits was established. For men the criterion was fitness for work. But the committee of inquiry decided that, if a woman could do her housework, she was not ill. So the criterion for eligibility for women was also fitness for work – but unpaid work in the private home, not paid work in the public market that was the basis for the contributory scheme under which the women were insured! This criterion for women was still being laid down in instructions issued by the Department of Health and Social Security in the 1970s.[65] The dual standard was further reinforced in 1975 when a non-contributory invalidity pension was introduced for those incapable of work but not qualified for the contributory scheme. Men and single women were entitled to the pension if they could not engage in paid employment; the criterion for married women was ability to perform 'normal household duties'.[66]

Wollstonecraft's Dilemma

So far, I have looked at the patriarchal structure of the welfare state, but this is only part of the picture; the development of the welfare state has also brought challenges to patriarchal power and helped provide a basis for women's autonomous citizenship. Women have seen the welfare state as one of their major means of support. Well before women won formal citizenship, they campaigned for the state to make provision for welfare, especially for the welfare of women and their children; and women's organizations and women activists have continued their political activities around welfare issues, not least in opposition to their status as 'dependents'. In 1953 the British feminist Vera Brittain wrote of the welfare state established through the legislation of the 1940s that 'in it women have become ends in themselves and not merely means to the ends of men', and their 'unique value as women was recognised'.[67] In hindsight, Brittain was clearly overoptimistic in her assessment, but perhaps the opportunity now exists to begin to dismantle the patriarchal structure of the welfare state. In the 1980s the large changes in women's social position, technological and structural transformations within capitalism, and mass unemployment mean that much of the basis for the breadwinner/dependent dichotomy and for the employment society itself is being eroded (although both are still widely seen as social ideals). The social context of Hegel's two dilemmas is disappearing. As the current concern about the 'feminization of poverty' reveals, there is now a very visible underclass of women who are directly connected to the state as claimants, rather than indirectly as men's dependents. Their social exile is as apparent as that of poor male workers was to Hegel. Social change has now made it much harder to gloss over the paradoxes and contradictions of women's status as citizens.

However, the question of how women might become full citizens of a democratic welfare state is more complex than may appear at first sight, because it is only in the current wave of the organized feminist movement that the division between the private and public spheres of social life has become seen as a major *political* problem. From the 1860s to the 1960s women were active in the public sphere: women fought not only for welfare measures and for measures to secure the private and public safety of women and girls, but for the vote and civil equality; middle-class women fought for entry into higher education, and the professions and women trade unionists fought for decent working conditions and wages and maternity leave. But the contemporary liberal-feminist view, particularly prominent in the United States, that what is required above all is 'gender-neutral' laws and policies, was not widely shared.[68] In general, until the 1960s the focus of attention in the welfare state was on measures to ensure that women had proper social support, and hence proper social respect, in carrying out their responsibilities in the private sphere. The problem is whether and how such measures could assist women in their fight for full citizenship. In 1942 in Britain, for example, many women welcomed the passage in the Beveridge Report that I have cited because, it was argued, it gave official recognition to the value of women's unpaid work. However, an official nod of recognition to women's work as 'vital' to 'the nation' is easily given; *in practice*, the value of the work in bringing women into full membership in the welfare state was negligible. The equal worth of citizenship and the respect of fellow citizens still depended on participation as paid employees. 'Citizenship' and 'work' stood then and still stand opposed to 'women'.

The extremely difficult problem faced by women in their attempt to win full citizenship I shall call 'Wollstonecraft's dilemma'. The dilemma is that the two routes toward citizenship that women have pursued are mutually incompatible within the confines of the patriarchal welfare state, and, within that context, they are impossible to achieve. For three centuries, since universal citizenship first appeared as a political ideal, women have continued to challenge their alleged natural subordination within private life. From at least the 1790s they have also struggled with the task of trying to become citizens within an ideal and practice that have gained universal meaning through their exclusion. Women's response has been complex. On the one hand, they have demanded that the ideal of citizenship be extended to them,[69] and the liberal-feminist agenda for a 'gender-neutral' social world is the logical conclusion of one form of this demand. On the other hand, women have also insisted, often simultaneously, as did Mary Wollstonecraft, that *as women* they have specific capacities, talents, needs and concerns, so that the expression of their citizenship will be differentiated from that of men. Their unpaid work providing welfare could be seen, as Wollstonecraft saw women's tasks as mothers, as women's work *as citizens*, just as their husbands' paid work is central to men's citizenship.[70]

The patriarchal understanding of citizenship means that the two demands are incompatible because it allows two alternatives only: either women become (like) men, and so full citizens; or they continue at women's work, which is of no value for citizenship. Moreover, within a patriarchal welfare state neither demand can be met. To demand that citizenship, as it now exists, should be fully extended to women accepts the patriarchal meaning of 'citizen', which is constructed from men's attributes, capacities and activities. Women cannot be full citizens in the present meaning of the term; at best, citizenship can be extended to women only as lesser men. At the same time, within the patriarchal welfare state, to demand proper social recognition and support for women's responsibilities is to condemn women to less than full citizenship and to continued incorporation into public life as 'women', that is, as members of another sphere who cannot, therefore, earn the respect of fellow (male) citizens.

The example of child endowments on family allowances in Australia and Britain is instructive as a practical illustration of Wollstonecraft's dilemma. It reveals the great difficulties in trying to implement a policy that both aids women in their work and challenges patriarchal power while enhancing women's citizenship. In both countries there was opposition from the right and from laissez-faire economists on the ground that family allowances would undermine the father's obligation to support his children and undermine his 'incentive' to sell his labour-power in the market. The feminist advocates of family allowances in the 1920s, most notably Eleanor Rathbone in Britain, saw the alleviation of poverty in families where the breadwinner's wage was inadequate to meet the family's basic needs as only one argument for this form of state provision. They were also greatly concerned with the questions of the wife's economic dependence and equal pay for men and women workers. If the upkeep of children (or a substantial contribution toward it) was met by the state outside of wage bargaining in the market, then there was no reason why men and women doing the same work should not receive the same pay. Rathbone wrote in 1924 that 'nothing can justify the subordination of one group of producers – the mothers – to the rest and their deprivation of a share of their own in the wealth of a community.'[71] She argued that family allowances would, 'once and for all, cut away the maintenance of children and the reproduction of the race from the question of wages.'[72]

But not all the advocates of child endowment were feminists – so that the policy could very easily be divorced from the public issue of wages and dependence and be seen only as a return for and recognition of women's private contributions. Supporters included the eugenicists and pronatalists, and family allowances appealed to capital and the state as a means of keeping wages down. Family allowances had many opponents in the British union movement, fearful that the consequence, were the measure introduced, would be to undermine the power of unions in wage bargaining. The opponents included women trade unionists who were suspicious of a policy that could be used to try to persuade women to leave paid employment. Some unionists also argued that social services, such as housing, education and health, should be developed first, and the TUC adopted this view in 1930. But were the men concerned, too, with their private, patriarchal privileges? Rathbone claimed that 'the leaders of working men are themselves subsconsciously biased by prejudice of sex. . . . Are they not influenced by a secret reluctance to see their wives and children recognised as separate personalities?'[73]

By 1941 the supporters of family allowances in the union movement had won the day, and family allowances were introduced in 1946, as part of the government's wartime plans for post-war reconstruction. The legislation proposed that the allowance would be paid to the father as 'normal household head', but after lobbying by women's organizations, this was overturned in a free vote, and the allowance was paid directly to mothers. In Australia the union movement accepted child endowment in the 1920s (child endowment was introduced in New South Wales in 1927, and at the federal level in 1941). But union support there was based on wider redistributive policies, and the endowment was seen as a supplement to, not a way of breaking down, the family wage.[74] In the 1970s, in both countries, women's organizations again had to defend family allowances and the principle of redistribution from 'the wallet to the purse'.

The hope of Eleanor Rathbone and other feminists that family allowances would form part of a democratic restructuring of the wage system was not realized. Nevertheless, family allowances are paid to women as a benefit in their own right; in that sense they are an important (albeit financially very small) mark of recognition of married women as independent members of the welfare state. Yet the allowance is paid to women as *mothers*, and the key question is thus whether the payment to a mother – a private person – negates her standing as an independent citizen of the welfare state. More generally, the question is whether there can be a welfare policy that gives substantial assistance to women in their daily lives *and* helps create the conditions for a genuine democracy in which women are autonomous citizens, in which we can act *as women* and not as 'woman' (protected/dependent/subordinate) constructed as the opposite to all that is meant by 'man'. That is to say, a resolution of Wollstonecraft's dilemma is necessary and, perhaps, possible.

The structure of the welfare state presupposes that women are men's dependents, but the benefits help to make it possible for women to be economically independent of men. In the countries with which I am concerned, women reliant on state benefits live poorly, but it is no longer so essential as it once was to marry or to cohabit with a man. A considerable moral panic has developed in recent years around 'welfare mothers', a panic that obscures significant features of their position, not least the extent to which the social basis for the ideal of breadwinner/ dependent has crumbled. Large numbers of young working-class women have little or no hope of finding employment (or of finding a young man who is employed). But there is a source of social identity available to them that is out of the reach of their male counterparts. The socially secure and acknowledged identity for women is still that of a mother, and for many young women, motherhood, supported by state benefits, provides 'an alternative to aimless adolescence on the dole' and 'gives the appearance of self-determination'. The price of independence and 'a rebellious motherhood that is not an uncritical retreat into femininity'[75] is high, however; the welfare state provides a minimal income and perhaps housing (often substandard), but child-care services and other support are lacking, so that the young women are often isolated, with no way out of their social exile. Moreover, even if welfare state policies in Britain, Australia and the United States were reformed so that generous benefits, adequate housing, health care, child-care and other services were available to mothers, reliance on the state could reinforce women's lesser citizenship in a new way.

Some feminists have enthusiastically endorsed the welfare state as 'the main recourse of women' and as the generator of 'political resources which, it seems fair to say, are mainly women's resources.'[76] They can point, in Australia for example, to 'the creation over the decade [1975–85] of a range of women's policy machinery and government subsidized women's services (delivered by women for women) which is unrivalled elsewhere.'[77] However, the enthusiasm is met with the rejoinder from other feminists that for women to look to the welfare state is merely to exchange dependence on individual men for dependence on the state. The power and capriciousness of husbands is being replaced by the arbitrariness, bureaucracy and power of the state, the very state that has upheld patriarchal power. The objection is cogent: to make women directly dependent on the state will not in itself do anything to challenge patriarchal power relations. The direct dependence of male workers on the welfare state and their indirect dependence when their standard of living is derived from the vast system of state regulation of and subsidy to capitalism – and in Australia a national arbitration court – have done little to undermine class power. However, the objection also misses an important point. There is one crucial difference between the construction of women as men's dependents and dependence on the welfare state. In the former case, each woman lives with the man on whose benevolence she depends; each woman is (in J. S. Mill's extraordinarily apt phrase) in a 'chronic state of bribery and intimidation combined'.[78] In the welfare state, each woman receives what is hers by right, and she can, potentially, combine with other citizens to enforce her rightful claim. The state has enormous powers of intimidation, but political action takes place collectively in the public terrain and not behind the closed door of the home, where each woman has to rely on her own strength and resources.

Another new factor is that women are now involved in the welfare state on a large scale as employees, so that new possibilities for political action by women also exist. Women have been criticizing the welfare state in recent years not just as academics, as activists, or as beneficiaries and users of welfare services, but as the people on whom the daily operation of the welfare state to a large extent depends. The criticisms range from its patriarchal structure (and, on occasions, especially in health care, misogynist practices), to its bureaucratic and undemocratic policy-making processes and administration, to social work practices and education policy. Small beginnings have been made on changing the welfare state from within; for example, women have succeeded in establishing Well Women Clinics within the NHS in Britain and special units to deal with rape victims in public hospitals in Australia. Furthermore, the potential is now there for united action by women employees, women claimants and women citizens already politically active in the welfare state – not just to protect services against government cuts and efforts at 'privatization' (which has absorbed much energy recently), but to transform the welfare state. Still, it is hard to see how women alone could succeed in the attempt. One necessary condition for the creation of a genuine democracy in which the welfare of *all* citizens is served is an alliance between a labour movement that acknowledges the problem of patriarchal power and an autonomous women's movement that recognizes the problem of class power. Whether such an alliance can be forged is an open question.

Despite the debates and the rethinking brought about by mass unemployment and attack on the union movement and welfare state by the Reagan and Thatcher governments, there are many barriers to be overcome. In Britain and Australia, with stronger welfare states, the women's movement has had a much closer relationship with working-class movements than in the United States, where the individualism of the predominant liberal feminism is an inhibiting factor, and where only about 17 per cent of the work force is now unionized. The major locus of criticism of authoritarian, hierarchical, undemocratic forms of organization for the last twenty years has been the women's movement. The practical example of democratic, decentralized organization provided by the women's movement has been largely ignored by the labour movement, as well as in academic discussions of democracy. After Marx defeated Bakunin in the First International, the prevailing form of organization in the labour movement, the nationalized industries in Britain and in the left sects has mimicked the hierarchy of the state – both the welfare and the warfare state. To be sure, there is a movement for industrial democracy and workers' control, but it has, by and large, accepted that the 'worker' is a masculine figure and failed to question the separation of (public) industry and economic production from private life. The women's movement has rescued and put into practice the long-submerged idea that movements for, and experiments in, social change must 'prefigure' the future form of social organization.[79]

If prefigurative forms of organization, such as the 'alternative' women's welfare services set up by the women's movement, are not to remain isolated examples, or if attempts to set them up on a wider scale are not to be defeated, as in the past, very many accepted conceptions and practices have to be questioned. Recent debates over left alternatives to Thatcherite economics policies in Britain, and over the Accord between the state, capital and labour in Australia, suggest that the arguments and demands of the women's movement are still often unrecognized by labour's political spokesmen. For instance, one response to unemployment from male workers is to argue for a shorter working week and more leisure, or more time but the same money. However, in women's lives, time and money are not interchangeable in the same way.[80] Women, unlike men, do not have leisure after 'work', but do unpaid work. Many women are arguing, rather, for a shorter working day. The point of the argument is to challenge the separation of part- and full-time paid employment and paid and unpaid 'work'. But the conception of citizenship needs thorough questioning, too, if Wollstonecraft's dilemma is to be resolved; neither the labour movement nor the women's movement (nor democratic theorists) has paid much attention to this. The patriarchal opposition between the private and public, women and citizen, dependent and breadwinner is less firmly based than it once was, and feminists have named it as a political problem. The ideal of full employment so central to the welfare state is also crumbling, so that some of the main props of the patriarchal understanding of citizenship are being undermined. The ideal of full employment appeared to have been achieved in the 1960s only because half the citizen body (and black men?) was denied legitimate membership in the employment society. Now that millions of men are excluded from the ideal (and the exclusion seems permanent), one possibility is that the ideal of universal citizenship will be abandoned, too, and full citizenship become the prerogative of capitalist, employed and armed men. Or can a genuine democracy be created?

The perception of democracy as a class problem and the influence of liberal feminism have combined to keep alive Engels' old solution to 'the woman question' – to 'bring the whole female sex back into public industry'.[81] But the economy has a patriarchal structure. The Marxist hope that capitalism would create a labour force where ascriptive characteristics were irrelevant, and the liberal-feminist hope that anti-discrimination legislation will create a 'gender-neutral' workforce, look utopian even without the collapse of the ideal of full employment. Engel's solution is out of reach – and so, too, is the generalization of masculine citizenship to women. In turn, the argument that the equal worth of citizenship, and the self-respect and mutual respect of citizens, depend upon sale of labour-power in the market and the provisions of the patriarchal welfare state is also undercut. The way is opening up for the formulation of conceptions of respect and equal worth adequate for democratic citizenship. Women could not 'earn' respect or gain the self-respect that men obtain as workers; but what kind of respect do men 'achieve' by selling their labour-power and becoming wage-slaves? Here the movement for workplace democracy and the feminist movement could join hands, but only if the conventional understanding of 'work' is rethought. If women as well as men are to be full citizens, the separation of the welfare state and employment from the free welfare work contributed by women has to be broken down and new meanings and practices of 'independence', 'work' and 'welfare' created.

For example, consider the implications were a broad, popular political movement to press for welfare policy to include a guaranteed social income to all adults, which would provide adequately for subsistence and also participation in social life.[82] For such a demand to be made, the old dichotomies must already have started to break down – the opposition between paid and unpaid work (for the first time all individuals could have a genuine choice whether to engage in paid work), between full- and part-time work, between public and private work, between independence and dependence, between work and welfare – which is to say, between men and women. If implemented, such a policy would at last recognize women as equal members of the welfare state, although it would not in itself ensure women's full citizenship. If a genuine democracy is to be created, the problem of the content and value of women's contribution as citizens and the meaning of citizenship has to be confronted.

To analyze the welfare state through the lens of Hegel's dilemma is to rule out such problems. But the history of the past 150 years and the contemporary record show that the welfare of all members of society cannot be represented by men, whether workers or capitalists. Welfare is, after all, the welfare of all living generations of citizens and their children. If the welfare state is seen as a response to Hegel's dilemma, the appropriate question about women's citizenship is: how can women become workers and citizens like men, and so members of the welfare state like men? If, instead, the starting point is Wollstonecraft's dilemma, then the question might run: what form must democratic citizenship take if a primary task of all citizens is to ensure that the welfare of each living generation of citizens is secured?

The welfare state has been fought for and supported by the labour movement and the women's movement because only public or collective provision can maintain a proper standard of living and the means for meaningful social participation for all citizens in a democracy. The implication of this claim is that democratic citizens are both autonomous and interdependent; they are autonomous in that each enjoys the means to be an active citizen, but they are interdependent in that the welfare of each is the collective responsibility of all citizens. Critics of the class structure of the welfare state have often counterposed the fraternal interdependence (solidarity) signified by the welfare state to the bleak independence of isolated individuals in the market, but they have rarely noticed that both have been predicated upon the dependence (sub-ordination) of women. In the patriarchal welfare state, independence has been constructed as a masculine prerogative. Men's 'independence' as workers and citizens is their freedom from responsibility for welfare (except insofar as they 'contribute' to the welfare state). Women have been seen as responsible for (private) welfare work, for relationships of dependence and interdependence. The paradox that welfare relies so largely on women, on dependents and social exiles whose 'contribution' is not politically relevant to their citizenship in the welfare state, is heightened now that women's paid employment is also vital to the operation of the welfare state itself.

If women's knowledge of and expertise in welfare are to become part of their contribution as citizens, as women have demanded during the twentieth century, the opposition between men's independence and women's dependence has to be broken down, and a new understanding and practice of citizenship developed. The patriarchal dichotomy between women and independence-work-citizenship is under political challenge, and the social basis for the ideal of the full (male) employment society is crumbling. An opportunity has become visible to create a genuine democracy, to move from the welfare state to a welfare society without involuntary social exiles, in which women as well as men enjoy full social membership. Whether the opportunity can be realized is not easy to tell now that the warfare state is overshadowing the welfare state.

NOTES

1 R. Williams, *Keywords: A Vocabulary of Culture and Society*, rev. ed. (Oxford University Press, New York: 1985), p. 333.

2 I have presented a theoretical elaboration of a modern conception of 'patriarchy' as the systematic exercise by men of power over women in *The Sexual Contract* (Polity Press, Cambridge, 1988; Stanford University Press, Stanford CA, 1988). For a brief discussion of some of the issues, see chap. 2.

3 Women were formally enfranchised as citizens in 1902 in Australia, 1920 in the USA and 1928 in Britain (womanhood franchise in 1918 was limited to women over 30 years old).

4 On Scandinavia see, e.g., *Patriarchy in a Welfare Society*, ed. H. Holter (Universitetsforlaget, Oslo, 1984), esp. H. Hernes, 'Women and the Welfare State: The Transition from Private to Public Dependence'; and *Unfinished Democracy: Women in Nordic Politics* ed. E. Haavio-Mannila et al. (Pergamon Press, Oxford and New York, 1985).

5 Z. Eisenstein, *Feminism and Sexual Equality* (Monthly Review Press, New York, 1984), p. 125.

6 B. Nelson, 'Women's Poverty and Women's Citizenship: Some Political Consequences of Economic Marginality', *Signs*, 10(2) (1984), p. 221.

7 S. Erie, M. Rein and B. Wiget, 'Women and the Reagan Revolution: Thermidor for the Social Welfare Economy', in *Families, Politics and Public Policy: A Feminist Dialogue on Women and the State*, ed. I. Diamond (Longman, New York, 1983), p. 96.

8 Ibid., p. 100.

9 S. Kamerman, 'Women, Children and Poverty: Public Policies and Female-Headed Families in Industrialized Countries', *Signs*, 10(2) (1984), p. 250.

10 J. Smith, 'The Paradox of Women's Poverty: Wage-Earning Women and Economic Transformation', *Signs*, 10(2) (1984), p. 291.

11 B. Ehrenreich and F. Fox Piven, 'The Feminization of Poverty', *Dissent* (Spring 1984), p. 162.

12 L. Bryson, 'Women as Welfare Recipients: Women, Poverty and the State', in *Women, Social Welfare and the State*, ed. C. Baldock and B. Cass (Allen & Unwin, Sydney, 1983), p. 135.

13 B. Cass, 'Rewards for Women's Work', in *Women, Social Science and Public Policy*, ed. J. Goodnow and C. Pateman (Allen & Unwin, Sydney, 1985), p. 92. Cass also notes that women and their children were overrepresented among the poor making claims on colonial and post-colonial charities in Australia (p. 70). Similarly, in Britain, from 1834 during the whole period of the New Poor Law, the majority of recipients of relief were women, and they were especially prominent among the very poor; see D. Groves, 'Members and Survivors: Women and Retirement Pensions Legislation', in *Women's Welfare Women's Rights*, ed. J. Lewis (Croom Helm, London and Canberra, 1983), p. 40.

14 L. Doyal, 'Women and the National Health Service: the Carers and the Careless', in *Women, Health and Healing*, ed. E. Lewin and V. Olesen (Tavistock, London, 1985), pp. 237, 253.

15 H. Land, 'Beggars Can't Be Choosers', *New Statesman* (17 May 1985), p. 8.

16 Ehrenreich and Fox Piven, 'The Feminization of Poverty', p. 165; also Erie et al., 'Women and the Reagan Revolution', pp. 100–3.

17 D. Moon, 'The Moral Basis of the Democratic Welfare State', in *Democracy and the Welfare State*, ed. Amy Gutmann (Princeton University Press, Princeton, NJ, 1988).

18 For examples see T. Brennan and C. Pateman, ' "Mere Auxiliaries to the Commonwealth": Women and the Origins of Liberalism,' *Political Studies*, 27 (1979), pp. 183–200; and also chap. 1.

19 I have taken the term from J. Keane and J. Owens, *After Full Employment* (Hutchinson, London, 1986), p. 11.

20 Ibid., pp. 15–18, 89–90.

21 G. W. F. Hegel, *Philosophy of Right*, tr. T. M. Knox (Clarendon Press, Oxford, 1952) §171.

22 T. H. Marshall, 'Citizenship and Social Class', reprinted in *States and Societies*, ed. D. Held et al. (New York University Press, New York, 1983), p. 253.

23 Ibid., pp. 250–1, 257.

24 The graphic phrase is Judith Stiehm's, in 'Myths Necessary to the Pursuit of War' (unpublished paper), p. 11.

25 See especially F. Cobbe, 'Wife Torture in England', *The Contemporary Review*, 32 (1878), pp. 55–87. Also, for example, Mill's remarks when introducing the amendment to enfranchise women in the House of Commons in 1867, reprinted in *Women, the Family and Freedom:*

The Debate in Documents, ed. S. Bell and K. Offen vol. 1 (Stanford University Press, Stanford, CA, 1983), p. 487.

26 For more detail, see chap. 4.

27 D. Deacon, 'Political Arithmetic: The Nineteenth-Century Australian Census and the Construction of the Dependent Woman', *Signs*, 11(1) (1985), p. 31 (my discussion draws on Deacon); also H. Land, 'The Family Wage', *Feminist Review*, 6 (1980), p. 60.

28 T. Skocpol, 'The Limits of the New Deal System and the Roots of Contemporary Welfare Dilemmas', in *The Politics of Social Policy in the United States* ed. M.Weir, A. Orloff and T. Skocpol (Princeton University Press, Princeton, NJ, 1988).

29 Nelson, 'Women's Poverty and Women's Citizenship', pp. 222–3.

30 M. Owen, 'Women – A Wastefully Exploited Resource', *Search*, 15 (1984), pp. 271–2.

31 Thompson was a utilitarian, but also a feminist, cooperative socialist, so that he took his individualism more seriously than most utilitarians. In *Appeal of One Half the Human Race, Women, against the Pretensions of the Other Half, Men, to Retain Them in Political, and then in Civil and Domestic Slavery* (Source Book Press, New York, 1970 [first published 1825]), Thompson, writing of the importance of looking at the distribution of interests, or 'the means of happiness', argues that the 'division of interests' must proceed 'until it is brought home to every *individual* of every family.' Instead, under the despotism of husbands and fathers, 'the interest of each of them is promoted, in as far only as it is coincident with, or subservient to, the master's interest'. (pp. 46–7, 49)

32 As Beatrix Campbell has reminded us, 'we protect men from the shame of their participation in women's poverty by keeping the secret. Family budgets are seen to be a *private* settlement of accounts between men and women, men's unequal distribution of working-class incomes within their households is a right they fought for within the working-class movement and it is not yet susceptible to *public* political pressure within the movement'. (*Wigan Pier Revisited: Poverty and Politics in the 80s*, Virago Press, London, 1984, p. 57) Wives are usually responsible for making sure that the children are fed, the rent paid and so on, but this does not mean that they always decide how much money is allocated to take care of these basic needs. Moreover, in times of economic hardship women are often short of food as well as money; wives will make sure that the 'breadwinner' and the children are fed before they are.

33 L. J. Weitzman, *The Divorce Revolution* (The Free Press, New York, 1985), chap. 10, esp. pp. 337–40.

34 Deacon, 'Political Arithmetic', p. 39.

35 Cited in A. Phillips, *Hidden Hands: Women and Economic Policies* (Pluto Press, London, 1983), p. 76.

36 See M. Barrett and M. McIntosh, 'The "Family Wage": Some

Problems for Socialists and Feminists', *Capital and Class*, 11 (1980), pp. 56–9.

37 Ibid., p. 58.

38 Smith, 'The Paradox of Women's Poverty', p. 300.

39 Phillips, *Hidden Hands*, p. 21.

40 The perception is common to both women and men. (I would argue that women's perception of themselves is not, as is often suggested, a consequence of 'socialization', but a realistic appraisal of their structural position at home and in the workplace.) For empirical evidence on this view of women workers see, e.g., A. Pollert, *Girls, Wives, Factory Lives* (Macmillan, London, 1981); J. Wacjman, *Women in Control: Dilemmas of a Workers' Cooperative* (St Martin's Press, New York, 1983).

41 C. Baldock, 'Public Policies and the Paid Work of Women', in Baldock and Cass, *Women, Social Welfare and the State*, pp. 34, 40.

42 Land, 'The Family Wage', p. 62.

43 B. Cass, 'Redistribution to Children and to Mothers: A History of Child Endowment and Family Allowances', in Baldock and Cass, *Women, Social Welfare and the State*, p. 62.

44 Campbell, *Wigan Pier Revisited*, pp. 130–1.

45 A. Hacker, ' "Welfare": The Future of an Illusion', *New York Review of Books*, 28 February 1985, p. 41.

46 Ehrenreich and Fox Piven, 'The Feminization of Poverty', p. 163.

47 S. Hewlett, *A Lesser life: The Myth of Women's Liberation in America* (William Morrow, New York, 1986), p. 76.

48 Women's Bureau, Department of Employment and Industrial Relations, *Women At Work* (April 1986).

49 I. Bruegel, 'Women's Employment, Legislation and the Labour Market', in Lewis, *Women's Welfare*, p. 133 and table 7.4.

50 'Skill' is another patriarchal category; it is men's work that counts as 'skilled'. See the discussion in C. Cockburn, *Brothers: Male Dominance and Technological Change* (Pluto Press, London, 1983), pp. 112–22.

51 Doyle, 'Women and the National Health Service', pp. 250–4; and A. Oakley, 'Women and Health Policy', in Lewis, *Women's Welfare*, p. 120 and table 6.3.

52 *Women at Work*, April 1986.

53 Phillips, *Hidden Hands*, p. 15.

54 Bruegel, 'Women's Employment', p. 135.

55 Hewlett, *A Lesser Life*, p. 72.

56 Smith, 'The Paradox of Women's Poverty', pp. 304, 307; quotation, p. 306.

57 J. Dale and P. Foster, *Feminists and the Welfare State* (Routledge & Kegan Paul, London, 1986), p. 112.

58 H. Land, 'Who Cares for the Family?', *Journal of Social Policy* 7(3) (1978), pp. 268–9. Land notes that even under the old Poor Law twice

as many women as men received outdoor relief, and there were many more old men than women in the workhouse wards for the ill or infirm; the women were deemed fit for the wards for the able-bodied.

59 Campbell, *Wigan Pier Revisited*, p. 76.

60 Nelson, 'Woman's Poverty and Women's Citizenship', pp. 229–30.

61 Both quotations are taken from Land, 'The Family Wage', p. 72.

62 Cited in Dale and Foster, *Feminists and the Welfare State*, p. 17.

63 H. Land, 'Who Still cares for the Family?', in Lewis, *Women's Welfare*, p. 70.

64 M. Davis, *Maternity: Letters from Working Women* (Norton, New York, 1978) (first published 1915).

65 Information taken from Land, 'Who Cares for the Family?', pp. 263–4.

66 Land, 'Who Still Cares for the Family?', p. 73.

67 Cited in Dale and Foster, *Feminists and the Welfare State*, p. 3.

68 There was considerable controversy within the women's movement between the wars over the question of protective legislation for women in industry. Did equal citizenship require the removal of such protection, so that women worked under the same conditions as men; or did the legislation benefit women, and the real issue become proper health and safety protection for both men and women workers?

69 I have discussed the earlier arguments in more detail in 'Women and Democratic Citizenship', The Jefferson Memorial Lectures, Univesity of California, Berkeley, 1985, Lecture I.

70 For example, Wollstonecraft writes, 'speaking of women at large, their first duty is to themselves as rational creatures, and the next, in point of importance, as citizens, is that, which includes so many, of a mother.' She hopes that a time will come when a 'man must necessarily fulfil the duties of a citizen, or be despised, and that while he was employed in any of the departments of civil life, his wife, also an active citizen, should be equally intent to manage her family, educate her children, and assist her neighbours.' *A Vindication of the Rights of Woman*, (Norton, New York, 1975), pp. 145, 146.

71 Cited in Land, 'The Family Wage', p. 63.

72 Cited in Cass, 'Redistribution to Children and to Mothers', p. 57. My discussion draws on Land and Cass. In the USA during the same period, feminists supported the movement for mothers' pensions. Unlike mothers eligible for family allowances, mothers eligible for pensions were without male breadwinners. The complexities of mothers' pensions are discussed by W. Sarvesy, 'The Contradictory Legacy of the Feminist Welfare State Founders', paper presented to the annual meeting of the American Political Science Association, Washington, DC, 1986.

73 Cited in Cass, 'Redistribution', p. 59.

74 Ibid., pp. 60–1.

75 Campbell, *Wigan Pier Revisited*, pp. 66, 78, 71.

76 F. Fox Piven, 'Women and the State: Ideology, Power, and the Welfare State', *Socialist Review* 14(2) (1984), pp. 14, 17.
77 M. Sawer, 'The Long March through the Institutions: Women's Affairs under Fraser and Hawke', paper presented to the annual meeting of the Australasian Political Studies Association, Brisbane, 1986, p. 1.
78 J. S. Mill, 'The Subjection of Women', in *Essays on Sex Equality*, ed. A. Rossi (University of Chicago Press, Chicago, 1970), p. 137.
79 See S. Rowbotham, L. Segal and H. Wainright, *Beyond the Fragments: Feminism and the Making of Socialism* (Merlin Press, London, 1979), a book that was instrumental in opening debate on the left and in the labour movement in Britain on this question.
80 See H. Hernes, *Welfare State and Woman Power: Essays in State Feminism* (Norwegian University Press, Oslo, 1987), chap. 5, for a discussion of the political implications of the different time-frames of men's and women's lives.
81 F. Engels, *The Origin of the Family, Private Property and the State* (International Publishers, New York, 1942), p. 66.
82 See also the discussion in Keane and Owens, *After Full Employment*, pp. 175–7.

9

Feminism and Democracy

A feminist might dispose briskly of the subject of this chapter. For feminists, democracy has never existed; women have never been and still are not admitted as full and equal members and citizens in any country known as a 'democracy'. A telling image that recurs throughout the history of feminism is of liberal society as a series of male clubs – usually, as Virgina Woolf points out in *Three Guineas*, distinguished by their own costumes and uniforms – that embrace parliament, the courts, political parties, the military and police, universities, workplaces, trade unions, public (private) schools, exclusive clubs and popular leisure clubs, from all of which women are excluded or to which they are mere auxiliaries. Feminists will find confirmation of their view in academic discussions of democracy which will usually take it for granted that feminism and the structure of the relationship between the sexes are irrelevant matters. In the scope of a short essay it is hardly possible to demolish the assumption of two thousand years that there is no incompatibility between 'democracy' and the subjection of women or their exclusion from full and equal participation in political life. Instead, I shall indicate why feminism provides democracy – whether in its existing liberal guise or in the form of a possible future participatory or self-managing democracy – with its most important challenge and most comprehensive critique.

The objection that will be brought against the feminists is that after a century or more of legal reforms and the introduction of universal suffrage women are now the civil and political equals of men, so that feminism today has little or nothing to contribute to democratic theory and practice. This objection ignores much that is crucial to an understanding of the real character of liberal-democratic societies. It ignores the existence of widespread and deeply held convictions, and of social practices that give them expression, that contradict the (more or less) formally equal civic status of women. The objection is based on the liberal argument that social inequalities are irrelevant to political equality. Thus, it has to ignore the problems that have arisen from the attempt to universalize liberal principles by extending them to women while at the same time maintaining the division between private and political life which is central to liberal democracy, and is also a division between women and men. If liberal theorists of democracy are content to avoid these questions, their radical critics, along with advocates of participatory democracy, might have been expected to confront them enthusiastically. However, although they have paid a good deal of attention to the class structure of liberal democracies and the way in which class inequality undercuts formal political equality, they have rarely examined the significance of sexual inequality and the patriarchal order of the liberal state for a democratic transformation of liberalism. Writers on democracy, whether defenders or critics of the status quo, invariably fail to consider, for example, whether their discussions of freedom or consent have any relevance to women. They implicitly argue as if 'individuals' and 'citizens' are men.

It is frequently overlooked how recently democratic or universal suffrage was established. Political scientists have remained remarkably silent about the struggle for womanhood suffrage (in England there was a continuous organized campaign for forty-eight years from 1866 to 1914) and the political meaning and consequences of enfranchisement. Women's position as voters also appears to cause some difficulty for writers on democracy. Little comment is excited, for example, by Schumpeter's explicit statement, in his extremely influential revisionist text, that the exclusion of women from the franchise does not invalidate a polity's claim to be a 'democracy'. In Barber's fascinating account of direct democracy in a Swiss canton, womanhood suffrage (gained only in 1971) is treated very equivocally. Barber emphasizes that women's enfranchise-ment was 'just and equitable' – but the cost was 'participation and community'. Assemblies grew unwieldy and participation diminished, atomistic individualism gained official recognition and the ideal of the citizen-soldier could no longer be justified.[1] The reader is left wondering whether women should not have sacrificed their just demand for the sake of men's citizenship. Again, in Verba, Nie and Kim's recent cross-national study of political participation it is noted, in a discussion of the change in Holland from compulsory to voluntary voting, that 'voting rights were universal'. The footnote, on the same page, says that in both electoral systems there was 'a one man one vote system'.[2] Did women vote? Unrecognized historical ironies abound in discussions of democracy. Feminists are frequently told today that we must not be offended by masculine language because 'man' really means 'human being', although when, in 1867 in support of the first women's suffrage bill in Britain, it was argued that 'man' (referring to the householder) was a generic term that included women the argument was firmly rejected. Another recent example of the way in which women can be written out of democratic political life can be found in Margolis's *Viable Democracy*. He begins by presenting a history of 'Citizen Brown', who is a man and who, we learn, in 1920 obtained 'his latest major triumph, the enfranchisement of women'.[3] Thus the history of women's democratic struggles disappears and democratic voting appears as the sole creation – or gift – of men.

Such examples might be amusing if they were not symptomatic of the past and present social standing of women. Feminism, liberalism and democracy (that is, a political order in which citizenship is universal, the right of each adult individual member of the community) share a common origin. Feminism, a general critique of social relationships of sexual domination and subordination and a vision of a sexually egalitarian future, like liberalism and democracy, emerges only when individualism, or the idea that individuals are by nature free and equal to each other, has developed as a universal theory of social organization. However, from the time, 300 years ago, when the individualist social contract theorists launched the first critical attack on patriarchalism the prevailing approach to the position of women can be exemplified by the words of Fichte who asks:

> Has woman the same rights in the state which man has? This question may appear ridiculous to many. For if the only ground of all legal rights is reason and freedom, how can a distinction exist between two sexes which possess both the same reason and the same freedom?

He replies to this question as follows:

> Nevertheless, it seems that, so long as men have lived, this has been differently held, and the female sex seems not to have been placed on a par with the male sex in the exercise of its rights. *Such a universal sentiment must have a ground, to discover which was never a more urgent problem than in our days.*[4]

The anti-feminists and anti-democrats have never found this 'urgent problem' difficult to solve. Differential rights and status have been and are defended by appeal to the 'natural' differences between the sexes, from which it is held to follow that women are subordinate to their fathers or husbands and that their proper place is in domestic life. The argument from nature stretches back into mythology and ancient times (and today often comes dressed up in the scientific garb of sociobiology) and its longevity appears to confirm that it informs us of an eternal and essential part of the human condition. But, far from being timeless, the argument has specific formulations in different historical epochs and, in the context of the development of liberal-capitalist society, it appears in a form which obscures the patriarchal structure of liberalism beneath the ideology of individual freedom and equality.

It is usually assumed that the social contract theorists, and Locke in particular, provided the definitive counter to the patriarchal thesis that paternal and political power are one and the same, grounded in the natural subjection of sons to fathers. Locke certainly drew a sharp distinction between natural or familial ties and the conventional relations of political life, but although he argued that sons, when adult, were as free as their fathers and equal to them, and hence could only justifiably be governed with their own consent, it is usually 'forgotten' that he excluded women (wives) from this argument. His criticism of the patriarchalists depends upon the assumption of natural individual freedom and equality, but only men count as 'individuals'. Women are held to be born to subjection. Locke takes it for granted that a woman will, through the marriage contract, always agree to place herself in subordination to her husband. He agrees with the patriarchalists that wifely subjection has 'a Foundation in Nature' and argues that in the family the husband's will, as that of the 'abler and the stronger', must always prevail over 'that of his wife in all things of their common Concernment'.[5] The contradiction between the premise of individual freedom and equality, with its corollary of the conventional basis of authority, and the assumption that women (wives) are naturally subject has since gone unnoticed. Similarly, there has been no acknowledgement of the problem that if women are naturally subordinate, or born into subjection, then talk of their consent or agreement to this status is redundant. Yet this contradiction and paradox lie at the heart of democratic theory and practice. The continuing silence about the status of wives is testament to the strength of the union of a transformed patriarchalism with liberalism. For the first time in history, liberal individualism promised women an equal social standing with men as naturally free individuals, but at the same time socio-economic developments ensured that the subordination of wives to husbands continued to be seen as natural, and so outside the domain of democratic theorists or the political struggle to democratize liberalism.

The conviction that a married women's proper place is in the conjugal home as a servant to her husband and mother to her children is now so widespread and well established that this arrangement appears as a natural feature of human existence rather than historically and culturally specific. The history of the development of the capitalist organization of production is also the history of the development of a particular form of the sexual division of labour (although this is not the history to be found in most books). At the time when the social contract theorists attacked the patriarchal thesis of a natural hierarchy of inequality and subordination, wives were not their husband's equals, but nor were they their economic dependants. Wives, as associates and partners in economic production, had an independent status. As production moved out of the household, women were forced out of the trades they controlled and wives became dependent on their husbands for subsistence or competed for individual wages in certain areas of production.[6] Many working-class wives and mothers have had to continue to try to find paid employment to ensure the survival of their families, but by the mid-nineteenth century the ideal, the natural and respectable, mode of life had come to be seen as that of the middle-class, breadwinning paterfamilias and his totally dependent wife. By then the subjection of wives was complete; with no independent legal or civil standing they had been reduced to the status of property, as the nineteenth-century feminists emphasized in their comparisons of wives to the slaves of the West Indies and American South. Today, women have won an independent civil status and the vote; they are, apparently, 'individuals' as well as citizens – and thus require no special attention in discussions of democracy. However, one of the most important consequences of the institutionalization of liberal individualism and the establishment of universal suffrage has been to highlight the practical contradiction beween the formal political equality of liberal democracy and the social subordination of women, including their subjection as wives within the patriarchal structure of the institution of marriage.

It is indicative of the attitude of democratic theorists (and political activists) towards feminism that John Stuart Mill's criticism of the argument from (women's) nature, and the lessons to be learned from it, are so little known. The present revival of the organized feminist movement has begun to rescue *The Subjection of Women* from the obscurity into which Mill's commentators have pushed it, although it provides a logical extension of the arguments of his academically acceptable *On Liberty*. *The Subjection* is important for its substantive argument, but also because the ultimately contradictory position that Mill takes in the essay illustrates just how radical feminist criticism is, and how the attempt to universalize liberal principles to both sexes pushes beyond the confines of liberal-democratic theory and practice.

In *The Subjection* Mill argues that the relation between women and men, or, more specifically, between wives and husbands, forms an unjustifed exception to the liberal principles of individual rights, freedom and choice, to the principles of equality of opportunity and the allocation of occupational positions by merit that, he believes, now govern other social and political institutions. In the modern world, consent has supplanted force and the principle of achievement has replaced that of ascription – except where women are concerned. Mill writes that the conjugal relation is an example of 'the primitive state of slavery lasting on, . . . It has not lost the taint of its brutal origin.' (p. 130)[7] More generally, the social subordination of women is 'a single relic of an old world of thought and practice, exploded in everything else' (p. 146). Mill opens *The Subjection* with some pertinent comments on the difficulty feminists face in presenting an intellectually convincing case. Domination by men is rooted in long-standing customs, and the idea that male supremacy is the proper order of things derives from deep feelings and sentiments rather than rationally tested beliefs (and, it might be added, men have a lot to lose by being convinced). Thus feminists must not expect their opponents to 'give up practical principles in which they have been born and bred and which are the basis of much of the existing order of the world, at the first argumentative attack which they are not capable of logically resisting.' (p. 128) Mill is very conscious of the importance of the appeal to nature. He notes that it provides no criterion to differentiate the subordination of women from other forms of domination because all rulers have attempted to claim a grounding in nature for their position. He also argues that nothing at all can be said about the respective natures of women and men because we have only seen the sexes in an unequal relationship. Any differences in their moral and other capacities will become known when men and women can interact as independent and equal rational beings.

However, despite Mill's vigorous attack on the appeal to custom and nature, he ultimately falls back on the very argument that he has carefully criticized. His failure consistently to apply his principles to domestic life has been noted by recent feminist critics, but it is less often pointed out that his inconsistency undermines his defence of womanhood suffrage and equal democratic citizenship. The central argument of *The Subjection* is that husbands must be stripped of their legally sanctioned despotic powers over their wives. Most of the legal reforms of the marriage law that Mill advocated have now been enacted (with the significant exception of marital rape, to which I shall return), and the implications of his unwillingness to extend his criticism to the sexual division of labour within the home are now fully revealed. Mill argues that because of their upbringing, lack of education and legal and social pressures, women do not have a free choice whether or not to marry: 'wife' is the only occupation open to them. But although he also argues that women must have equal opportunity with men to obtain a proper education that will enable them to support themselves, he assumes that, if marriage were reformed, most women would *not* choose independence.

Mill states that it is generally understood that when a woman marries she has chosen her career, like a man when he chooses a profession. When a woman becomes a wife, 'she makes choice of the management of a household, and the bringing up of a family, as the first call on her exertions, . . . she renounces, . . . all [occupations] not consistent with the requirement of this.' (p. 179) Mill is reverting here to ascriptive arguments and the belief in women's natural place and occupation. He is falling back on the ancient tradition of patriarchal political theory that, as Susan Okin has shown in *Women in Western Political Thought*,[8] asserts that whereas men are, or can be, many things, women are placed on earth to fulfil one function only; to bear and rear children. Mill neatly evades the question of how, if women's task is prescribed by their sex, they can be said to have a real choice of occupation, or why equal opportunity is relevant to women if marriage itself is a 'career'. Mill compares an egalitarian marriage to a business partnership in which the partners are free to negotiate their own terms of association, but he relies on some very weak arguments, which run counter to liberal principles, to support his view that equality will not disturb the conventional domestic division of labour. He suggests that the 'natural arrangement' would be for wife and husband each to be 'absolute in the executive branch of their own department . . . any change of system and principle requiring the consent of both.' (p. 169) He also suggests that the division of labour between the spouses could be agreed in the marriage contract – but he assumes that wives will be willing to accept the 'natural' arrangement. Mill notes that duties are already divided 'by consent . . . and general custom' (p. 170) modified in individual cases; but it is exactly 'general custom', as the bulwark of male domination, that he is arguing against in the body of the essay. He forgets this when he suggests that the husband will generally have the greater voice in decisions as he is usually older. Mill adds that this is only until the time of life when age is irrelevant; but when do husbands admit that this has arrived?[9] He also forgets his own arguments when he suggests that more weight will be given to the views of the partner who brings the means of support, disingenuously adding 'whichever this is' when he has already assumed that wives will 'choose' to be dependent by agreeing to marry.

Anti-feminist movements and propagandists in the 1980s also claim that the domestic division of labour supported by Mill is the only natural one. They would not be disturbed by the implications of this arrangement for the citizenship of women but advocates of democracy should be. Mill championed womanhood suffrage for the same reasons that he supported votes for men; because it was necessary for self-protection or the protection of individual interests and because political participation would enlarge the capacities of individual women. The obvious problem with his argument is that women as wives will largely be confined to the small circle of the family and its daily routines and so will find it difficult to use their vote effectively as a protective measure. Women will not be able to learn what their interests are without experience outside domestic life. This point is even more crucial for Mill's arguments about political development and education through participation. He writes (p. 237) in general terms of the elevation of the individual 'as a moral, spiritual and social being' that occurs under free government, but this is a large claim to make for the periodic casting of a vote (although the moral transformation of political life through enfranchisement was a central theme of the womanhood suffrage movement). Nor did Mill himself entirely believe that this 'elevation' would result from the suffrage alone. He writes that 'citizenship', and here I take him to be referring to universal suffrage, 'fills only a small place in modern life, and does not come near the daily habits or inmost sentiments.' (p. 174) He goes on to argue that the family, 'justly constituted', would be the 'real school of the virtues of freedom'. However, this is as implausible as the claim about the consequences of liberal-democratic voting. A patriarchal family with the despotic husband at its head is no basis for democratic citizenship; but nor, *on its own*, is an egalitarian family. Mill argues in his social and political writings that only participation in a wide variety of institutions, especially the workplace, can provide the political education necessary for active, democratic citizenship. Yet how can wives and mothers, who have 'chosen' domestic life, have the opportunity to develop their capacities or learn what it means to be a democratic citizen? Women will therefore exemplify the selfish, private beings, lacking a sense of justice or public spirit, that result when an individual is confined to the narrow sphere of everyday family life.[10] Mill's failure to question the apparently natural division of labour within the home means that his arguments for democratic citizenship apply only to men.

It might be objected that it is unreasonable and anachronistic to ask of Mill, writing in the 1860s, that he criticize the accepted division of labour between husband and wife when only very exceptional feminists in the nineteenth century were willing to question the doctrine of the separate spheres of the sexes. But if that objection is granted,[11] it does not excuse the same critical failure by contemporary democratic theorists and empirical investigators. Until the feminist movement began, very recently, to have an impact on academic studies, not only has the relation between the structure of the institution of marriage and the formal equality of citizenship been ignored, but women citizens have often been excluded from empirical investigations of political behaviour and attitudes or merely referred to briefly in patriarchal, not scientific, terms.[12] A reading of *The Subjection* should long ago have placed these matters in the forefront of discussions of democracy. Perhaps the appearance of empirical findings showing, for example, that even women active in local politics are inhibited from running for office because of their responsibility for child-care and a belief that office-holding is not a proper activity for women,[13] will be taken more seriously than the feminist writings of even eminent philosophers.

The problems surrounding women's citizenship in the liberal democracies may have been sadly neglected, but the failure of democratic theorists to confront the woman and wife question runs much deeper still. Democratic citizenship, even if interpreted in the minimal sense of universal suffrage in the context of liberal civil rights, presupposes the solid foundation of a practical, universal recognition that all members of the polity are social equals and independent 'individuals', having all the capacities implied by this status. The most serious failure of contemporary democratic theory and its language of freedom, equality and consent and of the individual, is that women are so easily and inconspicuously excluded from references to the 'individual'. Thus the question never arises whether the exclusion reflects social and political realities. One reason why there is no consciousness of the need to ask this question is that democratic theorists conventionally see their subject matter as encompassing the political or public sphere, which for radical theorists includes the economy and the workplace. The sphere of personal and domestic life – the sphere that is the 'natural' realm of women – is excluded from scrutiny. Despite the central role that consent plays in their arguments, democratic theorists pay no attention to the structure of sexual relations between men and women and, more specifically, to the practice of rape and the interpretation of consent and non-consent which define it as a criminal offence. The facts about rape are central to the social realities which are reflected in and partly constituted by our use of the term 'individual'.

Among Mill's criticism of the despotic powers of nineteenth-century husbands is a harsh reminder that a husband had the legal right to rape his wife. Over a century later a husband still has that right in most legal jurisdictions. Locke excludes women from the status of 'free and equal individual' by his agreement with the patriarchal claim that wives were subject to their husbands by nature; the content of the marriage contract confirms that, today, this assumption still lies at the heart of the institution of marriage. The presumed consent of a woman, in a free marriage contract, to her subordinate status gives a voluntarist gloss to an essentially ascribed status of 'wife'. If the assumption of natural subjection did not still hold, liberal-democratic theorists would long ago have begun to ask why it is that an ostensibly free and equal individual should *always* agree to enter a contract which subordinates her to another such individual. They would long ago have begun to question the character of an institution in which the initial agreement of a wife deprives her of the right to retract her consent to provide sexual services to her husband, and which gives him the legal right to force her to submit. If contemporary democratic theorists are to distance themselves from the patriarchal assumptions of their predecessors they must begin to ask whether a person can be, at one and the same time, a free democratic citizen and a wife who gives up a vital aspect of her freedom and individuality, the freedom to refuse consent and say 'no' to the violation of the integrity of her person.

A woman's right of refusal of consent is also a matter of more general importance. Outside of marriage rape is a serious criminal offence, yet the evidence indicates that the majority of offenders are not prosecuted. Women have exemplified the beings whom political theorists have regarded as lacking the capacities to attain the status of individual and citizen or to participate in the practice of consent, but women have, simultaneously, been perceived as beings who, in their personal lives, always consent, and whose explicit refusal of consent can be disregarded and reinterpreted as agreement. This contradictory perception of women is a major reason why it is so difficult for a woman who has been raped to secure the conviction of her attacker(s). Public opinion, the police and the courts are willing to identify enforced submission with consent, and the reason why this identification is possible is that it is widely believed that if a woman says 'no' her words have no meaning, since she 'really' means 'yes'. It is widely regarded as perfectly reasonable for a man to reinterpret explicit rejection of his advances as consent.[14] Thus women find that their speech is persistently and systematically invalidated. Such invalidation would be incomprehensible if the two sexes actually shared the same status as 'individuals'. No person with a secure, recognized standing as an 'individual' could be seen as someone who consistently said the opposite of what they meant and who, therefore, could justifiably have their words reinterpreted by others. On the other hand, invalidation and reintepretation are readily comprehensible parts of a relationship in which one person is seen as a natural subordinate and thus has an exceedingly ambiguous place in social practices (held to be) grounded in convention, in free agreement and consent.

Political theorists who take seriously the question of the conceptual foundations and social conditions of democracy can no longer avoid the feminist critique of marriage and personal life. The critique raises some awkward and often embarrassing questions, but questions that have to be faced if 'democracy' is to be more than a men's club writ large and the patriarchal structure of the liberal-democratic state is to be challenged. The assumptions and practices which govern the everyday, personal lives of women and men, including their sexual lives, can no longer be treated as matters remote from political life and the concerns of democratic theorists. Women's status as 'individuals' pervades the whole of their social life, personal and political. The structure of everyday life, including marriage, is constituted by beliefs and practices which presuppose that women are naturally subject to men – yet writers on democracy continue to assert that women and men can and will freely interact as equals in their capacity as enfranchised democratic citizens.

The preceding argument and criticism is relevant to discussions of both liberal democracy and participatory democracy, but particularly to the latter. Liberal theorists continue to claim that the structure of social relations and social inequality is irrelevant to political equality and democratic citizenship, so they are no more likely to be impressed by feminists than by any other radical critics. Advocates of participatory democracy have been reluctant to take feminist arguments into account even though these arguments are, seen in one light, an extension of the participatory democratic claim that 'democracy' extends beyond the state to the organization of society. The resistance to feminism is particularly ironical because the contemporary feminist movement has, under a variety of labels, attempted to put participatory democratic organization into practice.[15] The movement is decentralized and anti-hierarchical and tries to ensure that its members collectively educate themselves and gain independence through consciousness-raising, participatory decision-making and rotation of tasks and offices.

Feminists deny the liberal claim that private and public life can be understood in isolation from each other. One reason for the neglect of J. S. Mill's feminist essay is that his extension of liberal principles to the institution of marriage breaches the central liberal separation, established by Locke, between paternal and political rule; or between the impersonal, conventional public sphere and the family, the sphere of natural affection and natural relations. Proponents of participatory democracy have, of course, been willing to challenge commonplace conceptions of the public and the private in their discussions of the workplace, but this challenge ignores the insights of feminism. It is rarely appreciated that the feminists and participatory democrats see the division between public and private very differently. From the feminist perspective participatory democratic arguments remain within the patriarchal-liberal separation of civil society and state; domestic life has an exceedingly ambiguous relation to this separation which is a division within public life itself. In contrast, feminists see domestic life, the 'natural' sphere of women, as private, and thus as divided from a public realm encompassing both economic and political life, the 'natural' arenas of men.[16]

By failing to take into account the feminist conception of 'private' life, by ignoring the family, participatory democratic arguments for the democratization of economic life have neglected a crucial dimension of democratic social transformation (and I include my *Participation and*

Democratic Theory[17] here). It is difficult to find any appreciation of the significance of the integral relation between the domestic division of labour and economic life, or the sexual division of labour in the workplace, let alone any mention of the implications of the deeper matters touched on in this essay, in writings on industrial democracy. It is the feminists, not the advocates of workplace democracy, who have investigated the very different position of women workers, especially married women workers, from that of male employees. Writers on democracy have yet to digest the now large body of feminist research on women and paid employment or to acknowledge that unless it is brought into the centre of reflection, debate and political action, women will remain as peripheral in a future participatory 'democracy' as they are at present in liberal democracies.

I have drawn attention to the problem posed by the assumption that women's natural place is a private one, as wife and mother in the home, for arguments about the educative and developmental consequences of political participation. It might be argued that this problem is much less pressing today than in Mill's time because many married women have now entered the public world of paid employment and so they, if not housewives, already have their horizons widened and will gain a political education if enterprises are democratized. In Australia, for example, in 1977 women formed 35 per cent of the labour force and 63 per cent of these women were married.[18] The reality behind the statistics, however, is that women's status as workers is as uncertain and ambiguous as our status as citizens and both reflect the more fundamental problem of our status as 'individuals'. The conventional but implicit assumption is that 'work' is undertaken in a workplace, not within the 'private' home, and that a 'worker' is male – someone who has his need for a clean place of relaxation, clean clothes, food and care of his children provided for him by his wife. When a wife enters paid employment it is significant for her position as 'worker' that no one asks who peforms these services for her. In fact, married women workers do two shifts, one in the office or factory, the other at home. A large question arises here why members of enterprises who are already burdened with two jobs should be eager to take on the new responsibilities, as well as exercise the opportunities, that democratization would bring.

The relative importance of the two components of the wife's double day, and so the evaluation of women's status as workers, is reflected, as Eisenstein notes, in the popular use of 'the term "working mother" which simultaneously asserts women's first responsibility to motherhood and her secondary status as worker.'[19] Again, the question has to be asked how workers of secondary status could, without some very large changes being made, take their place as equal participants in a democratized workplace. The magnitude of the changes required can be indicated by brief reference to three features of women's (paid) worklife. The sexual harassment of women workers is still a largely unacknowledged practice but it reveals the extent to which the problem of sexual relations, consent and women's status as 'individuals' is also a problem of the economic sphere.[20] Second, women still have to win the struggle against discrimination by employers and unions before they can participate as equals. Finally, it has to be recognized that the workplace is structured by a sexual division of labour which poses still further complex problems for equality and participation. Women are segregated into certain occupational categories ('women's work') and they are concentrated in non-supervisory and low-skilled and low-status jobs. It is precisely workers in such jobs that empirical research has shown to be the least likely to participate.

The example of the workplace, together with the other examples discussed in this essay, should be sufficient to show the fundamental importance to democratic theory and practice of the contemporary feminist insistence that personal and political life are integrally connected. Neither the equal opportunity of liberalism nor the active, participatory democratic citizenship of *all* the people can be achieved without radical changes in personal and domestic life. The struggles of the organized feminist movement of the last 150 years have achieved a great deal. An exceptional woman can now become Prime Minister – but that particular achievement leaves untouched the structure of social life of unexceptional women, of women as a social category. They remain in an uncertain position as individuals, workers and citizens, and popular opinion echoes Rousseau's pronouncement that 'nature herself has decreed that women, . . . should be at the mercy of man's judgement'.[21] The creation of a free and egalitarian sexual and personal life is the most difficult to achieve of all the changes necessary to build a truly democratic society precisely because it is not something remote from everyday life that can be applauded in abstract slogans while life, and the subjection of women, goes on as usual. Democratic ideals and politics have to be put into practice in the kitchen, the nursery and the bedroom; they come home, as J. S. Mill wrote (p. 136) 'to the person and hearth of every male head of a family, and of everyone who looks forward to being so.' It is a natural biological fact of human existence that only women can bear children, but that fact gives no warrant whatsoever for the separation of social life into two sexually defined spheres of private (female) existence and (male) public activity. This separation is ultimately grounded in the mistaken extension of the argument from natural necessity to child-rearing. There is nothing in nature that prevents fathers from sharing equally in bringing up their children, although there is a great deal in the organization of social and economic life that works against it. Women cannot win an equal place in democratic productive life and citizenship if they are deemed to be destined for a one ascribed task, but nor can fathers take an equal share in reproductive activities without a transformation in our conception of 'work' and of the structure of economic life.

The battle joined 300 years ago when the social contract theorists pitted conventionalist arguments against the patriarchalists' appeal to nature is far from concluded, and a proper, democratic understanding of the relation of nature and convention is still lacking. The successful conclusion of this long battle demands some radical reconceptualization to provide a comprehensive theory of a properly democratic practice. Recent feminist theoretical work offers new perspectives and insights into the problem of democratic theory and practice, including the question of individualism and participatory democracy, and an appropriate conception of 'political' life.[22] It has been hard to imagine what a democratic form of social life might look like for much of the past century. Male-dominated political parties, sects and their theoreticians have attempted to bury the old 'utopian' political movements which are part of the history of the struggle for democracy and women's emancipation, and which argued for prefigurative forms of political organization and activity. The lesson to be learned from the past is that a 'democratic' theory and practice that is not at the same time feminist merely serves to maintain a fundamental form of domination and so makes a mockery of the ideals and values that democracy is held to embody.

NOTES

1 B. R. Barber, *The Death of Communal Liberty* (Princeton University Princeton, NJ, 1974), p. 273. The comment on citizen-soldiers is very revealing. There is no reason why women should not be armed citizens and help defend the *patrie* (as guerrilla fighters and armies have shown). However, one of the major arguments of the anti-suffragists in Britain and the USA was that the enfranchisement of women would fatally weaken the state because women by nature were incapable of bearing arms. I have commented on these issues in C. Pateman, 'Women, Nature and the Suffrage', *Ethics*, 90(4) (1980), pp. 564–75. Some other aspects of the patriarchal argument from nature are discussed below.

2 S. Verba, N. Nie and J.-O. Kim, *Participation and Political Equality* (Cambridge University Press, Cambridge, 1978), p. 8.

3 M. Margolis, *Viable Democracy* (Penguin Books, Harmondsworth, Middlesex, 1979), p. 9.

4 J.G. Fichte, *The Science of Rights*, tr. A. E. Kroeger (Trubner, London, 1889), 'Appendix', §3.1, p. 439 (my emphasis).

5 J. Locke, *Two Treatises of Government*, ed. P. Laslett 2nd edn, (Cambridge University Press, Cambridge, 1967), 1, §47, 48; II, §82.

6 For amplification of these necessarily brief comments see T. Brennan and C. Pateman, ' "Mere Auxiliaries to the Commonwealth": Women and the Origins of Liberalism', *Political Studies*, 27 (1979), pp. 183–200: R. Hamilton, *The Liberation of Women: A Study of Patriarchy and Capitalism* (Allen & Unwin, London, 1978); H. Hartmann, 'Capitalism, Patriarchy and Job Segregation by Sex', *Signs*, 1(3), pt 2 (1976), pp. 137–70; A. Oakley, *Housewife* (Penguin Books, Harmondsworth, Middlesex, 1976), chaps. 2, 3.

7 Page references in the text are to J. S. Mill, 'The Subjection of Women', in J. S. Mill and H. Taylor, *Essays on Sex Equality*, ed. A. Rossi (Chicago University Press, Chicago, IL, 1970).

8 S. Okin, *Women in Western Political Thought* (Princeton University Press, Princeton, NJ, 1979).

9 It is worth noting that Mill implicitly distinguishes between the actions and beliefs of individual husbands and the power given to 'husbands' over 'wives' within the structure of the institution of marriage. He notes that marriage is not designed for the benevolent few to whom the defenders of marital slavery point, but for every man, even those who use their power physically to ill-treat their wives. This important distinction is still frequently overlooked today when critics of feminism offer examples of individual 'good' husbands personally known to them.

10 Mill, and many other feminists, see the lack of a sense of justice (a consequence of confinement to domestic life) as the major defect in women's characters. The assertion that the defect is natural to women is central to the belief – ignored by writers on democracy – that women are inherently subversive of political order and a threat to the state; on this question see chap. 1.

11 It need not be granted. *The Subjection of Women* owes a good deal to William Thompson's (much neglected) *Appeal of One Half the Human Race, Women, Against the Pretensions of the Other Half, Men, to Retain them in Political, and Hence in Civil and Domestic, Slavery* (Source Book Press, New York, 1970), originally published in 1825. Thompson was very willing to question these matters in his vision of a cooperative-socialist and sexually egalitarian future.

12 For an early critique see, for example, M. Goot and R. Reid, 'Women and Voting Studies: Mindless Matrons or Sexist Scientism', *Sage Professional Papers in Contemporary Sociology*, 1 (1975); more recently, for example, J. Evans, 'Attitudes to Women in American Political Science', *Government and Opposition*, 15(1) (1980), pp. 101–14.

13 M. M. Lee, 'Why Few Women Hold Public Office: Democracy and Sexual Roles', *Political Science Quarterly*, 91 (1976), pp. 297–314.

14 A detailed discussion of the paradoxical manner in which political theorists have treated women's consent, and references to the empirical evidence on which these comments are based, can be found in chap. 4. In some legal jurisdictions, for example the states of New

South Wales, South Australia and Victoria in Australia, rape within marriage is now a criminal offence. Legal reform is extremely welcome, but the wider social problem remains.

15 On the other hand, the experience of women in the 'participatory democratic' New Left was a major impetus to the revival of the feminist movement. The New Left provided an arena for political action, the development of skills, and was ideologically egalitarian – but it remained male supremacist in its organization and, especially, its personal relations: see S. Evans, *Personal Politics* (Knopf, New York, 1979).

16 For some comments on the ambiguous place of the family, see chap. 1; on the wider question of public and private, see chap. 6.

17 C. Pateman, *Participation and Democratic Theory* (Cambridge University Press, Cambridge, 1970).

18 A steady increase in the employment of married women has been one of the most striking features of the post-war development of capitalism. However, it is worth re-emphasizing that (working-class) wives have always been in the paid workforce. In Britain in 1851 about a quarter of married women were employed (Oakley, *Housewife*, p. 44). Moreover, domestic service, until the late 1930s, was a major occupation for (usually single) women. One reason that Mill is able to overlook the fundamental importance of wives' (private) child-rearing duties for their public status is that middle-class mothers had other women to look after their children; similarly, upper- and middle-class suffragettes could go to prison secure in the knowledge that domestic servants were caring for their homes and children (on this point see J. Liddington and J. Norris, *One Hand Tied Behind Us: The Rise of the Women's Suffrage Movement*, Virago, London, 1978).

19 Z. R. Eisenstein, *The Radical Future of Liberal Feminism* (Longman, New York, 1980), pp. 207–8.

20 On sexual harassment see, for example, C. A. Mackinnon, *Sexual Harassment of Working Women* (Yale University Press, New Haven, CT, 1979).

21 J.-J. Rousseau, *Emile*, tr. B. Foxley (Dent, London, 1911), p. 328.

22 See, for example, the discussion by R. P. Petchesky, 'Reproductive Freedom: Beyond "A Woman's Right to Choose" ', *Signs*, 5(4) (1980), pp. 661–85.

Index